FAMILY HEALTH:
A Literature Review

Sue Sharpe
Melanie Mauthner
Merry France-Dawson

Social Science Research Unit
Institute of Education
London WC1

0752108336

Acknowledgements

We would like to express our thanks to the HEA and especially to Rhiannon Barker for advice and feedback throughout the final draft of this review, and also to Janet Holland for her encouragement and support.

Published by the Health Education Authority
ISBN 07521 0833 X

© Health Education Authority, 1996

First published 1996

Health Education Authority
Hamilton House,
Mabledon Place,
London WC1H 9TX

Typeset by Type Generation Ltd, London
Printed in Great Britain

Contents

Foreword

This research report was commissioned by the Health Education Authority (HEA), as part of a wider programme of research to coincide with the United Nation's International Year of the Family in 1994. The research programme aimed to provide a greater insight into the mechanisms of family health, thus informing parents and professionals about effective ways of taking forward health promotion work with young people.

The HEA has a national remit for health education in England. It advises the Secretary of State, organises national health education campaigns and works with health service commissioners and providers to help them implement national health promotion targets. Good research-based evidence is key to improving health and healthcare, and for this reason the HEA bases its campaigns on thorough needs assessment and evaluation.

Over the last decade the HEA has worked with parents and professionals to improve and promote the health of children. Emphasis is put on offering appropriate support to parents in the complex and sometimes stressful task of promoting the health and education of children and young people. Projects have focused on increasing the uptake of child immunisations, reduction of child accidents, and advice and support for pregnant mothers and first time parents. We have also produced training materials for those working in parenting education and initiated inter-agency collaboration through workshops, seminars and the provision of resource databases. The research reported on here forms part of the on-going needs assessment in the area of parent and child health. Previous initiatives include a report on health promotion for children under 5 and a review of the literature assessing the effectiveness of health promotion interventions on infant mortality and morbidity.

The HEA encounters a constant demand from health professionals to provide materials to support parents, yet appropriate health education messages, and the style and manner in which they are relayed, are increasingly open to question. This report highlights the importance of recognising the environmental, social and economic constraints which influence parental behaviour and shows how parental roles and needs change as children grow and develop. It also stresses that there is no 'blueprint' defining the ideal parent. Different parents adopt different parenting styles which may work to equal effect; individual styles need to be respected and supported. Such messages are particularly important in an environment where parents are probably under more intense pressure from the media and a range of professionals than at any other time, to create a healthy, nurturing and moral environment for their young.

Kathy Elliot

Executive summary

Communication and health in the family context is an area that has been sparsely covered in health research and promotion. As a private domain, the family is not as easily accessed as the school or the workplace. Yet it is potentially an extremely effective location for the dissemination of health information and advice. This review brings together research studies that focus on, or have some relation to, families and communication on a range of health issues. The review also identifies areas that would benefit from further research.

This report is divided into two parts, with four chapters in Part I, and nine chapters in Part II. The first three sections provide a context to exploring specific health issues. The first section covers studies of family communication in general, and their limitations. The second section describes concepts of health and approaches to health behaviour, and the links between individuals' lay beliefs and social circumstances, and their health behaviours. Health variations among different social groups is the subject of the third section, including between social classes, where differences appear to be widening, ethnicity, gender and family status. The relationship between these variables and specific health issues is considered throughout the review. There is a need for more work in the area of ethnicity, which is relatively briefly covered in this review.

To complete the background (and Part I), Chapter 4 provides an overview of the range of methodologies and techniques that have been used to research families, communication and health issues. It covers both quantitative and qualitative research methods and highlights the strengths of each: quantitative methods are useful for collecting demographic information and measuring the prevalence of any health risk-taking behaviour, and other individual behaviours; while qualitative techniques shed light on the dynamic processes involved in communication and other family interactions. Some methods are more appropriately applied to certain health areas than others. For example, small-scale qualitative studies may be more appropriate for exploring the processes underlying family communication patterns, while larger studies, both cross sectional and longitudinal, may be more useful for collecting prevalence data on smoking and drinking behaviour.

Part II reviews research relating to family communication in the nine health areas under consideration: alcohol: smoking; sexual health; diet; physical activity; parenthood education; childhood accidents; immunisation; and men's health. These health topics vary in length, reflecting the amount of the research on families and communication in each area. For instance, relatively few studies have been carried out specifically on families and physical activity. The greater magnitude and separate consideration of smoking and sexual health not only reflect that these are well-researched areas, but also relate to the historical development of this review, with its initial focus on these two issues. The review subsequently took on an increasingly broader brief, but this process could not be infinite, and thus some gaps remain. Mental health is one such omission, but its importance is recognised and discussed as it arises within many sections. It is recommended that a separate literature review relating to mental health and family dynamics and communication be carried out in the future.

For each health topic, attention is drawn to areas that appear to have been under-researched, and recommendations are made for further studies.

Part II begins with a section on **alcohol**. Drinking is a social activity that makes it a complicated target for health education, and children, for instance, usually have their earliest experiences of drinking at home with the family. The detrimental effects of alcohol can be short- and long-term, and vary at different stages of the life cycle. Men generally drink more than women, but women's drinking has shown some increase over the past few years. Drinking patterns also vary by geographical region, age, and social class. In Britain, a significant number of people grow up in families with parents who are problem drinkers. Parental attitudes and behaviour towards alcohol can be important influences on children and young people. Young people's drinking does not appear to have increased, but to have changed its pattern, with an increase in 'binge drinking' behaviour amongst both young men and women.

Smoking has long been a concern for health education and there are a plethora of studies that attempt to trace the nature and impact of different influences on smoking behaviour. Smoking behaviour patterns show some gender differences, in that although smoking prevalence has shown a significant decline among the adult population and young men, girls' and young women's smoking has not followed the same pattern, and some research suggested that more girls than boys were taking up smoking. There are also social-class variations in smoking behaviour, and smoking levels have decreased more slowly among the lower social-class groups. Health education has been particularly concerned with the possible influences on children's smoking behaviour, and many studies, both cross-sectional and longitudinal, have tried to find links between the attitudes and behaviour of parents, siblings, and peers. Recent studies demonstrate strong links between parents' behaviour and patterns of smoking in children but reviews of family smoking studies have tended to show inconsistent results and clear conclusions remain elusive.

There has been an increasing interest in **sexual health** issues for a number of reasons, including concerns with teenage pregnancies and the increase in HIV/AIDS. The sexual health issues examined here are not limited to the processes of sexual intercourse and reproduction, but also cover aspects of children growing up, such as puberty and physical development, body image, emotions and emotional relationships. Sex education has become a topical issue, with concerns about its treatment at home as well as in the school curriculum. Studies on young men's and women's sexual experiences suggest that there are a number of contradictions that they each face in acquiring sexuality. Despite the apparent openness in the ways that sex is discussed in the media, family communication about sex and sexual health remains a problematic area between many parents and children, and may also be difficult between adult sexual partners.

Nutrition and diet is a topic strongly related to class, income, gender and ethnicity. Eating a healthy diet appears to be linked to three main factors: knowledge and attitudes about diet and healthy eating; personal influences such as food aversions, habits and beliefs; and external factors such as price, accessibility, time, culture, and food scares. Women are more likely to be classified as healthy eaters than men. Food can be a highly charged symbol of relations between parents and children and communication patterns around this subject may reflect related issues of family conflict and control. Social pressures from outside and inside the family can contribute to the development of eating disorders especially among young women. Families have the potential to shape future eating habits of young people. However, health messages directed at families need to be aware of the different needs of each family member and the pressures placed on the main food provider, usually a woman.

Most work on **physical activity** has involved studies of people's individual participation in sport and exercise. This shows the influence of gender and age: for instance, men are more physically active than women, and boys more active than girls; and taking regular exercise in youth increases the likelihood of doing so later in life. For men, it has been suggested that participation in sport, or even watching sport as a spectator, can act positively in relation to stress and mental health. Although little work has focused on the family and physical activity, research suggests that young children may be getting less exercise through spending more time on computers, combined with restricted mobility because of parents' increased fears about safety outside the home.

The section on **parenthood education** focuses on parenting skills during the period leading up to and soon after the birth of a new baby. Greater research emphasis has generally been placed on antenatal rather than postnatal care and information, particularly in the context of the medical and physical health issues involved. Parenthood education has tended to neglect the important social and emotional changes that may be involved at this time. Not enough attention is paid to the parenthood education of men as fathers, nor to the teaching of parenting skills to both girls and boys at school. Teenage motherhood (and fatherhood) is another area of parenting that needs more specific attention. Research suggests that care should be taken to ensure that the 'parenting needs' defined by health professionals are the same as those that parents want for themselves.

Although many **childhood accidents** occur outside the home, involving motor vehicles and child pedestrians, many children are also at risk from accidents in their own family homes. Material resources relating to factors such as social class, family size and unemployment contribute to a higher risk of accidents, as well as environmental hazards, in certain households. Accidental death in childhood has the steepest social-class gradient of all causes of death. Some research suggests that mothers and fathers have different roles and levels of awareness about home safety measures for young children, and that families may vary in adopting pro-active or reactive approaches to home safety. This area has provoked much research and a diversity of interventions, the efficiency of which have been inconsistent, but reflect the need to take account of behavioural, material and environmental perspectives.

Although a generally high proportion of the population respond positively to **immunisation** programmes, there are a number of families in certain circumstances, or with certain sets of beliefs, who do not have their children vaccinated against childhood diseases. These factors are generally related to class or unstable housing situations; or simply to inefficient follow-up procedures at clinics. However, a minority of parents choose not to immunise their children, and some recent studies have explored their attitudes and health beliefs, and the dilemmas of parental decision-making in this area. These studies highlight the need to broaden and improve information and health education on this issue (and take in both sides of the debate), and to raise awareness, especially in high-risk groups.

Men's health has been included here as a separate topic because it is an area that has been hitherto neglected, both by men and by health professionals and authorities. Efforts are now underway to research relevant areas of men's health, as well as to promote increased health awareness in men themselves, especially younger men.

Factors such as the increased incidence of testicular cancer in young men, and a lowering in the sperm count have caused medical concern in recent years. Men's sexual health risks have also come into focus with the increase incidence of HIV/AIDS. Mortality and morbidity statistics have long shown gender differences: men die earlier than women, and from different diseases; and there are wide health differences between men from different social classes. However, little research has looked at aspects of men's health in more detail, or at men's attitudes to their own health. Marriage and employment serve as protective factors for men's health, while the male lifestyle tends to involve health risks such as alcohol, drugs, and accidents. Masculinity and the male gender role has tended to make it socially and psychologically harder for men to seek medical advice or help, and men as fathers have tended to leave responsibility for most aspects of family health to their partners.

Introduction

This literature review highlights research carried out on families and health with special reference to communication about health issues and serves as a guide to further research in this area. The review focuses on how parents and children talk about health issues together and how they discuss and transmit health messages from the media, health professionals, friends and personal experience (Fitzpatrick 1990). The 'family' has become a matter for political and social debate with concern about the break-up of the traditional nuclear family growing in recent years (Brannen and O'Brien 1995a).

A wide range of health topics is covered in the review: immunisation and childhood accidents, parent education, nutrition, physical activity, sexual health, smoking, alcohol and men's health. Its main perspective is that of parent-child communication, though it also touches on the questions of health inequalities and use of health services (DoH 1995). The reason for the review's span across such a wide range of health topics lies in its history: it incorporates findings from two earlier reviews on smoking and sexual health, hence these topics are addressed more fully (Sharpe and Oakley 1992; Mauthner 1992). A further review on family communication about general health was also carried out in 1992 and later revised (Mauthner *et al.* 1995). These three separate reviews formed part of the original pilot study, *The Family and Health Education Project* which subsequently led the HEA to commission a large national programme of research on the family (see Hey *et al.* 1993): *The Family Health Research Programme* included six studies on various aspects of family communication about health which ran during 1994–1995.*

Some health areas have received greater attention than others, reflecting the nature of the original brief for this review. One important area, that of stress and mental health, has not been given a separate section, but is raised within the discussion of individual health topics throughout the review. Its relevance is not to be underestimated, and this topic deserves a section of its own at a later stage. Mental health and stress-related illness are clearly important in studying the quality of family life and communication and there is a substantial literature in this area (Rutter and Smith 1995; Rutter *et al.* 1994; Brannen *et al.* 1994; Sweeting and West 1995; Rogers *et al.* 1996; OPCS 1995a). The issue of drug misuse is another area not included in the original remit. However, the HEA is currently embarking on a programme of drugs education and research, and a more complete study looking at family communication and drug misuse may be warranted at a later date.

---

*These are: Brannen and Storey 1996: Holland *et al.* 1996; Prout 1996; Rogers *et al.* 1996; Beattie *et al.* (forthcoming) 1996; Brynin and Scott (forthcoming) 1996. Summaries of the first four of these studies can be found in Hogg *et al.* (1996)

An interdisciplinary approach was adopted to collect the material. A number of electronic searches (for instance, of Psych. Lit., Medline, Popline, Sociological Abstracts, the Social Science Citation Index, and Unicorn (HEA)) and hand searches of journals were carried out over the years. Research on marriage and the family, child and adolescent development, gender and communication, health and illness was drawn from sociological and psychological studies (see Fitzpatrick 1988a; Noller and Fitzpatrick 1988; Callan and Noller 1987). This wide trawl was necessary to make up for the paucity of research on how health beliefs and attitudes are formed and discussed both within the family and in general. There is far less information about healthy families than there is about illness and family life (Textor 1989; Northouse and Northouse 1987; Jansen *et al.* 1989; Brannen *et al.* 1994). Whereas research on general health highlights the links between health, class and inequalities (Martin and McQueen 1989), few studies have focused on parent–child communication, sexual health being one exception (Warman 1986; Allen 1987; Nolin 1988).

One reason for the absence of studies on family communication lies in the practical difficulties involved. 'Quality' data on families is difficult and expensive to collect due to the problems of accessing a private domain and the time required to study interactions. In health education the debate has centred on the relative contributions of individual behaviour change versus public health and social policy on health outcomes (Bechhofer 1989).

There is little research on health care work within families or on the health of whole family groups other than a few intervention studies in parent education and nutrition (Pugh and Poulton 1987; Perry *et al.* 1988; Nicklas *et al.* 1988; Cade and O'Connell 1991). Research has tended to prioritise infancy (Mayall and Watson 1989; Loveland-Cherry 1984; Pratt 1976). Research linking children's behaviour with that of their parents has mainly concentrated on young people's cigarette and alcohol consumption but little work has been done with young children (Prout 1986). There is also a lack of qualitative research on children's health knowledge, with some exceptions (Backett and Alexander 1991; Farquhar 1990; Mayall 1995; Turner *et al.* 1995). The HEA is currently commissioning more research in this area. Once again, studies have tended to examine children's illness rather than health, and more work has been done in schools than other settings (Minuchin 1988; Bribace and Walsh 1980). There is also a gap in the literature between studies in developmental psychology and family research.

Prior to the HEA *Family Health Research Programme*, there was little sociological work on how families discuss health issues except for studies on the transmission of health beliefs from one generation to another and parents' and children's different ideas about health (Blaxter and Patterson 1982a; Backett and Alexander 1991; Kitzinger and Kitzinger 1989; Brannen *et al.* 1994). For this reason, the review includes a wide range of material from studies in development psychology on communication and interaction patterns (Noller and Fitzpatrick 1988); sociological studies on health and deprivation (Whitehead 1988); and cultural/behavioural studies on health practices (HEA 1989).

The main theme of this review is family communication patterns about various health topics. Chapter 1 explores family communication patterns in general; Chapter 2 examines concepts of health and lay health beliefs; Chapter 3 describes findings on families and health variations; Chapter 4 looks at the range of different methods used. In Part II, Chapters 5–13 review studies on alcohol, smoking, sexual health, diet and nutrition, physical activity, parenthood education, childhood accidents, immunisation, and men's health. Recommendations for further research are made at the end of each chapter in Part II.

PART I: CONTEXT AND METHODOLOGICAL BACKGROUND

1. Family communication about health

Communication between family members on health issues is not easy to research. It may involve focused discussion, but it is just as likely to be embedded within other topics or concerns. Communication may be verbal or non-verbal, and take place in a (methodologically) 'uncontrolled' situation, and thus be difficult to measure. Studies of communication amongst families and couples focus on how individuals: define their relationships; share information, attitudes and opinions; negotiate rules and roles; express feelings; make plans and decisions; and resolve problems and conflict (Fitzpatrick and Badzinski 1985; Callan and Noller 1987; Noller and Fitzpatrick 1988; Finch and Mason 1993; Holland *et al.* 1996). Effective or 'quality' communication has been defined as that which leads to self-disclosure, sharing, confirmation, listening and decision-making, and in this context, that which also determines physical and mental health (Callan and Noller 1987; Hanson 1986). This section looks at processes of communication, power relations in the family, and studies on communication between family members.

VERBAL AND NON-VERBAL COMMUNICATION

In studying gender and conversation Tannen (1991, 1995) analysed gender, body language and power relations and explored women's and men's assumptions about self-sufficiency and intimacy. She found that, for men, talking meant an exchange of information, whereas for women, its main function was interaction. Non-verbal behaviour has included speed of talking, pitch, loudness and voice quality (Callan and Noller 1987). Silverstein and Bengtson (1991) examined whether close and affectionate parent–child relationships reduced the mortality of older parents, and found that positive non-verbal communication was associated with the well-being of parents who felt emotionally close to their adult children.

Other studies have observed the gender differences that exist in ease of communication about personal issues inside and outside the family (Sharpe 1994;

Rogers *et al.* 1996; Holland *et al.* 1996). Boys and men tend to find it more difficult to talk about their emotions, or to seek help and advice on sensitive issues or problems, such as aspects of sexuality and sex education (see the chapters below on sexual health and men's health).

Talking about illness

Studies of verbal and non-verbal communication have taken place in various family therapeutic (including medical) situations (Barnes 1990). Communication studies on cancer, mental illness, eating disorders and alcoholism have shown how families communicate in terms of illness rather than well-being (Ferris and Marshall 1987; Steinglass 1987; Shisslak *et al.* 1990; Spitzack 1990; Throwe 1986). This once more identifies health issues with the presence of illness and disease, rather than the freedom from them.

In reviewing the literature on family communication during experiences with cancer, Northouse and Northouse (1987) found that the most salient issues for family members were concealment of feelings, acquisition of information, and feelings of helplessness. A number of studies have found that in terms of family communication, parents who have children with cancer and other chronic illnesses coped in similar ways. They shared the same strategies, such as family participation, and the same difficulties, such as different family members receiving different information (Birenbaum 1990; Shapiro and Shumaker 1987; Jansen *et al.* 1989; McWhinney 1989). One study described the use of audio-visual techniques to help cancer patients and their families express their fears, concerns and confusion, which enabled them to draw strength from their new knowledge and shared concerns and cope with the situation better, together (Rosenbaum and Rosenbaum 1986).

Family power relations

Apart from marital relationships, relatively little research has been carried out on power relations in the family, that is, who initiates, sets the agenda and controls family conversations or on how health messages are mediated in the family (Millar and Rogers 1988). One exception involves the area of family therapy where issues of gender and power are being addressed (Perelberg and Miller 1990). Umberson (1987) used two lifestyle measures to analyse the links between marital status, social control, and health behaviour. Umberson found that there were two ways in which family health behaviour could be socially controlled: a) indirectly, by family members acting as role models; and b) directly, through regulation, sanctions and physical intervention. These health behaviours can be transmitted verbally by suggesting healthy behaviours, dissuading or regulating others through threats or sanctions, or non-verbally by controlling the amount and type of food consumed by someone or by administering prescribed treatments.

Decision-making processes and gendered power relations in the family operate at several levels: there is the communication involved in decision-making in the family that reflects wider gendered power relations which structure both public and private domains (Ribbens and Edwards 1995); and there are different modes of decision-making and the exercise of power which lead to different types of relationships between family members. In a study of communication within families, Holland *et al.* (1996) identified four such modes or types of negotiation or decision-making processes: authoritarian, democratic, trade-offs, and issues on which children decide. Rogers *et al.* (1996) found that the parents in their study had a lot to say about discipline, and their responses also revealed deeper issues of power and emotions. They observed that for some respondents, this topic became the main vehicle for discussing emotional issues or questions of power between generations or between male and female parents.

PARENT–CHILD COMMUNICATION

Most research has focused on marital and parent–child communication patterns, but even here health issues have rarely been mentioned. Issues that have received attention include family interaction processes, men's lack of educaton for parenthood, and the difficulties parents have in communicating with their children about sexuality (Callan and Noller 1986; Combes and Schonveld 1992; Nolin 1988; Warman 1986; Holland *et al.* 1996).

Parents

Perhaps the dearth of studies on how families talk about general health issues is related to some assumption that this is more a topic of conversation for mothers (Callan and Noller 1987). Neither in research nor in areas such as the media have men been asked about their role as fathers as frequently as women are interviewed as mothers. Men often experience at least two psychological barriers in talking about fatherhood. The first is the traditional male role which determines that men do not talk about childbirth or satisfaction in having children. In the study by Combes and Schonveld (1992) men felt that, unlike women, there were few or no obvious places for them to discuss their feelings about becoming a father. A second difficulty is that researchers have assumed that all men are unable to reveal their true feelings about fatherhood and the impact of marriage and family life on their lives.

In this context, relatively little work has been done specifically on how fathers perceive their role in health education (Mayall and Watson 1989), but one study on family communication about health (Holland *et al.* 1996) noted fathers' lower awareness (than mothers') of the state of individual members' health, and their reluctance to get involved in talking to children about personal issues related to sexual health. The authors also observed how both children and mothers to some extent colluded in marginalising fathers through children often choosing to take their health issues or problems to their mothers.

Two studies describe how parents, especially mothers, directly or indirectly transmit their health attitudes and values to their children. The first adopts a sociological approach (Blaxter and Patterson 1982a), the second, an anthropological approach (Kitzinger and Kitzinger 1989).

Blaxter and Patterson (1982a) studied three generations of women in a sample of working-class families in Scotland. They compared grandmothers' and mothers' views and experiences of health, analysing mother–daughter pairs for similarities and discrepancies. Mother–daughter pairs were found to have different attitudes. Daughters 'saw many services as a "right" and expected a great deal of medication for their (own) children. Few (daughters) retained the deferential model characteristic of their mothers: they had adopted new attitudes to meet new circumstances.' They found that there was a fine line between 'advice', 'interference' and 'over-protectiveness' in the way lay beliefs were transmitted. It appeared that such inter-generational changes were inextricably bound up with changes in lifestyle, circumstances, the provision of services and public attitudes, and that these were more important than direct familial transmission.

Taking an anthropological approach, Kitzinger and Kitzinger (1989) focused on the range of issues raised by 3–12-year-olds that were of concern to them, and how their parents responded. For instance, mothers felt they had dealt with questions about birth most successfully, whereas subjects like rape, sexual abuse, masturbation and menstruation were more difficult to explain (Kitzinger and Kitzinger 1989). Mothers may involve children as young as three years old in decision-making using praise and encouragement rather than punishment to instill self-confidence. These are methods that also help children develop responsibility, independence and, relating to sexual issues, the ability to make decisions about ownership of their own bodies. Children were seen as needing to explore and understand complex feelings of curiosity, excitement, fear, shame, guilt and rejection. In addition to children's need for factual information, the importance of parents communicating attitudes and emotions was stressed (Kitzinger and Kitzinger 1989).

Children

There has been increasing interest in recognising and endorsing children's contributions to various social and economic worlds and to the construction of their own childhood, instead of perceiving them as dependants, and passive recipients of knowledge (Qvortrup 1985; Mayall 1995; Brannen and O'Brien 1996). Work by Kalnins *et al.* (1992) on health education as empowering people to alter the conditions affecting their health, serves to influence how children's health is perceived, and how health promotion programmes are designed for them. They stress the need for a shift from thinking about children as recipients of health promotion efforts, to accepting them as active participants in the process.

Few studies have tried to study children's views about health in the context of their everyday lives, as such research is difficult to conduct (Mayall 1994). Communication with children is not easy because it involves exchanges between partners unequal in age and status (McGurk and Glachan 1988; Bury 1993; Alderson and Mayall 1994; Mauthner forthcoming). Data is rarely collected directly from children themselves. Kalnins *et al.* (1992) suggest that children have to be seen as partners in health promotion rather than a special group needing protection, and that there has to be a belief in their competence (see also Brannen and O'Brien 1995b). They believe that we have fallen into the trap of focusing most on correcting the negative aspects of children's health behaviours rather than encouraging what is positive.

Research on children's own perceptions of family life has shown that with regard to their relationships inside and outside the family, children want affection, enhancement of their sense of worth, security and help from their parents when necessary (Furman and Buhrmester 1985). This study found that mothers were seen as the most important source of love and intimacy. Children wanted the same kind of affirmation for affection and enhancement from grandparents, but there was less emphasis on security and help. Friends were needed for companionship and intimacy.

Although there has been considerable research on the transmission of sex education and sexual health, rather less has been carried out on how families transmit information about general health topics to children and young people (Mayall and Watson 1989) or what children learn about general health (Wilkinson 1988). The HEA Family Research Programme attempted to address this imbalance, and Hogg *et al.* (1996) provide a summary of key points arising from the qualitative studies in this programme. Quantitative data linking parental attitudes and opinions with child health data is forthcoming (Brynin and Scott 1996). Another study that looked at children's perception of health issues was an HEA project in primary schools (Williams and Moon 1987). Primary school children were asked to describe, using the 'draw and write' technique, what they did to look after themselves in relation to various health issues such as diet and safety.

Backett and Alexander (1991) looked at 11–15-year-old children's perceptions of health and illness as part of a larger in-depth qualitative study of health in family groups which included interviews with all family members. They interviewed children aged 4–12 years, and found that children gave both 'public' and 'private' accounts of health and illness, held apparently inconsistent views about health, showed limited knowledge or understanding of parents' health-related behaviour and that their attitudes, beliefs and practices did not always coincide. Backett and Alexander (1991) also found that children appear to be more aware of the negative effects of 'unhealthy' eating than of the positive benefits of 'healthy' foods, and that they value and enjoy activities which they also think of as 'unhealthy' (Backett 1990). Furthermore, when comparing children's perceptions to those of their parents, they found that children tended to consider their parents in terms of healthy rather than unhealthy behaviour. There were also discrepancies between siblings', children's, and parents' reports regarding parents' health-related behaviours, such as smoking. Peers were seen as healthy because of their high levels of activity and physical ability, but unhealthy because of poor eating habits, especially the eating of sweets.

Adolescents

Although little is known about how they become responsible for making decisions about health-related behaviour, adolescents tend to be seen as a risk-taking group (Mayall and Watson 1989; Harding 1989). Studies which prevail in this area have focused on demographic variables such as age, sex, and class to account for behaviour differences. However, there are some exceptions (Brannen *et al.* 1994; Beattie *et al.* 1982; Bewley *et al.* 1984; Dodd 1991; Brynin and Scott 1996). Evidence from a study on adolescents' health-related beliefs and behaviour has shown that smoking patterns are gender- and class-related (Oakley *et al.* 1992). Harding (1989) has suggested that adolescents' health decisions may be regarded as partly determined by forces over which they have little or no control, such as unemployment, and inadequate housing.

Using an ethnographic approach, Bewley *et al.* (1984) examined adolescent attitudes to health and illness among 16–20-year-olds in an inner-city area and found that family disharmony was an important contributing factor compounded by poor housing and lack of educational and employment opportunities. They argued that this situation severely undermined traditional health education approaches. Macfarlane *et al.* (1987) administered a health questionnaire to young people in secondary schools, exploring their attitudes to health and illness and their views about family cohesion. In this context, Sweeting and West (1995) believe that family communication incorporates what they define as 'family culture', which is 'patterns of family activity, typically comprising family cohesiveness, support and affection, parenting styles and family roles and relationships' (Sweeting and West 1995: 164), and family conflict is included within these patterns. The authors suggest that these factors making up the 'family culture' may have an even greater impact on adolescent health than the material conditions of a family. This is supported by some research findings (West 1988; West *et al.* 1990) that show little class variation in health during adolescence.

In examining psychosocial disorders in young people, Rutter and Smith (1995) have observed the effects of increased levels of conflict and tension in families with teenage children, and link this to several trends: greater social isolation of teenagers from their parents; teenagers' financial dependence on parents for longer periods, and today's emphasis on individual consumption and gratification. Although there is a consensus in the literature, as in Sweeting and West (1995), linking conflict between teenagers and their parents with negative consequences like low self-esteem, delinquency and poor psychological adjustment, Rogers *et al.* (1996) point to the importance of considering the meaning of constructs such as family centredness and conflict, as their study showed that not all conflict was seen as negative, depending on whether the effects of conflict are seen to have a positive or negative outcome.

Rogers *et al.* (1996) also took note of the distancing that occurs between parents and teenagers in actual shared time and activities, and how this is experienced as a distancing in communication, especially as young people start to feel they can talk better to their friends than their parents. Some families try to maintain shared meal-times to conserve this opportunity for communication. They suggest that parents retain more communication with girls than boys, and that teenagers tend to take different problems to different parents; for instance, emotional problems are taken to mothers, and financial problems to fathers. Brannen *et al.* (1994) suggest that mothers tend to create a 'talking relationship' with their teenage children, while fathers may have more of a joking relationship.

Although relatively little research has been carried out on adolescent health and family communication processes, or on the actual processes by which adolescents decide on their health behaviour, various large-scale studies and surveys have examined teenagers' attitudes and behaviour around health issues (HEC 1987; HEA 1992a; HEA 1992b; Owen and Bolling 1995; Brynin and Scott 1996). Two MORI surveys (HEA 1992a; 1992b) looked at 9–15-year-olds' views on alcohol, drugs, exercise and smoking; and 16–19-year-olds' views on diet, alcohol, smoking, drugs and sexual behaviour, including questions about who they talk to about certain issues. Other HEA studies have tracked teenage health behaviours such as smoking, over a period of time (Owen and Bolling 1995). More ambitiously, a cross-national study of the health of schoolchildren was started by researchers in England, Finland and Norway in 1982 and developed as a WHO collaborative study involving ten countries (Aaro *et al.* 1986).

SPOUSE COMMUNICATION

Most research on spouse communication focuses on psychological aspects of health such as the quality of interaction, and communication problems. Fitzpatrick (1988b) analysed methods of negotiation, conflict avoidance and withdrawal in different marriage situations, and what couples gained from greater openness and/or from therapy. Differences have been found in terms of verbal and non-verbal communication between husbands and wives in emotional situations (Noller 1984; Noller and Gallois 1986). The impact of friends and family on marital relationships may have some importance but this has received little attention (Dickson-Markman and Markman 1988).

Problems in communication identified between couples include inattentiveness, vagueness, lack of clarity, over-generalisation, early anticipation of what is about to be said, negative reactions and coercion (Dickson-Markman and Markman 1988; Noller and Gallois 1986; Fitzpatrick 1988b). Strategies for conflict avoidance include ignoring the issues, refusing to discuss them, competitiveness or co-operation. A lot of attention has been devoted to improving the communication skills of couples and families. Furthermore, there is evidence to suggest that a supportive marriage can have a positive influence on the mother-child relationship and on 'sensitive parenting' (Engfer 1988; Easterbrooks and Emde 1988).

Couple and parenting educational programmes have been set up in the United States, and generally targeted individuals rather than families or couples, and aimed to teach parents to communicate more effectively with their children and to solve family problems (Miller *et al.* 1975; Dinkmeyer and McKay 1976; Gordon and Davidson 1981). Skills programmes take a directive approach, emphasising active listening, eye contact, appropriate body language (such as leaning towards the other person), understanding the other person's point of view and expressing one's own point of view in a non-defensive way (Callan and Noller 1987).

RECOMMENDATIONS FOR FURTHER RESEARCH

1. In the light of evidence suggesting that aspects of family conflict and closeness are important for adolescent health behaviours such as smoking, drinking, and mental health, further research is needed to explore the extent to which communication between family members is a form of well-being and may serve to

enhance health. Rogers *et al.* (1996) have suggested that some conflict in families may be seen as being positive, not just as negative interaction. Therefore characteristics of family culture and communication could be explored more deeply in relation to the health of all members of the family (Sweeting and West 1995).

2. The issue of how and through which channels health messages are brought into the family is an important one for health educators. Focused studies looking at this question in relation to specific health topics may be of value.

3. Research could usefully look more specifically at power relations and decision-making in the family (Holland *et al.* 1996) and relate these to other processes of control and resistance around health behaviours. The issue of control over health definitions and redefinitions, both within the family and in relation to the medical establishment, may also benefit from further examination.

4. Children's perspectives are important, for example as on health, parent–child relationships, and the processes involved in the relationship between children's early home environment and their health-related behaviour in adulthood (Backett and Alexander 1991; Kalnins *et al.* 1992). Children's acquisition of knowledge, the sources of their knowledge and their perceptions of appropriate health-care behaviour need more attention (Mayall and Watson 1989).

5. More research on adolescents' perceptions of health including their own definitions of health, responsibility and risk is needed (Harding 1989).

6. Specific attention should be given to the role of fathers as health educators within the family, on both general and sexual health issues.

7. More research could be done generally on the influence of ethnicity on family structure and how this affects various health topics.

2. Health concepts, beliefs and approaches

Research on health and families embraces different ideas about health and various approaches to studying the family. From a theoretical perspective, most approaches to the family are drawn from sociology, such as functionalism, which suggests that the family, like other social institutions, fulfils certain functions necessary for the regulation and maintenance of society (Parsons 1952). Other theoretical perspectives that have been applied to family research include symbolic interactionism (Burr *et al.* 1979), social exchange theory (Nye 1979), and systems theory (Bertalanffy 1969; Kantor and Lehr 1975). The consensual model of the family has been challenged from a feminist theoretical standpoint with the view that conflict, repression and 'plays for power' exist within families, which highlights age and gender differences, and the contradictory ways that the family can be both nurturing and supportive, and controlling and oppressive (Callan and Noller 1987; Leonard and Delphy 1992; VanEvery 1995).

This section discusses some concepts of health and the ways that individuals and families perceive health and illness; and briefly examines the public and private domains of health.

HEALTH AND HEALTH BEHAVIOUR

Some researchers have claimed that 'we know little of what health is' (Brannen *et al.* 1994), and certainly there seem to be differing notions which either perceive health as residing in the individual, or in the social environment. These have different implications for health promotion, since if the individual is responsible for his/her health, then health promotion should be aimed at individual behaviour and lifestyle, whereas if health is dependent on social conditions, then this demands a different approach and solution. In the context of medicine, health has traditionally been seen as concerned with the treatment of suffering (Stacey 1991), and to some commentators, health appears to be equated with figures on morbidity, mortality and life expectancy.

The government's 1992 White Paper, *The Health of the Nation*, identified key population health targets, all of which showed a systematic, consistent and large differential by socio-economic class. The inequal social distribution of ill-health and patterns of mortality have been linked to the concept of health as health behaviour but this explanation alone will not account for the widening socio-economic variations in health in advanced industrial societies. Health behaviour and interactions take place within a complex social environment. Health involves a learning process which begins in the family of origin and evolves according to need (Klesse and Sontag 1989).

Historically, health promotion has played a secondary role to health care in the national provision of health services, but more recent health service reforms, such as *The Health of the Nation*, have placed greater emphasis on prevention and health promotion, looking to a more pro-active approach to health, rather than a reactive one.

LAY BELIEFS ABOUT HEALTH

Lay definitions of health and illness are necessary to the understanding of whether ordinary people believe themselves to be ill or not, and if they do, whether this would lead them to consult doctors, and whether they choose to follow advised courses of treatment (Backett *et al.* 1994). Common-sense views of health and illness are passed from generation to generation and variations in lay perceptions may be seen between and within social and cultural groups, over time and locations, between individuals and even in the same person at different times (Stacey 1988; Pill and Stott 1986; Lewis 1986; Currer 1986). People define health in ways which give explanations of their 'material, social and bodily circumstances' (Stacey 1988).

Health definitions from different cultures include characteristics of 'health' such as having energy and athleticism, ability to work hard, having a zest for life, not being ill, and being free from emotional and physical stress (Blaxter 1983; Cornwell 1984; D'Houtaud and Field 1986; Pill and Stott 1986; Blaxter 1990). In some situations, health can be a socially constructed entity which is 'negotiated', for example, when someone feels ill but medical investigation cannot uncover a cause, or when doctors and their clients disagree about the significance of symptoms (Naidoo and Wills 1994). This can lead to patients being branded as hypochondriacs and to the withholding of sickness certification.

Arksey (1994) used the example of repetitive strain injury (RSI) to demonstrate how medical knowledge and beliefs can be influenced by lay knowledge and beliefs. She showed how clients with this condition were able to convince medical practitioners that RSI was a condition worthy of medical discussion and acceptance as an illness. Another example of health 'negotiation' is for a person to have no signs or symptoms of ill-health, but be labelled as 'sick' after screening or medical examination reveals health problems.

Illness generally refers to what may or may not be the symptoms of disease: pain, discomfort, disability and malaise. For lay people, the focus for the concept of illness is subjective. For example, many illnesses have obvious signs of an underlying physical problem, while others have no discernible symptoms, such as some types of benign tumours. People may describe themselves as 'being ill' when they see the doctor, but may have a 'disease' after consultation. 'Illness' is something they have; 'disease' is what their organs have. Individuals have their own perceptions and understanding of the origin of their illnesses. Their attempts to find meaning regarding their illnesses and, for example what the best source of treatment would be, are shaped by their particular understandings. The same ill health conditions and/or symptoms may therefore be interpreted differently by members of different cultures, and their responses to their experiences may also be quite different.

Lay perceptions of the causation of illness include the effects of poverty, poor home and working environments, infection by 'germs' and viruses, genetic predisposition, psychological stresses and strains and lack of 'moral fibre' (Blaxter 1983; Cornwell 1984; D'Houtaud and Field 1986). Prevention of ill health may be seen as a matter of individual discipline and control, except in cases of certain types of infection, and in chronic or inherited illness (Blaxter 1983; Helman 1981, 1986; D'Houtaud and Field 1986). Personal perceptions of risk may also be much influenced by lay health beliefs. Work by Warwick *et al.* (1988a, 1998b) explored how young people construct beliefs about AIDS and HIV infection in particular and health and illness in general. They found many misconceptions about HIV and AIDS, and showed how mainstream medical explanations may be insufficient to allay anxiety and help individuals to acquire a realistic perception of risk. Other studies have also looked at the sources of young people's beliefs about AIDS (Abrams *et al.* 1990; Abraham *et al.* 1991).

It has been suggested that there is growing popular dissatisfaction with biomedical practice in the West, as early successes in curing ill-health precipitated by infection have not been matched by successes in curing chronic ill-health (Bakx 1991). In addition, biomedical practice has been seen as a means of exercising professional power over lay people, with medical professionals also tending to differentiate how they perceive health and illness among men and women (Stacey 1986; 1988; Hillier 1986; Graham and Oakley 1985; Oakley 1993).

People's common-sense views of health may be reinforced by biomedical definitions of health. It has been argued by van Dalen *et al.* (1994) that while there was little social differentiation in concepts of health held in Britain, the biomedical model predominated, but over the last seventy years or so, biomedical viewpoints have moved away from a curative to a more preventive mode as certain types of behaviour were seen to be strongly associated with particular illness conditions. Thus the prevailing medical view today is that many deaths from these 'socially defined' conditions are preventable. For example, smoking is associated with various types of cancer, obesity with heart conditions and so on. As these views become known, they are adopted by ordinary people who modify their perceptions of health to include the notion of 'candidacy' (Davison *et al.* 1991). Davison *et al.* discussed the results of ethnographic research in which lay people identified candidates for heart attacks by making associations between their lifestyles and heart conditions:

> *He was a bugger for his fry-ups and his cream cakes, so he had to be well up for it, like.*
> (Davison *et al.* 1991: 8)

There was also discernible puzzlement when the candidacy explanation did not seem to fit:

> *Fit, skinny, young. The last person you'd expect to have a coronary.*
> (Davison *et al.* 1991:8)

Davison and his co-workers suggest that the development of lay beliefs is a collective activity with many sources of input. These include: the mass media; official bodies and government information; evidence from illness and deaths within the family and among friends, neighbours and colleagues; and deaths of celebrities whose demise is very well publicised and discussed. This has potential for influencing lay beliefs in terms of health promotion and health education.

Backett *et al.* (1994) explored people's evaluation of health and healthy lifestyle through analysing the findings from three qualitative social science projects. They believe that the evidence that many people tend to ignore 'healthy lifestyle' advice indicates that more needs to be known about how relatively simple health promotion messages are understood and evaluated by the lay public. They suggested that lay evaluation processes use subtle ideas of balance to weigh up the desirability of behavioural change and that the practice of trading-off positive and negative aspects of health-related behaviour is widespread. There are important differences between lay people and health professionals and scientists in the ways they weigh up evidence on health. For the lay person, health and illness evaluation is inseparable from social and cultural experience. Although people tend to talk about illness and health in ways which parallel that of the biomedical mode, the logic by which they approach it is more rooted in socio-economic models (Blaxter 1983; Cornwell 1984). Some ethnic groups embrace models of health and illness that include symbolic, kinship, witchcraft/magical, and religious models of health and illness (Kleinman 1986; Herzlich and Pierret 1986; Lewis 1986; Young 1986).

Similarly, Rogers *et al.* (1996), in their work on families and mental health, discuss the issue of how lay people understand what mental health is and what causes it, and note how in contrast to some health professionals, they tend to attribute mental health problems to social conditions and family variables. People's private and public accounts of emotional issues, and the difference in type and style of language, can create a barrier between lay and professional understandings.

An examination of lay beliefs and decisions about medical treatment led Donovan and Blake (1992) to observe that a large number of patients are non-compliant about the medical advice or instructions they receive. They queried the concept of compliance in this context and noted how patients carry out a cost-benefit analysis of each treatment, weighing up the costs and risks against the benefits as they perceive them. Their perception and the social circumstances within which they lived were shown to be crucial to their decision-making. Therefore what may appear to a doctor to be an irrational act of non-compliance may be a very rational action from the patient's point of view and this has implications for doctor–patient communication and interaction. Forrest (1995) also noted the rational nature of the reasons held by a group of mothers in her study who had refused vaccination for their children, and how pressures to conform tended to alienate them from their GPs and lead them to seek alternative support and advice.

In considering people's lay beliefs and the ways that they reach decisions about their own health and health behaviour, health education has to take account of various theories and approaches, and most health promotion is based on some model of behaviour change. One of these is the Health Beliefs Model (Becker 1974), which sees individual decisions to take preventative health action as dependent on the perception of a number of factors, such as the seriousness of the disease and their susceptibility to it, and also the costs and benefits involved. Others include the Health Action Model (Tones 1987) and the Theory of Reasoned Action (Ajzen and Fishbein 1980) which focus on additional factors in health decision-making processes, such as a motivational system of values and drives. Another approach that has proved popular is the Stages of Change Model (Prochaska and Di Clemente 1984) which looks at how change happens at an individual level. It suggests that there are several distinct stages that a person may pass through when altering health behaviour such as smoking. These are: pre-contemplation; contemplation; preparation; action; maintenance; and relapse. Evidence suggests that individuals may stay in any stage for a different length of time, but that every stage is gone through at some time. Furthermore, Prochaska and Di Clemente build into this model the possibility that having made the change, an individual may well relapse, but this forms part of the learning process about themselves and their behaviour, and the next time will afford a greater chance of success.

PUBLIC AND PRIVATE DOMAINS OF HEALTH

Primary health care goes on extensively inside and outside the home, in both the private and the public domains. Although men clearly have an important role as doctors, male nurses, other roles within the health service, and as fathers in the family, it is still the case that women have the major role in health care and health education. Women's roles in the public domain, such as in hospitals, echo their roles in their homes and families, as carers of personal and public health concerns (Oakley 1994; Graham 1984) In addition, the main responsibility for caring for the sick and elderly falls to women. Wives/partners and mothers are seen as the primary source of socialisation for other family members in the development of positive health strategies (Graham 1984; Mayall 1994) and may serve as models for their family's health behaviour and lifestyle. The labour of caring for a family may be sustained in various ways to cope with the stress that may be involved, some of which may be harmful to health, such as the use of tobacco, alcohol and psychotropic drugs (Ettorre and Riska 1993; Graham, 1984).

The socialisation of children's understanding of the division of health care labour between themselves and others within the context of the home has been described in studies by Mayall (1994), Bendelow and Oakley (1993), and Oakley (1994). These studies of children's perceptions of health and illness have suggested that children as young as nine years old have recognised the roles of caring for others and making the home comfortable as essentially female (Mayall 1994). Gender differences are also evident with respect to perceived health risks, with boys focusing on lifestyle factors whereas girls, who tended to have more health concerns, combined lifestyle with other factors ranging from homelessness to nuclear war (Oakley 1994; Bendelow and Oakley 1993). This was also seen in a study on young people and family health which found that young men were more likely than young women to see health as being a matter of individual control (Brannen *et al.* 1994).

In the public domain of health, men have traditionally occupied the higher medical occupations, as doctors, medical consultants and specialists, although the number of women doctors has increased considerably and continues to do so. While it is true that family health concerns are primarily the perogative of mothers, men as fathers have an increasingly important and changing role to play (Lewis and O'Brien 1987; Sharpe 1994; Fulop 1992). Outside the home, men's health is often threatened through the conditions and hazards in the workplace, particularly in manual and industrial occupations. As described in Chapter 13, the 'unhealthy' characteristics of macho lifestyle behaviours related, for instance, to alcohol, drugs, accidents, and violent incidents or crimes, and the effects of unemployment on their mental state, are increasing health risk factors for men.

3. Families and health variations

In the 1980s, a new public health movement concerned with the effects of the social environment on physical and mental health drew attention to factors which were largely beyond individual control, and which highlighted important health issues beyond that of the provision of services (Martin and McQueen 1989). This section focuses on health inequalities in families, with particular reference to gender, class and ethnic differences, and variations in accessing health services.

HEALTH INEQUALITIES

Social differentials in health and life expectancy have been documented since official statistics were published 150 years ago. Despite many social changes, it has been of great concern to find that not only do these large and systematic differences still exist between social groups, but that these gaps are widening (Marmot and McDowell 1986; Marmot 1994; Phillimore *et al.* 1994; McLoone and Boddy 1994; HEA 1995d; DOH 1995). They also vary geographically and, for instance, the North of England has a higher mortality rate than the South, especially for certain illnesses (Eames *et al.* 1993). Such inequalities in health are correlated with and caused by poverty and related social conditions such as housing (Townsend and Davidson 1982; Whitehead 1987). These differences are reflected in perinatal, neonatal, infancy, childhood and adult mortality rates for different classes and racial groups: for example, men and women of occupational class V are more likely to die before retirement age than their counterparts in occupational class I (Balarajan 1991; OPCS 1990a; OPCS 1991a; OPCS 1992a). Furthermore, unemployed people in social classes IV and V also have higher mortality and morbidity rates than the unemployed in higher occupational class groups (Moser *et al.* 1986a, 1986b; Balarajan 1991; Balarajan *et al.* 1991; OPCS 1990a; OPCS 1992a).

Social class

Socio-economic status, as measured by occupation, class, assets (such as house and car ownership) or employment, is associated with almost all health outcomes (Townsend and Davidson 1982; Whitehead 1988). There are strong associations between high mortality rates and poor countries, while within more affluent countries income disparity and unemployment are associated with high mortality and morbidity (Power 1994; Morris *et al.* 1994). In Britain, increased mortality rates between the 1981 and 1991 censuses have been linked to relative poverty (McLoone and Boddy 1994; Sloggett and Joshi 1994). The Black Report (Townsend and Davidson 1982) proposed four types of explanations for social class differences in mortality: artefactual, social selection, behavioural or cultural, and material circumstances. Most evidence has found the first two to be weak influences on this class effect (Fox *et al.* 1985; Goldblatt 1989; Davey Smith *et al.* 1994). Harding (1995) claims that the persistence of a class gradient at all ages and for a range of causes of death suggests that a broader approach is needed, and argues for an explanation of class differences based on an interaction of socio-economic, behavioural and psychosocial factors over the life course in promoting these outcomes (MacIntyre1994).

It is therefore clear that people occupying the lower levels of occupational class experience higher rates of death and ill-health. The Registrar General's Classification of occupations is a crude measure of social class, but despite its occupational and gender bias, it appears to reflect pervasive health differences in the population (Cameron and Jones 1984; MacIntyre 1986, 1994). Blaxter (1990) used data from the Health and Lifestyle Survey and found that social circumstances are more important than lifestyle habits in determining health. Work by other researchers including Graham (1984), Davey Smith *et al.* (1990), Packer *et al.* (1994) and Phillimore *et al.* (1994) have confirmed Blaxter's findings. However, health professionals have still tended to concentrate on behavioural explanations for health differentials (Davey Smith *et al.* 1990; Townsend *et al.* 1988).

MacIntyre argues that socio-economic differentials in health exist in all societies and are apparent throughout the social scale. She further argues that this suggests that there is no threshold of absolute deprivation below which people have more ill-health, but rather that there is a linear relationship between socio-economic circumstances and health even among the better-off (MacIntyre 1994). A study of Whitehall civil servants carried out by Marmot *et al.* (1993) also demonstrated such health differentials. This research showed that socio-economic differences in health status within this group persisted over a twenty-year period. An inverse association was found between employment grade and prevalence of angina, electro-cardiogram evidence of ischaemia, and symptoms of chronic bronchitis.

Children in low-income families and in single-parent families have significant health problems. Early effects of poverty on their health include higher neonatal and post-neonatal mortality, lower birthweight, and a higher incidence of infectious illness, accidents and dietary deficiencies than that seen for children whose family income is higher (Allen 1994). Children and their families in these cases may also have poorer access to health care (Thorogood *et al.* 1993; Vineis *et al.* 1993). There are further implications for long-term health and development as poor families have limited access to resources which help to maintain good health in families (Allen 1994; Bartley *et al.* 1994). A longitudinal analysis of birthweight from the 1958 British cohort study found a link between low birthweight and a number of health problems in adulthood (Bartley et al 1994). In adolescence, things are not quite so clear-cut in the sense that some research findings point to a lack of class differences in health during this time (West 1988; West *et al.* 1990), and it has been suggested that for teenagers, family functioning, family culture and parenting styles may be more important factors (Brannen *et al.* 1994; Sweeting and West 1995).

Gender

In industrialised countries, women live longer than men and have a lower mortality rate in all age groups. In Britain there are differences in the way women use the National Health Service (NHS). They make more use than men of the NHS for a number of reasons, which are usually related to their role as mothers and their responsibilities for family health. In terms of class, there is evidence of marked differences in women's use of GP services, in-patient and out-patient hospital facilities, and preventive services (Townsend and Davidson 1986; Doyal 1985, 1995). The NHS has not equalised women's access to medical care (Doyal 1985, 1995).

Although men are at risk from a large range of illnesses and their life expectancy is well known to be lower than women's (Calman 1993; Waldron 1993; Craig 1995), men are generally less concerned with their own health, and less willing to ask for help, or to go and see the doctor than women. Masculinity and the male gender role has been shown to contribute to this and to other ways that men use the health services differently to women, such as being slower to take up medical services (Blaxter 1990). (Aspects of men's health are examined separately in Chapter 13.)

Despite the fact that they live longer than men, women are more likely to suffer from both acute and chronic ill-health (Graham 1984; Whitehead 1988). Housing conditions, dampness, overcrowding and a lack of basic amenities have all been identified as factors which create health problems in general, but especially for women and young children (Packer *et al.* 1994; McLoone and Boddy 1994; Phillimore *et al.* 1994; Power 1994; Bartley *et al.* 1992; Arber 1991; Popay *et al.* 1993). Women who are economically inactive may see themselves as being less healthy than women in paid work, although the reverse was found for lone mothers who were in paid employment (Macran *et al.* 1994; Arber *et al.* 1985). Macran *et al.* (1994) also found that working men in the household may inadvertently take dangerous substances from the workplace to the home. Domestic violence, usually occurring against women or children is also a potential source of physical and emotional damage (Graham 1984; Leonard and Delphy 1992; Gelles 1994).

Research has looked at the influence of paid and unpaid work on women's health, and Oakley argued that being a 'captive wife or mother' can seriously undermine women's health, as new mothers who were previously publicly employed had to abandon many activities when the baby arrived (Oakley 1980). This loss of 'place in the public domain' meant that childbirth was also seen as bereavement. However, the alternative of retaining paid work and combining it with the unpaid posts of wife and mother placed another set of strains on women's mental and physical health as their capacity for leisure activity diminished. In the area of drug use, some researchers (Ettore and Riska 1993; Etorre 1992) have suggested that women's use of psychotropic drugs has been seen as more of a social problem than men's use of drugs because it implies instability in the family (Ettore and Riska 1993).

Studies of the family have shown that both men and women suffer from mental stress but that it has tended to originate from different sources. Men's anxieties are more based on concern with work and keeping a job, or with actually being unemployed (Briscoe 1989; Lewis 1988), while women's stress factors are more often from childcare, housing and money worries (Holland *et al.* 1996). Several studies have examined how women cope with the stress of caring for the family while often striving to ensure good health for family members on a limited budget. To make their lives easier, women with young children may rely on strategies which go against health advice. For example, sweets may to be used to keep children quiet on shopping trips and during other stressful occasions, breastfeeding may be abandoned to allow more time for other members of the family, and babies' milk may be mixed with cereal to help cope with crying and sleep problems (Charles and Kerr 1985). Cigarette smoking is used by some mothers with young children as a way of easing tension in the home, especially if they are on low incomes (Jacobson 1986; Popay and Bartley 1989; Graham 1992, 1993a). Graham points out that contradictory health actions may be the only way mothers can stay sane and act responsibly towards their family. Such studies illustrate a complex relationship between individual behaviour and structural and material factors in family health. It is not just adult men and women who suffer from stress. Levels of stress in adolescents have increased over recent years (Rutter and Smith 1995) and, for example, research by Sweeting and West (1995) suggests that family conflict has a greater negative effect on teenage girls' health and self-esteem than on that of boys.

Ethnicity

It is beyond the scope of this review to deal with all aspects of ethnicity and health. However, there are a number of important issues related to families, communication and health among different ethnic groups. In 1993 the Department of Health issued guidance to purchasers, looking at key health promotion targets in relation to minority ethnic groups (DoH 1993). The health targets outlined in *The Health of the Nation* which focus on coronary heart disease and stroke, cancers, mental illness, HIV/AIDS and sexual health, and accidents pose considerable but not uniform risks for ethnic minority groups (DHSS 1992). African–Caribbeans are at greater risk from strokes, and men and women born in the Asian sub-continent have a significantly higher mortality rate from coronary heart disease (Balarajan and Raleigh 1993). African–Caribbeans are also 3–6 times more likely than whites to be diagnosed as schizophrenic (DOH 1995). Early literature on black families and health focused on ill-health conditions affecting black and minority ethnic communities such as blood- and diet-related illness (Douglas 1992).

The first *Black and Minority Ethnic Groups Health and Lifestyles Survey* was set up to examine factors contributing to health status, and to assess health needs and barriers to maintaining good health among ethnic minority groups (HEA 1994a; see also HEA 1994b, 1995c). A second *Black and Minority Ethnic Groups Health and Lifestyles Survey* focused on risk factors associated with cardiovascular disease. The survey assesses knowledge, attitudes and behaviour concerning physical activity, diet, weight and smoking, and results will be available in 1996. Findings from several qualitative studies commissioned by the

HEA to examine health beliefs about coronary heart disease among the South Asian population will also be available in 1996. Other recent research on ethnicity and health is reviewed by Ahmad and Chaplin (1994).

While ethnicity is increasingly used as a variable in epidemiological research there are serious problems in its use (Bhopal *et al.* 1991; Senior and Bhopal 1994; Sheldon and Parker 1994; Bradby 1995). Difficulties include problems to do with the classification and heterogenity of the study populations, lack of clarity about the purpose of research and ethnocentrism affecting the use and interpretation of the data (Senior and Bhopal 1994). Some studies have been mainly descriptive and have not been used to develop and evaluate strategies to improve health care (Sheldon and Parker 1994). Research into the health of minority ethnic groups is often restricted by methodological difficulties. Chaturvedi and McKeigue (1994) review the available sources of mortality and morbidity data and assess their uses and limitations for research involving minority ethnic groups.

Many studies of ethnic differences have addressed the links between poverty, racism, cultural difference and admission rates to psychiatric hospitals which are higher for African–Caribbeans than for other population groups (Littlewood and Cross 1980; Littlewood and Lipsedge 1982; Knight 1982; Ineichen 1986). Other research has focused on the higher mortality and perinatal mortality rates for black women from Africa, the Caribbean and Indian subcontinent than for white Britons (Marmot *et al.* 1983, 1984; Townsend and Davidson 1986; Whitehead 1988). There is a paucity of data on morbidity rates of black people which makes it difficult to compare ill-health amongst this group generally with the ethnic majority population (Whitehead 1988). Furthermore, it may be that black children have a higher than average morbidity associated with material deprivation (Amin 1992).

There are variations in the uptake and effectiveness of services: socially disadvantaged groups and ethnic minority members make less use of preventive services – immunisation, cervical screening, antenatal care – and survival rates from some conditions are poorer among socially disadvantaged groups (Leon and Wilkinson 1989; Kogevinas 1990). While some work has examined poor access to services – language barriers, lack of public transport and inconvenient opening hours – there has been little analysis of class or of links between the economic status of black communities and poor health (Torkington 1991; Amin 1992). Access to appropriate health care for members of minority ethnic groups may also be hindered by racism (Wilson 1983; Mares *et al.* 1985). Research also shows clear links between cultural attitudes to health and low use of health services (Douglas 1992; Forna 1992; Dickinson and Bhatt 1994). Studies on the uptake of breast screening by Asian, Chinese and African–Caribbean women suggested that transient populations, length of residence in the UK and family attitudes were factors influencing the use of screening services (McAllister and Bowling 1993; Hoare *et al.* 1994). Recent research on Chinese people in Britain suggested that emergency services are used more than primary care and preventive health services (Watt *et al.* 1993).

The problems that many Asian mothers had in making use of the health services were highlighted in the 'Stop Rickets' campaign launched in 1979. This led to a Department of Health/Save the Children Fund initiative to improve the health of

Asian mothers and babies via the launch of The Asian Mother and Baby Campaign (AMBC) in 1984 (DHSS 1987; Rocheron 1988; Rocheron *et al.* 1989). This campaign aimed to encourage early diagnosis of pregnancy and uptake of maternity services, improve communication between mothers and health professionals, help health professionals gain the co-operation of Asian families, help Asian families to become more aware of the services and to ensure that the services provided are accessible and acceptable. It achieved only limited success (Rocheron and Dickinson 1990). Research on ethnicity and health has to take account of specific family and cultural beliefs and practices to be relevant. For instance, the relative cohesiveness of Asian families, and their sensitive attitudes to health issues such as sexuality and sex education (Holland 1993a) through religious or cultural beliefs, will affect the outcomes of any intervention. Therefore communication within the family will also be tempered in both process and content by these and other factors, such as gender roles and parenting styles.

A number of intervention studies have incorporated some cultural considerations in their approach (McAvoy and Raza 1991; Jemmott and Jemmott 1992; Quirk *et al.* 1993; Hoare *et al.* 1994; Abdulrahim *et al.* 1994). McAvoy and Raza (1991) found that a recognisably Muslim assistant had some success in improving the uptake of cervical cancer screening among women of New Commonwealth and Pakistani descent whom she visited at home. Videos and leaflets in appropriate languages were produced. Jemmott and Jemmott (1992) used the results of interviews with members of the target group when designing and developing their intervention. Quirk *et al.* (1993) evaluated an AIDS prevention programme which was given by a trained peer using a professionally produced rap video based on lyrics written and performed by local teenagers. However, Hoare *et al.* (1994) found that home visiting by Bangladeshi and Pakistani women to increase breast screening clinic attendance resulted in no improvement in uptake rates compared to the control group.

Several projects have examined ways of meeting the needs of minority ethnic groups through experiments in health advocacy. One project carried out in Hackney had similar aims to the AMBC and focused on the needs of Asian and Turkish women (Cornwell and Gordon 1984). The advocates had very clearly defined roles which included giving 'health education and antenatal talks, taking information when women first booked in, staying with women who had difficult labours and a range of other activities' (Watson 1984), and the project achieved some success (Parsons and Day 1992). While changes cannot be directly attributed to health advocacy, improved communication could have improved clinical practice.

Results from the Bristol Inner City Health Project and a series of linked interventions with Asian women are reported by Harding (1988a, 1988b, 1989). Harding documents a multi-stage evaluation of an Asian Women's Group during a one-year pilot programme in order to enable them to continue with a sewing class and to develop health promotion. Beneficial outcomes for the women included: greater knowledge about health services, reduced social isolation, increased confidence and greater visibility for Asian women and children's health issues (Harding 1998a). Another scheme piloted 'patient-led advocacy' in order to extend an existing interpreting and advocacy service to non-English-speaking women using ante- and post-natal clinics at a health centre (Harding 1988b). A third project set up and evaluated an Asian self-help group for families of children with special needs, and showed that parents gained knowledge and self-confidence in dealing with their children's needs (Harding 1989).

Research indicates that a range of issues need to be addressed regarding ethnicity and health. More research is especially needed into communication patterns in families from a wide range of cultural and ethnic backgrounds. Cultural considerations are key to all health promotion and interventions targeted at the family.

Family status

There is evidence to suggest that married men are significantly more healthy than single men while the reverse seems to be the case for women (Miles 1991). Relatively little research has been conducted on the health or health care within single-parent families (Mayall and Watson 1989). Children in one-parent families have a higher rate of hospitalisation, a higher GP consultation rate and have more health problems than children in two-parent families (Jennings and Sheldon 1985; Burghes 1994). In addition, insecurity around housing, financial pressure, lack of adult company at home and the burden of bringing up children alone, all contribute to the stress of being a single parent (Miles 1991).

SOURCES OF INFORMATION ABOUT HEALTH

In the last two decades there have been considerable changes in people's attitudes to health. The 'health revolution' has led to an increased awareness of health issues and to more and better informed individuals (Eshuys *et al.* 1990). An increasing lay network of health advice has also developed, and lay referral systems operate alongside official channels of health communication. Moreover, the increasing profile that complementary medicine (such as homeopathy, herbalism, acupuncture, osteopathy) is taking through both personal and doctors' recommendations is giving people a sense of more choice, control and even understanding in relation to their health treatment, although this is not a course open to everyone because of the financial costs involved (West 1990; Sharma 1991; BMA 1992).

Health promotion and research in the family

Health promotion and health education have focused on a wide variety of areas. The HEA *Health and Lifestyle Surveys* have been used, along with other national and regional surveys, to look at health issues and assess needs. The HEA *Health and Lifestyle Survey* (HEA 1995d) was geared to the targets for health improvement specified in the government White Paper The Health of the Nation (1992), which focused on key areas of: coronary heart disease and strokes; cancers; mental illness; HIV/AIDS and sexual health; and accidents. A family health research programme commissioned by the HEA includes several projects that explore how the family might be used more effectively as a vehicle in health education (Holland *et al.* 1996; Brannen and Storey 1996; Prout 1996; Rogers *et al.* 1996; Brynin and Scott forthcoming 1996; Beattie *et al.* forthcoming 1996).

Health messages are relayed through a number of settings (such as home, workplace, school), and are generally aimed at changing people's health behaviour and lifestyles. Research and campaigns have targeted the family, frequently via mothers in their role as gatekeepers of family health (Doherty and Campbell 1988). Certain family health promotion programmes have targeted women specifically, for example, in relation to: pregnancy, to help to produce healthy infants; infectious disease control and child care; the prevention of children's accidents; teaching children healthy behaviours; and providing them and their husbands with 'healthy' foods in order to reduce coronary heart disease and some cancers (Garcia *et al.* 1994; Amos 1993; Towner *et al.* 1993). This may place heavy responsibilities on women which do not take the nature of their social and economic conditions into account (Amos 1993; Rose 1990; Graham 1988; Ruzek 1987).

Health messages

Most people understand that risk-taking behaviour and lifestyles can contribute to ill health and this concept has widespread public support (Graham 1990). However, it is also well known that health messages are not always acted upon. Backett *et al.* (1994) looked at the way that patients perceived the desirability of behavioural change and noted important differences in how they weigh up evidence on health compared with the ways health professionals and scientists do so. This is relevant for understanding the ways that health messages are received and perceived by the general public. Where people indulge in 'risky' health behaviour as expressed in certain lifestyles in which smoking, drinking, and drug taking are the norm, health messages will be processed according to how they fit in with other social and cultural experiences.

A lot of health education research and promotion examines how and where people access health information and the effectiveness of these sources. Most commonly identified sources include the media – television, magazines and newspapers (especially for food and health), books, health professionals, family, friends and personal experience (HEA 1989). Television is frequently cited as the most useful source of information about a range of health topics including health and fitness and preparation for parenthood (Eadie and Leathar 1988; Prendergast and Prout 1987). Prendergast and Prout reviewed parenthood education in secondary schools and found that pupils obtained much of their knowledge on birth, fertility, incest, baby battering and divorce from television programmes. They argued that television offered up-to-date information, different viewpoints and stimulated discussion, and concluded that: 'So much is said against television that we may actually forget its potential and actual value as an educational resource' (Prendergast and Prout 1987:155).

Recent new contracts for GPs include giving them greater health education and preventative responsibilities, although some may argue that doctors are inappropriate as health educators because of their emphasis on curative rather than preventive measures (Calnan and Johnson 1983; Chew 1986). There is some evidence of differences between patients' ideas and beliefs and those of their doctors (Wallace and Haines 1984). Discrepancies between patients' expectations and perceptions of GPs' interests were also evident for smoking, drinking and weight (Campbell *et al.* 1985). Furthermore, a study on food and low-income groups found that doctors were rarely mentioned as direct sources of information on healthy eating (HEA 1989).

Dissemination of health messages

The main vehicle for health messages has been through health education promotional programmes. The Health Education Authority and regional health authorities have run campaigns around healthy eating ('Food for Health'), drinking ('Drinkwise'), smoking ('No Smoking Day'), AIDS ('National AIDS Week'), dental health ('National Smile Week') and exercise (Spray and Greenwood 1989). Schools have been targeted as sites for the promotion of 'healthy' behaviour, and school-based alcohol education programmes have used young people's own language and relevant experiences (Tacade 1985). Workplaces and primary health care settings are also important for disseminating health education messages.

USE OF HEALTH SERVICES

The quality of services provided and low take-up rate are two problems of health service use, for instance, in family planning, antenatal and postnatal care. Evidence shows that social groups who have the greatest need for such services use them the least, and in the case of antenatal care, these people are the most likely to be late attenders. Work by Green and France-Dawson (1993) has suggested that late referrals to antenatal booking clinics may be a problem for some minority ethnic groups.

Other factors that contribute to under-use of health services include access to clinics, insensitivity of health staff, especially to the particular needs of different ethnic communities, poor provision for the homeless and problems with transport to and from clinics (Townsend and Davidson 1986; Conway 1988; Whitehead 1988; Torkington 1991).

The evidence shows that inequalities in health care are associated with class, gender and race, and affect certain groups more than others. For example, one-parent families could benefit from access to health promotion and other health services. More attention is beginning to be paid to health-related issues in families from minority ethnic backgrounds, and an HEA (1994a) research programme to assess the knowledge, attitudes, behaviours and health status of the five largest minority groups in England (African–Caribbeans; Bangladeshis; Indians/East African Asians; Pakistanis; and Black Africans) has revealed important differences in health status and lifestyle between different ethnic groups. The relatively high proportion who describe their health status as poor, compared to the general UK population, highlights the need to tailor health education and services in ways that will better reach and serve these groups.

4. Methodologies used in family research

Research into family health issues has used a wide variety of methodologies, depending on the assumptions made and the sort of information required. Different approaches are appropriate for different health topics, such as the collection of frequency data on people's attitudes and health behaviours, to a more in-depth look at family dynamics and individual psychological processes This section examines some of the methodological approaches used in family research, many of which are common to research in general; and some of the issues involved, such as the difficulty of negotiating access, managing 'sensitive' topics; the relationship between participant and researcher; and finding a 'shared' vocabulary (Fitzpatrick 1988a; Noller and Callan 1991).

The methods used to access family discourses on health have encompassed the disciplines of sociology, psychology, and ethnography. In general, research tends to have either a quantitative or a qualitative emphasis, that is, either a collection of data using a questionnaire design which defines or delimits the information but grants the greater reliability generated by large numbers, or a more in-depth study, often involving interviews, which looks at smaller samples or case histories to explore and analyse the processes involved. Some studies, however, have found it more fruitful to adopt a mixed-method approach.

The choice of sample size depends on whether the project adopts a quantitative or qualitative methodology. It may vary between large-scale surveys, small samples and individual families for case studies. Larger samples are necessary for demonstrating links between variables and are essential for proving the generality of principles (Hinde and Hinde 1988). However, although the effects may be statistically significant they may explain little of the variance. Small samples can be useful for exploring the importance of specific variables and for studying processes. It may also be possible to expose family processes more readily by studying extreme groups, exaggerating differences. 'Extreme groups' can provide principles which would be more difficult to detect in a more homogeneous sample and it may be possible to apply data collected for generalisations to 'more normal families' (Hinde and Hinde 1988).

QUALITATIVE METHODOLOGY

Qualitative work enlivens and illuminates the material provided by surveys and facilitates exploration of social phenomena (Roche 1991). These methods access indirect and non-verbal family discourses rather than specific attitudes and behaviours in the general population. They are especially suitable for studying processes and provide scope for internal corroboration of accounts. While a small homogeneous sample raises questions of validity, a very high response rate can enhance the internal validity compared to large surveys which have low response rates (Kotva and Schneider 1990).

Present-day social epidemiology consists mainly of surveys of people's health experiences. More subjective approaches are now being explored which include participant observation, life histories, case studies, semi-structured and unstructured interviews. An advantage of these methods is that they are more sensitive to influences on behaviour, provide a complex look at a complex world, avoid over-simplification, favour the perspective, knowledge and understanding of the participant, and can be highly creative for collecting and interpreting data (Callan and Noller 1987). Qualitative research methods are particularly appropriate to family research and to studying sensitive issues. They may be able to penetrate the 'public discourse', unravelling some of the inherent contradictions of family life. They are very suitable for studying children, and as no single method is appropriate for this, several instruments have to be designed to accommodate specific age groups according to their varying levels of verbal expression (Kreppner 1988).

There are various methods involved in qualitative research, and the main ones described here include: participant observation; interviews; focus groups; diaries; documents, oral and life histories, stories and drama role plays; visual techniques; and telephone interviews.

Participant observation

Participant observation includes a wide range of roles and activities – from total participation to total observation – and various forms of involvement – from overt to covert. Many researchers combine participant observation with interviews to compare parents' accounts of how they behave, with their actual behaviour. Data may be collected by making notes, recording interactions or writing summaries (Callan and Noller 1987). Participant observation enables researchers to record the research process, such as negotiating access, establishing trust and parents' and children's reactions. However, the issue of the nature of the researcher's role in observation work remains unresolved (Bell and Roberts 1984). One example of participant observation might be to live in the family home or to attend a child clinic to watch how adults and children interact (Kreppner 1988).

Observation is best suited to analysing the operation of family decision-making processes (Gudykunst *et al.* 1988). Families can be videotaped while performing a decision-making task (planning a holiday for instance) and the tapes then coded (Noller and Callan 1991). Timed observation has been used by family researchers (Brannen *et al.* 1991; Elkes and Crocitto 1987). One disadvantage of this method lies in proving its validity, since 5–10 minute staged behaviour interactions have been questioned as accurate representations of authentic behaviours (Noller and Callan 1991).

Interviews

Interviews are usually intensive or in-depth, last quite a long time, and require a rapport to develop between the interviewer and the interviewee. As the interview progresses, trust can lead to the disclosure of intimate details by the interviewee thus contributing to social knowledge. The in-depth interview is generally semi-structured or unstructured, and follows an interview guide rather than a strict question-and-answer format (Dodd 1991; Elkes and Crocitto 1987). The advantage of the interview guide is that it lets participants set the agenda (Thomson and Scott 1990; Oakley 1980). This format was appropriate, for instance, when Wheelock (1990) interviewed couples together about the domestic role of men, and Callan (1985) interviewed couples in their homes over nine years on voluntary and involuntary childlessness.

In-depth interviews are appropriate for the exploration of individual experiences. They are useful for the representation of subjectivity within academic discourse, and the facilitation of a non-hierarchical organisation of the research process (Oakley 1990). For example, Klesse and Sontag (1989) interviewed working-class mothers about their health motives and behaviour in everyday life in order to develop a 'health biography'. This approach allowed the researchers to access perceptions and information about health without being perceived as monitoring or policing individuals' health behaviours.

Interviewing in itself can have a supportive effect for participants (Finch 1984; Oakley 1990; Holland 1992). Oakley (1981) has argued that the boundaries between friendship, counselling, advisory education and interviewing cannot be clearly drawn. Some women of varying ages have indicated that the contact with the researcher broke the isolation of life at home (Oakley 1981; Finch 1984). This kind of interview, being informal, spontaneous and exploratory, can serve a therapeutic purpose. However, clear boundaries need to be established between researcher and those researched to protect both parties avoid raising false expectations.

Interviewing children
In-depth interviews can be one of the most fruitful methods for eliciting ideas, attitudes and information from children, along with participant observation (Mauthner, forthcoming). Within a long-term, in-depth study of family health, Backett and Alexander (1991) interviewed children aged 4–12 years in their homes, using creative techniques appropriate to their ages. Backett and Alexander also used nine different methods to prompt children to talk about health, including drawing, direct and indirect questions, and projective techniques. The drawing activity was based on the HEA Primary Schools Project 'Draw and Write Technique' and created a rapport at the start of the interview (Williams and Moon 1987). According to Backett and Alexander, the most useful techniques were the direct and indirect questions about self, peers and parents. They found that children had a wide-ranging view of health, although younger children tended to find the concept of health difficult, and made decisions based on preference. One unresolved issue was the fact that many health-related activities are done to and for them.

Interviews about sensitive health issues

Social research often involves exploring 'sensitive' subjects (Brannen 1988). A number of studies on sexual issues, for instance, have encountered this aspect of research. Warwick *et al.* (1988a; 1988b) combined semi-structured interviews with group interviews to examine lay beliefs about HIV infection and AIDS. In their study of young women's sexuality the Women's Risk and AIDS project (WRAP) team found that the interviews often took different forms. Thomson and Scott (1990) identified three types of 'social events' for what they call 'the management of taboo' or talking about a 'sensitive' area. These are the confessional type where admissions are made and moral guidance is sought, the doctor/patient type where the interviewer is treated as an expert, and the therapy/counselling type where the participant works out difficulties through rooting them in past experience. The interviews led the team to look at how young people talk about their sexuality and present their sexual identities. This process exposed contradictions in young women's experience of sexuality, in the labelling process and in their own evaluation of their experience. Thomson and Scott (1990) argue that this is more likely to produce valid knowledge than more straightforward 'factual' accounts. The interviews often enabled participants to evaluate their experiences which sometimes became part of the learning experience. Not only do interviews structured in this way give the participants a voice, they also contribute to the richness and depth of the data, revealing the complexities of sexual practices as well as their meanings.

Dyads and triads

Interviews tend to be conducted individually and it is quite unusual to carry out paired interviews. Research on couples usually involves separate interviews with each member, and studies on parent–child communication on sex education are conducted similarly. Dodd (1991) interviewed parent–adolescent dyads, mainly in the home, for a study of how adolescents negotiate their responsibility for health with parents. Gjerde (1986) interviewed family members in dyads and triads. The aim of the study was to compare parent–adolescent interaction in the presence of one spouse (triad) and without the spouse present (dyad). The exception to individual, pair or triad interaction is in the therapy situation where a therapist might conduct sessions with individual family members or pairs as well as seeing whole families together (Warner 1981). Otherwise there are no accounts of interviewing whole households together (Nolin 1988).

Focus groups

The focus group is a fairly recent development in interview techniques, which has been described in the United States as 'popular epidemiology' (Brown 1990; Morgan 1986; Krueger 1994). Through the use of this form of group discussion, access is gained to 'delicate' material about 'sensitive' issues and validates participants' experience. Focus groups are often held before carrying out individual interviews, in order to elicit the most relevant concerns expressed by the group about the subject under question, which can then be focused on in more depth in an individual situation. They have been used by several researchers working with families (Roberts 1991).

As well as validating participants' experiences, focus groups allow the participant, rather than the researcher, to determine or shape the discussion. Thom and Edmondson's research (1989) on women substance users used unstructured discussion groups enabling women of different cultural and ethnic backgrounds the freedom to define and elaborate on the issues they felt were the most relevant. Focus groups can also be used as a means of exchanging information and a forum for promoting attitude change. Boyle *et al.* (1989) who carried out discussion groups on 'health in the transition to the nineties' argued that these serve to increase individual participation, supplement passive mass health campaigns, and can act as a vehicle for health interventions. Within a study of family communication about sex, Nolin (1988) conducted small mixed discussion groups of adults, and of adolescents. Focus groups were useful to elicit information about boys' friendships, relationships and sexual behaviour in Wight's research (1991). He also observed how they talked to each other, and how the discussion groups created an atmosphere of trust before the boys were interviewed.

An extension of the focus group is memory work, in which respondents come together to analyse specific experiences. Kippax *et al.* (1990) used memory work to examine how women acted in sexual encounters. Participants wrote down their memories of episodes or events before discussing and theorising about them in a group.

Diaries

Asking participants in research projects to write diaries of their behaviour or attitudes over a specified period of time has been found to be especially appropriate for accessing 'sensitive' information. Some of the young women in the WRAP study of young women's negotiation of sexual experiences kept diaries of these events in their lives, in addition to questionnaires and interviews (Holland *et al.* 1990a; 1990b; 1991). Keeping a sexual diary was integral to Coxon's pioneering study (1989) of the sexual vocabularies of gay men, and has also been used to provide information about marital interactions (Dickson-Markman and Markman 1988). One drawback about using diaries is that participants may volunteer to keep them with some enthusiasm, but may not sustain doing so for very long, and therefore unless there is high personal commitment, there can be a low return.

Documents, oral and life histories, stories, drama role plays

Studies from a biographical perspective which take account of social processes in health and illness are slowly being developed. Family history archives are often combined with oral history or interviews. The problems with this approach include faulty recall, reliability and difficulties with organising the data. Mandelbaum (1982) suggests three ways of organising the data: 1) to focus on the personal/biological, cultural, social and psychological aspects; 2) to emphasise life transitions such as marriage, birth, illness and death or 3) to examine personal adaptations which arise from changing conditions in families and society. The changes that occur after such events can provide insights into the processes of the family lifespan (Hinde and Hinde 1988).

Graham (1984) took a biographical approach to health using story-telling. A rarely used method of drama role plays, on audio and videotape was used by Griffiths (1990) in her work with 13–14-year-old girls. She used a combination of dramatic improvisation, informal discussions and mother–daughter role plays to recreate adolescent experiences. The advantage of this 'collective story-telling' method is that it creates trust, is spontaneous, increases confidence and makes certain themes more immediate and accessible to young participants.

Visual techniques

Whereas visual materials such as television, family videos and photo albums have been little explored as prompts for initiating discussions around health in the family, some researchers have used video and/or audio recordings for analysing pair communication, counselling sessions and role plays. Dorval (1990) videotaped friends talking in same-sex dyads across a range of ages. He told them to consult each other and find a 'serious' topic to discuss. The gender differences in Dorval's videos were analysed by Tannen (1991), who noted differences between the male and female speakers in terms of content and body language.

Telephone

In some studies the telephone was used to collect data about frequency of conversation on certain topics over the past 24 hours. Family members were rung each night and asked to provide a list of their most recent conversations (Montemayor and Hanson 1985). In a study of parents, schools and sex education (NFER/HEA 1994), a follow-up telephone survey was carried out with parents to explore in greater depth the issues that had emerged from the earlier questionnaires that they had completed.

QUANTITATIVE METHODOLOGY

Quantitative methods, favoured by the psychological paradigm, include questionnaires, structured interviews, experiments, or coding and scoring of marital and family interactions. The focus is on objectivity and replicability. The researcher assigns counts or scores to observations or responses. Measures and procedures are objective in order to reduce the influence of the researcher's personal biases and values upon what is reported.

The information gathered in large-scale surveys can provide a context for subsequent more detailed qualitative work. Many studies rely on cross-sectional designs with fixed-response questions (Bowie and Ford 1989; Ford and Morgan 1989; MORI 1990; HEA 1992a, 1992b; Field *et al.* 1991). These kind of surveys have been well used to gather prevalence data on health behaviours such as smoking, drinking, physical activity, etc. However, they cannot be used to examine the nature and variation in the transmission process that stretches throughout the early years of a child's life. Furthermore, surveys institute the hegemony of the researcher over the researched and reduce personal experience to the anonymity of numbers (Oakley 1990). Longitudinal studies, such as repeating the survey research with either an equivalent group (such as an annual survey on attitudes of 15–16-year-olds at school), or following the same group through time (Brynin and Scott 1996), give some indication of the changes taking place, although they are more complicated and costly to implement.

Questionnaires

Surveys use questionnaires, which are self-administered, structured research instruments without the flexibility of the semi-structured or unstructured interviews and do not usually allow respondents to expand on certain topics. However, respondents have a greater say in deciding whether or not to participate. In the 1980s the survey was most popular data collection method in family studies. This method has been used to examine parent–child relationships, family power and violence, intra-family similarities in attitude and behaviour, marital quality, adolescent attitudes and behaviours on various health issues such as smoking, alcohol, diet, drugs, exercise and sexual activity (HEA 1992a, 1992b). They are cheaper to carry out than depth interviews, can elicit sensitive information, are easy to distribute and are less threatening for participants than other methods. Surveys can be used to measure attitudes, beliefs and values and they produce a large amount of data quickly, which can then be easily stored. They are used in all the national surveys of health-related behaviours done by census data-collecting organisations such as the Office of Population Censuses Surveys (OPCS).

An example of the different use of quantitative survey methods versus qualitative interview data can be drawn from research on smoking. Carrying out both self-completion questionnaires and interviews has been shown to elicit different reports of smoking behaviour from the same individual (Oakley *et al.* 1992). Thus although there are advantages in the use of large-scale surveys, they may provide only a limited picture of the smoking behaviour and characteristics of adults and children. It is generally too simplistic to infer causal links from survey data. Distributions and correlations do not reliably provide predictive relationships. This kind of information overlooks the complexities and irrationalities of everyday life, and the social context and psychological meanings attached to seemingly risky behaviours such as smoking, drinking or unprotected sex. While quantitative work is useful to examine broad trends, its use for looking at dynamic processes and social relationships that characterise people's lives is limited. According to Callan and Noller (1987) questionnaires are more useful for studying attitudes than behaviour.

The survey questionnaire is a very common research tool, and may be self-administered, or filled in by the researcher in a face-to-face situation. Questions are generally closed (respondents check off their chosen response), although some studies include a few open-ended questions which are categorised into some kind of quantifiable response scale later. Marriage and family researchers have developed a variety of scales to measure marital quality, love, trust in relationships, family power, family and marital systems and parent–child relationships (Olson and Rabunsky 1972; McDonald 1980). Questionnaires do not always have to be used on a large-scale basis, but are very useful for providing background information on the particular sample of people (family members, for instance) who are participating in a small-scale study. Questionnaires are also used in conjunction with observational methods to study spouse and family interaction, power in the family and parent–child relationships.

Self-administered questionnaires and scales are often used to measure parent–adolescent communication and to determine population norms before being compared with other published test norms (Barnes and Olson 1985; Youniss and Ketterlinus 1987; Elkes and Crocitto 1987). Questionnaires may consist of statements which are rated by participants and have been used to measure sexual attitudes, knowledge and behaviour, communication about sex and spouse communication (Sanders and Mullis 1988; Fisher 1987; Sanders and Mullis 1988; Wright *et al.* 1990; Fitzpatrick 1988a). They might include questions about the frequency of conversations between family members on various topics (Noller and Callan 1991) or on communication, information, and values and can be completed by young people and their parents (Warren and Neer 1986; Noller and Bagi 1985).

Brynin and Scott (1996) developed an innovative technique for quantitative interviews carried out with 11–15-year-olds. Questions were pre-recorded and children were provided with Walkmans to listen to the questionnaires. Responses were recorded on simple data sheets requiring low levels of literacy skills. Parents, if present, were not able to connect questions and answers, allowing the questionnaire to be carried out in confidence.

Self-report

A considerable amount of the literature on family communication about health and sexual health relies on self-report. For example, researchers have used self-report to study communication about sport (Biddle and Armstrong 1992) and alcohol consumption (Rowland and Maynard 1991). However, some studies have challenged its validity. There are problems of accuracy, and over- or under-estimation. For instance, in a study of alcohol use, Rowland and Maynard (1991) found that spouses tended to under-report alcohol consumption. It is also felt that young people are likely to under-report smoking and drinking because they perceive it to be socially unacceptable. However, other evidence does exist to suggest that adolescents do provide accurate reports of their smoking (Plant *et al.* 1985). In a study of self-perception, Noller and Bagi (1985) and Noller and Callan (1990) used the Parent–Adolescent Communication Inventory questionnaire to examine communication with the father alone, mother alone and both parents together.

Methods for studying interactions

Although most methods used to study interactions are qualitative, there are some quantitative methods that can be applied. These include self-report; repertory grids; coding of verbal and non-verbal behaviour from videotaped interactions; participant ratings; measuring physiological changes during interactions and comparing spouse interactions with others. Variables that have been measured in this way include problem-solving, conflict and anger, expressing emotion, controlling manoeuvres and 'talk-time' with the spouse or others (Noller and Fitzpatrick 1988).

MIXED-METHOD APPROACHES

Many health researchers have found it most fruitful to mix elements of qualitative and quantitative methods (Graham 1990; Finch and Mason 1993). Brannen *et al.* (1991) combined quantitative and qualitative methodologies in their longitudinal analysis of dual-earner households, social support and pregnancy, and adolescent health and parenting. There is no agreed best method for obtaining data on marriage and the family (Callan and Noller 1987). The methods chosen will depend on the research question, theoretical perspective, time and funds available, and the audience for which the findings are intended. Hogg *et al.* (1996) discuss the range of methodologies used in the HEA's Family Health Research Programme.

Generation studies

Some researchers have found multi-method approaches especially useful for studying and comparing different generations (Blaxter and Patterson 1982a); Finch and Mason 1993). Blaxter and Patterson's study (1982a) involved three generations of women and different methods were used for gathering data on health and social histories. These included self-reported data from mothers during a six-month longitudinal study of families' health; visits to collect demographic data; conducting discussions and limited observation work; examining children's health records; interviews with health visitors; interviews with the mothers and grandmothers; and data from an earlier study (Thompson and Illsley 1969) in which two-thirds of the grandmothers had taken part, used as independent data on the older generation's health behaviour. In a study of the links between affection and health, Silverstein and Bengtson (1991) mailed a questionnaire to three generations of the same families, who were studied over a 14-year period.

Communication studies

In a study of family communication, Holland *et al.* (1996) used a semi-structured questionnaire, self-report communication inventories, individual depth interviews and family groups interviews. Nolin (1988) combined a questionnaire and interviews in her study of parent–child communication about sex. Dickson-Markman and Markman (1988) used several different methodologies for their three studies of how friends and family affect couples' relationships, including self-report and diaries, and a longitudinal analysis of relationship development.

Noller and Callan (1991) used three methods for studying communication patterns: self-report questionnaires, diaries of conversations, and telephone check-ups. These methods require collecting data over time. Wright *et al.* (1990) has also emphasised the need for more longitudinal research in this area. In addition, some of the more experimental methods such as video, together with focus group discussions, might be usefully combined with single and pair depth interviews. There are many possibilities, and from a study of group work, Butler and Wintram have concluded that there is 'no one correct method, no one norm' (Butler and Wintram 1991).

METHODOLOGICAL ISSUES

After deciding on the appropriate methodology to use, there are still a few potential obstacles to overcome and decisions to be made. These include: negotiating access to the people being researched; finding a shared 'language' in an interview situation; adopting perspectives; taking account of inequalities of power in research situations; and issues of comparability and objectivity.

Negotiating access

Gaining access to the private domain of the family, or to talk to people about delicate issues such as sex, marital difficulties, and family relationships can prove problematic (Holland *et al.* 1996). Some people may be reluctant to take part in research because of their feelings about privacy and what they consider to be appropriate topics for public discussion. For example, in studies of young people's sexuality, there are difficulties in recruiting a sample and gaining access to participants within particular environments (Holland *et al.* 1991; Wight 1991; Dodd 1991). Some of the boys in Wight's study (1991) on sexual behaviour were reluctant to take part because of the topic of the research. In a study of mature mothers in full-time education, Edwards (1993) had to acknowledge 'racial' difference overtly and used snowballing methods in order to recruit her sample. In examining adolescent health and parenting, Dodd (1991) had difficulty persuading different members of the same household to participate. Parents often acted as 'gate-keepers', 'non-interferers' or 'facilitators' of the parental home when the researcher contacted selected teenagers. Holland *et al.* (1996) used health clinics to contact families, and found each clinic defined a different mode of accessing families on their register for the study.

Perspectives on the family

Noller and Callan (1991) favour methods that provide a multiple perspective on the family, gaining data from each family member. For example, parents' and adolescents' reports of abuse in the family were studied by Garbarino *et al.* (1984) using the Adolescent Abuse Inventory created by Sebes (1983), it was found that adolescent reports of the family were more valid than parental reports. Brynin and Scott (1996) revealed discrepancies in the reporting of health data between parents and children, lending support to the need to gain multiple perspectives.

Other studies have compared reports by individual family members and by other families and objective raters (Noller and Callan 1988; Noller and Bagi 1985). These researchers found a tendency for adolescents to rate the family more negatively than other family members whether they were responding to a self-report inventory or making ratings of family members from videotape interactions. Noller and Callan (1988) have explained this in terms of 'the generational stake hypothesis', that is, that parents who have large investment in their children are likely to want to see the family positively. On the other hand, the ratings of adolescents, who were beginning to distance themselves from the family, were more likely to be correlated with those of outsiders than with ratings made by their parents. While advocating a multiple perspective, Noller and Callan (1991) emphasise the complexities which arise when attempting to understand family communication by using these methods (Barnes and Olson 1985; Noller and Callan 1988).

A similar methodological issue is whether to adopt the insider or outsider viewpoint, for example, family members rating their own interactions on a videotape with their histories of relationships with family members, or outsiders making the ratings relating only to the video. In a study of peer communication, Dorval (1990) videotaped friends of different ages talking and asked scholars from different disciplines to analyse them.

According to Fitzpatrick (1988a), who studied spouse communication and its effect on marriage, the insider perspective can draw on either subjective data such as self-report assessments or objective data, such as a couple monitoring their own behaviour. The outsider perspective can draw on subjective data such as clinical insight or objective data like communication coding schemes. Fitzpatrick (1988a) argues that the best research model includes both perspectives.

Managing 'sensitive' topics

For the respondent, a sensitive issue can be of concern because of fears of incrimination, damaging their reputation and/or of psychological, emotional, personal and social consequences (Holland 1992). This can also have effects on the researcher. In exploring sexual behaviour, for instance, researchers might first address their own assumptions, and explore fears and beliefs with others in the research team before and/or after collecting their data, in order to 'desensitise' themselves to the topic (Ramazanoglu 1990; Wight 1991). A similar method, the 'flooding technique of awareness' is used in therapy to train therapists working with sexual issues in the family (Latham 1981). In some cases, the question of 'the management of taboo' has been the focus of the study itself (Thomson and Scott 1990).

There are very few studies on vocabularies in general, and little knowledge of how people talk about their sexual behaviour in naturally occurring situations (Silverman and Perakyla 1990). In another area of researching communication, which looked at the way teenage boys talk about sex, the researcher, rather than the participants, often ended up articulating the topic (Wight 1991).

The vocabulary of sensitive issues

The potential difference in language and vocabulary of the researcher and the researched can create a problem, especially on sensitive issues such as sexual, criminal, or deviant behaviour. In research on sexual behaviour, for example, interviewees are often reluctant to use a sexual vocabulary without its introduction and 'licensing' by the researcher, and this has highlighted the need for some appropriate and shared language for social research on AIDS. There is a gap between clinical terminology and vulgar colloquialisms: in the case of female sexuality, sexual language is either obscene or too technical (Spencer *et al.* 1988).

Therefore there may be no shared, acceptable sexual language with which both participants or researchers feel at ease, and there is no guarantee that researchers and researched share the same definitions of crucial words such as 'sex ' (Wight 1991; Holland *et al.* 1991). Researchers may be reluctant to ask sexually explicit questions, and therefore the validity of the answers may be questionable (Wight 1991). In looking at the ways teenage boys talk about sex, Wight deliberately used slang in his interviews to make the teenage boys feel more at ease, thereby avoiding ambiguity and confusion and giving them the chance to air their views.

Comparability

Various methods may not lend themselves easily to comparisons in terms of their results due to the wide range of demographic and geographic variables and sample size differences. The WRAP study on young women's sexuality (Holland *et al.* 1990a; 1990b; 1991) generated qualitative data that did not aim to be random or strictly representative but to select categories of participants considered to be of theoretical or empirical relevance to the study. However, the sample generated by the WRAP study was found to be comparable to random samples of young people generated in other studies of the age of first intercourse and levels of sexual activity (Ford and Morgan 1989; Bowie and Ford 1989; Ford 1991).

The participant–researcher relationship

This epistemological and methodological issue has generated debates on the relationship between 'subject' and 'object', 'objectivity' and 'subjectivity', the critique of 'neutrality' and the masculinist bias in sociology (Stanley 1990; Stanley and Wise 1983). Feminist sociology has emphasised the need to analyse relationships between participant and research, participant and researcher, and researcher and research (Holland and Ramazanoglu 1994). Edwards' (1993) advice to researchers is 'to recognise that their own sex, race and class, and other social characteristics, in interaction with interviewees' own social characteristics and experiences, can increase or lessen the sensitivity of their research topics.' Age is another factor to be considered in this context. Douglas (1992) also calls for methodologies to take account of the complexities of race, gender, class as well as culture and of the relationship of black women to their families, their communities, to paid and unpaid work. She notes that none of the white feminist writers exploring women's experiences of health examined the race dimension in the interview process and the power relations between white researchers and black participants which may affect that process. There are also methodological and theoretical problems, including access difficulties encountered by white researchers studying black people's health experiences (Donovan 1986; Thorogood 1988).

Ramazanoglu (1990) argues that although participants and researchers remain socially removed from one another, participants can be involved in the research process by the avoidance of structured interview schedules. Graham (1984) advocates using stories and story-telling around themes which allows participants to contribute to the structure of the interviews and avoids fracturing their experiences. A loose and flexible interview schedule enables participants to direct the conversation and set the agenda. Holland *et al.* (1990b) let young women give their own definitions of sexual relationships before negotiating meanings with the participants. The assurance of confidentiality and anonymity helps to address some of the needs of participants in the research process.

The research experience itself can sometimes have beneficial effects for participants. Some have involved respondents in the research process and asked them to evaluate both the experience of taking part in research, and the methods used (Dodd 1991; *et al.* Graham 1984; Brannen *et al.*). Researchers' techniques may allow participants to evaluate their experiences by giving feedback at the end of the interview, in a final questionnaire or through written summaries (Brannen *et al.* 1991; Butler and Wintram 1991). Some have allowed the opportunity for emotion in the research process, or provided 'reciprocity' in the self-disclosure process (Ramazanoglu 1990; Edwards 1993). Others have disseminated the findings back to the participants, individually or collectively (Brannen *et al.* 1991).

It is essential that researchers are aware of their own assumptions about factors like class explicit throughout the research design and process. Many studies deal with concepts and language more familiar to middle class people, and researchers tend to be middle class themselves, designing and interpreting the data according to their own perspectives. For instance, one cannot make the simple assumption that there are areas for the privacy of research in every type of family home (Dodd 1991; Brannen *et al.* 1994; Holland *et al.* 1996). Researchers studying sexual health and the family must also address the class nature of their assumptions, and it has been questioned whether families 'discuss' or 'debate' sexual health much at all (Mauthner 1994).

Researchers therefore need to analyse their own assumptions, the social relations between different members of a research team, and the link between theory, the production of knowledge and the research process, as the relationship between theory and methodology can be critical for the validity of the research (Butler and Wintram 1991; see also Thomson and Scott 1990; Holland *et al.* 1991; Holland and Ramazanoglu 1994).

Randomised control trials

There has been an increase in the use of randomised control trials to evaluate the outcomes of health education interventions. Essentially this represents the inclusion of the physical science paradigm in the health education evaluation procedures.

Randomised control trials are based on the medical model, which advocates the use of experimental and control groups: one section of the population under study is randomly assigned to the 'treatment' group and the other section becomes the control. Measurements are taken before and after the programme. Such trials are regarded as the best way of assessing whether observed outcome changes in the experimental or treatment group are a direct result of intervention. Reservations on the use of such trials in the health education arena focus on the ethics of withholding the intervention from a section of the target population, on the likelihood of contamination between groups, and the difficulties of assigning 'real life' populations to control conditions.

These trials have been used in many areas of health education including smoking, HIV/AIDS, reproductive health, workplace health substance abuse and many others. An example of the use of a randomised control trial in HIV/AIDs education was that conducted by Basen-Enguist (1994) where young people were randomly assigned to two treatment groups and a control group: one group received a peer-led safe sex workshop on HIV; another a lecture on HIV; and the third group received a lecture on an unrelated topic. The programme was partially effective. Another example of these trials was a parenthood education programme in Ireland in which the 'treatment' group of mothers were given child development information by non-professional mothers (Johnson *et al.* 1993), and this group showed significant changes.

PART II: GENERAL HEALTH TOPICS

In this part, the literature on the family and communication in relation to the following nine important health areas is reviewed: alcohol; smoking; sexual health; diet and nutrition; physical activity; parenthood education; childhood accidents; immunisation; and men's health. Men's health is considered here in a separate section because new interest and attention is being paid to this somewhat neglected issue, and it was felt that men's health is an area that needs to be highlighted. This is not, however, to detract from the continuing importance of women's health issues, which are considered throughout the review.

5. Alcohol

Alcohol plays a contradictory role in family life. On the one hand it is often used in family celebrations and associated with happy occasions; often a child's first experience of drinking alcohol is within the family. On the other hand, when drinking is inappropriate or done to excess it can be dangerous and the cause of many disorders (physical, social, and psychological).

EFFECTS OF ALCOHOL ON HEALTH

Alcohol is absorbed into the bloodstream through the stomach wall and small intestine. The body takes about one hour to absorb one unit of alcohol (ie 8g or 10ml of alcohol, equivalent to half a pint of ordinary beer, lager or cider, a small glass of wine, sherry or port, or a 25 ml measure of spirits). Women's bodies contain less water than men's, they metabolise alcohol in a different way, and they are generally smaller. These differences mean that women achieve a higher blood alcohol concentration than men. They feel the effects of alcohol faster and for longer. People who are unused to alcohol or young people who have not reached physical maturity may find that they are more affected by alcohol than others.

There are long-term and short-term health risks associated with alcohol. The long-term effects of excess drinking (either large quantities on various occasions, or cumulatively) include liver damage, raised blood pressure, certain types of stroke, throat and mouth cancers, stomach disorders, brain damage, problems with the nervous system, malnutrition, weight problems, sexual difficulties, and psychological problems. Research has also suggested an increased risk of breast cancer associated with drinking, especially in those with a history of the disease (Willet *et al.* 1987). Although alcohol is used for positive social reasons, it functions as a depressant, and therefore a common psychological effect is depression, which in some cases significantly increases the risk of suicide (Edwards *et al.* 1994).

The short-term risks from drinking, and especially drinking to excess, include alcohol poisoning, and accidents of various sorts, such as while driving or using other sorts of machinery. Drinking can impair judgements and vision (OPCS 1992); 15 per cent of all road accidents in 1993 were the result of drink driving (Department of Transport 1994). Fires and other accidents in the home are often associated with alcohol, as are 20 per cent of deaths by drowning (Tether and Harrison 1986). Alcohol also contributes to sexual risk-taking behaviour(Bagnall 1991, McEwan *et al.* 1992), and can be a contributory factor in incidents of violence and social disorder.

DEMOGRAPHIC FACTORS

Levels of alcohol consumption vary by a number of interesting geographical variations, for example, in East Anglia the levels of male drinking are relatively low, while women's are high. The proportion of women in England, Wales and Scotland regularly drinking over 14 units per week is 12, 11, and 8 per cent respectively (OPCS 1992b). Young people have different drinking cultures according to where they live (such as rural or inner-city areas in various parts of the country) and their cultural backgrounds (Gofton 1990; Wright and Buczkiewicz 1995; Newcombe *et al.* 1995). Their drinking patterns may also be affected by other aspects of family structure, for instance, research by Isohanni *et al.* (1994) in Finland suggests that parental loss or absence may be important factors leading to excessive haste in adopting adolescent culture including potentially dangerous habits.

Gender

Data from the General Household Survey from 1984 onwards show that a higher proportion of women than men in Britain are non-drinkers, and that women who drink consume less than men (OPCS 1992b). This applies over all age groups.

One study on alcohol consumption collected information by asking people whether they drank, and if so, how often (Blaxter 1987). The findings showed that a considerably higher proportion of women than men were non-drinkers or light drinkers, and that very few women said that they were 'heavy drinkers' (Miles 1991). In this and other surveys, definitions of drinking rely on different standards applied to each sex on the grounds of different physiological effects of alcohol consumption. Until the recent changes, quoted 'sensible' levels have been up to 21 units a week for a man and up to 14 units a week for a woman. These recommended levels have now been increased to a daily rate of 4 units for men and 3 units for women, making weekly totals of 28 and 21 units respectively. The intention is to focus more on controlling daily intake and reducing high-consumption drinking sessions (binge-drinking).

In 1992, men aged 16 or over were drinking an average 15.9 units a week, and about three times as much as women of the same age; 27 per cent of men and 11 per cent of women aged over 18 were drinking more than 21 units and 14 units per week respectively; and 6 per cent of men and 2 per cent of women were drinking more than 50 and 35 units a week respectively. The higher levels are considered dangerous to health by the medical profession. The proportion of men drinking above 21 units per week has remained quite steady since 1986 although there are signs of an increase for men aged 45 years or more. However, the proportion of women drinking more than 14 units per week rose from 9 per cent in 1984 to 11 per cent in 1992, and increased by 2 or 3 percentage points in all age groups over this period (OPCS 1994b).

There are differences between men's and women's drinking patterns throughout the life cycle. The proportion of women drinking above 14 units a week starts decreasing after the age of 25 while a third of men aged 16–44 drink more than 21 units per week (OPCS 1994b). Relatively higher rates of alcohol consumption among younger women is demonstrated in the UK and in several other countries (Fillmore 1987, Corti *et al.* 1989, Bennett *et al.* 1991). Young women aged 18–24 are more likely to exceed the recommended drinking levels than those aged 25–44 (14 and 7 per cent respectively). Younger women are more likely than older women to indulge in heavy episodic binge-drinking (Bennett *et al.* 1991) and to report being drunk regularly (HEA 1993d). However, both types of behaviour are more common amongst men than women. Women over 60 are more likely to be abstemious than younger women, and women under 40 are more likely to be regular drinkers (Miles 1991).

Various approaches have been suggested to understand the changing nature of women's drinking. These include:

1 **accessibility:** women have increased access to alcohol through pubs, wine bars and the like, and have become purchasers through supermarket sales. Women drink predominantly in their own homes, (Goddard and Iken 1988; SHE 1994) and may influence and be influenced by a trend towards home consumption and increased access to alcohol in the private sphere.

2 **stress:** caused by women's increased work/home roles and stressful life events.

3 **vulnerability:** the physiological and social vulnerability of women placing them at greater risk of problem drinking; and

4 **life cycle approach:** which suggests that different hypotheses for problem drinking are appropriate at different stages in women's life cycle (Fillmore 1987; Bradstock *et al.* 1988; Ettorre 1992; Lisansky Gomberg 1994; Wilsnack *et al.* 1994).

Women's drinking behaviour and the increase in women's alcohol-related problems have formed the focus of a number of other studies (Blaxter 1987; OHE 1987; Gillies 1989; Miles 1991). These studies have demonstrated that social attitudes change slowly. Although drinking by women of all ages has become more acceptable, drunkenness in women has not become more socially acceptable, while society maintains a degree of tolerance towards male intoxication. Negative attitudes towards women's drinking may also result in considerable under-reporting of alcohol consumption by women respondents in surveys, not only by women who think they drink 'too much' but by all women (Miles 1991). Information about drinking habits is difficult to collect as it is necessary to rely on a variety of sources to obtain greater response reliability.

Age and social class

Men in their mid-thirties are the group most likely to drink, together with unemployed men. Heavy drinking is more common among manual occupational groups than non-manual occupational groups (Whitehead 1988). For women, it is the single, under-25s in the higher income groups who tend to drink the most, and, in general, more single women (15 per cent) tend to drink over the recommended levels than married, separated and divorced women (12 per cent), or widows (5 per cent). Of women in professional or managerial households, 15 per cent drink more than recommended weekly amount compared to 8 per cent of women in households where the main income is from a semi-skilled or unskilled occupation. Women in full-time employment are more likely to drink at higher levels than economically inactive women (18 per cent compared to 9 per cent), and those in low-income households are less likely to drink than those with high income. Drinking therefore appears to be related to occupation, with women in professional, managerial and other non-manual employment being more likely to be regular drinkers than those doing manual work. In addition, housewives tend to drink more often when alone than when in social situations (Corrigan 1987). Generally speaking, it appears that women's drinking tends to decrease with their involvement in home and family, whereas men's drinking does not decrease, it even tends to increase.

In the younger age groups, research findings have suggested that 14-year-old-drinkers were more likely to be from social class I or II (Parker and Measham 1994). No other social class differences were recorded in relation to any other health-behaviour-related variable in this study. If the association between class and drinking among these young people was real, it may be explained by easy access to alcohol because this group had more available money or because they had access to well-stocked liquor cabinets in the home. At 16–18, regular drinkers are more likely to be male and (despite some stereotyping of working-class young people as being heavy drinkers) to come from social class group AB, but this group is also the group least likely to exceed sensible drinking levels. This may relate to income, and one study has shown that financial factors are important in accounting for variations in drinking at this age (Roberts 1988).

Ethnicity

In terms of the drinking behaviour of ethnic minority groups, the MORI surveys (HEA 1992a, 1992b) on children and young adults showed that African–Caribbean and white children were more likely to have tried alcohol and more likely to be regular drinkers than their Asian counterparts; and a similar trend was found with 16–19-year-olds. This is in part a reflection of the strict religious attitudes towards alcohol held by some Asian communities. Relatively little is known about patterns of alcohol consumption among adult ethnic minority groups (although an *HEA Health and Lifestyle Survey* is forthcoming).

EFFECTS OF ALCOHOL ON FAMILY LIFE

Sexual risks

The various effects of alcohol consumption on individuals and the family can be traced throughout the life cycle. Beginning with conception, research has shown that alcohol consumption increases the likelihood of taking sexual risks, and not taking sexual precautions, either against HIV infection, or for contraception (Bagnall 1991; McEwan *et al.* 1992; Donovan and McEwan, 1995).

Pregnancy

If a woman is pregnant, any alcohol she drinks can pass into her unborn child from her bloodstream through the placenta and have adverse effects on the baby, especially during the early stages of pregnancy. (Plant 1985a, 1985b; Waterson and Murray-Lyon 1990; Hawkes 1993). Fifteen minutes after alcohol is ingested by the mother, the blood-alcohol content of the foetus is equal to that of the mother (Hawkes 1993). Excessive alcohol consumption in pregnancy can lead to foetal alcohol syndrome (FAS), a combination of conditions which includes growth retardation, mental retardation and facial dysmorphology. Affected babies may also exhibit altered neonatal behaviour. The severity of signs and symptoms may differ in infants (Plant 1985a, 1985b; Matis and May 1991; Hawkes 1993). A young breastfeeding baby can also be affected through the passage of alcohol in breastmilk which may have effects on the baby's feeding, bowel movements or sleeping.

There may be more factors involved in FAS than alcohol alone: the socio-economic situation of the mother, her nutrition and the drinking behaviour of a partner have all been linked to FAS. One study of young adolescent pregnant women (Rhodes *et al.* 1994) suggested that those who live with partners or family who are drinking are also more likely to drink throughout their pregnancy. The use of alcohol by pregnant women who smoke also appears to enhance the effects of smoking, possibly by inhibiting the deposition of fat in the foetus and thereby contributing to the reduction in birthweight associated with smoking (Kokotailo *et al.* 1992).

The incidence of FAS in Britain is not clear: Some researchers say that FAS is rare (Waterson and Murray-Lyon 1990; Breeze 1985), others have suggested a higher incidence. (Plant (1985) gives figures of between 1 and 4 per thousand live births in Britain; and in America, figures are believed to be between 1.3 to 2.2 per thousand live births (Matis and May 1991)). Studies in the UK suggest that socio-economic factors are more important than stress factors in relation to alcohol consumption during pregnancy, and there is evidence of alcohol consumption being positively related to age, single marital status, unemployment, and smoking. These imply a more complex interaction of factors involving stress, low income, education and employment that denies any simple relationship (Heller *et al.* 1988).

Several studies suggest that women have a natural tendency to reduce their drinking during pregnancy (Plant 1985a, 1985b; Heller *et al.* 1988) and that awareness of the dangers of drinking while pregnant is high both in the UK and elsewhere (Breeze 1985; HEA 1990; Ihlen *et al.* 1993; Dufour *et al.* 1994). However, ordinary people are less knowledgeable about the specific effects alcohol has on the foetus, or the safe levels of alcohol consumption during pregnancy (McKnight and Merrett 1987; Fox *et al.* 1987; Waterson *et al.* 1989; Dufour *et al.* 1994). This shows the necessity to educate men as well as their pregnant partners about this issue, and to ensure their knowledge is accurate. Dufour *et al.* (1994) found that half their sample mistakenly thought that FAS meant that a child was born addicted to alcohol.

Effects of parental drinking on children

The home is a very common setting for the consumption of alcohol and surveys have shown that 1 in 10 children aged 11–15 years regularly (that is at least once a week) drink with their parents (HEA 1992b). A lot of work has focused on the effects of parental drinking on children within the family. It has been estimated that more than 2 million people in Britain grew up in families where one or more parents were problem drinkers (Gilvarry 1993). The ill effects of this have been well documented (Plant *et al.* 1989; Orford and Velleman 1990; Orford 1992; Straussner 1994; Dobkin *et al.* 1994; Webb and Baer 1995). The mechanisms by which harmful drinking patterns may be transmitted from one generation to the next are not so clear. Orford and Velleman (1990) suggest from their own research and from a review of the literature that children's vulnerability is more likely to arise from family disruption, discord, or a high degree of non-specific harmony rather than any alcohol-specific effects.

The role of parents in the development of their children's drinking behaviour has received substantial attention (Wilks and Callan 1984; Collins *et al.* 1990; Werch *et al.* 1991; Manning 1991; Jung 1995). Parental influence can be transmitted in different ways, through behaviour, attitudes, beliefs, family management techniques and parent–child communication (Werch *et al.* 1991). In the case of ethnic minority groups in the United States, acculturation theories have been applied to explain generational differences in drinking behaviours (Martin and Posner 1995).

Parental attitudes and behaviour can be important influences, and parental models can produce heavy drinking in children (Orford and Velleman 1990). The importance of family influence on sensible drinking, particularly parental consent and appropriate parental and family drinking was examined in a small qualitative study of 15–16-year-olds (Foxcroft *et al.* 1994). These young people identified poor family relationships and inappropriate parental drinking as negatively affecting their own drinking. Analyses of research studies in this area have suggested that it is family support, control, and structure that are the essential factors, and adolescents who tend to drink more come from less supportive and/or less controlling families, and from non-nuclear families (ie families without two parents in the household) (Baer 1987; Foxcroft and Lowe 1991). A subsequent review of studies also concluded that adolescents drink more if their parents drink more, and/or their parents approve of their drinking (Lowe *et al.* 1993). Testing this out on a large survey of young people in Humberside, the researchers concluded that family support, control models, and parental attitudes were independently and additively related to adolescents' drinking behaviour, the most salient of these being parental attitudes. There is some evidence (HEA 1995i) that over-strict parental controls on drinking, particularly amongst young people from some minority ethnic groups may also 'encourage' young people to drink more. In relation to parental strictness on smoking and alcohol, one study (Brannen *et al.* 1995) suggested that this is gender-related in the sense that parents are stricter about alcohol with girls, and about smoking with boys.

Family conflict

Drinking has been linked with family conflict and breakdown: it is claimed that 30 per cent of divorces and 40 per cent of domestic violence incidents are related to alcohol (Alcohol Concern 1991). Studies have reported an association between spouse or partner's drinking and women's alcohol use, usually the adverse effects on women of living with a heavy drinker, and how this contributes to onset and maintenance of heavy drinking (Baily 1990; Wilsnack *et al.* 1994).

YOUNG PEOPLE AND ALCOHOL

Social pressures to drink clearly increase during the teenage years (Pisano and Rooney 1988), and it is often suggested that family pressures recede in favour of peer pressures with increasing age. The nature and relative importance of parents' and peers' influence on adolescent drinking has been widely debated (see, for instance, Wilks *et al.* 1989; Green *et al.* 1991). Peer pressures can be important but they are changeable rather than fixed. In this context, young people go around with others who have similar drinking behaviour, and there is not a simple causal link. There is perhaps a danger of placing the blame for negative behaviour of 'good' young people, on their peers (Davies 1992, Coggans and McKellar 1994).

Although there have been some signs of a moral panic developing about young people and alcohol, British researchers challenge this as a predominantly US perspective. They suggest that young people's drinking is not increasing significantly, and there is a danger of pathologising what is a normal social activity and part of growing up (Sharp and Lowe 1989; May 1992; Lowe *et al.* 1993).

The 1990 HEA survey of Health and Lifestyles of 16–19-year-olds in England showed that most young people over the age of 16 see themselves as drinkers, and 52 per cent of them as regular drinkers (HEA 1992b). After the age of 17, young men are more likely to be drinkers than young women, whose peak age for drinking is 16–18 years (Plant *et al.* 1990; Goddard 1992; HEA 1992b). However, where once it was the case that young men drank more than young women, this difference appears to be diminishing in that young women's drinking is approaching the same level as that of young men.

One longitudinal study explored teenagers' reasons for their health behaviour choices, how these reasons changed as teenagers grew up and located their behaviours within the social context in which they occurred (Gillies 1989). It was found that 11- and 14-year-old 'weekly drinkers' were more likely to be male than female. Dislike of school appeared to be another related characteristic often expressed by 11-year-old drinkers who also smoked with their friends.

Isolating predictive factors for drinking in teenagers was the focus of another longitudinal study in the 1980s (Plant *et al.* 1985). In this study of alcohol, tobacco and drug misuse, the researchers noted that smoking at the age of 15 was a predictive factor for alcohol consumption four years later. They explored social aspects of smoking and drinking in youth, and found that alcohol was most often used in the company of friends, and at discos. None of the young people mentioned using alcohol as a coping strategy but rather it was used to promote changes of mood such as feelings of well-being thereby increasing sociability.

Other studies have shown a significant positive correlation between alcohol use and misuse by young people and their use of tobacco and illicit drugs (Plant *et al.* 1985; Diamond *et al.* 1988; Bean *et al.* 1988; Lader and Matheson 1990; Green *et al.* 1991; HEA 1992b). In one longitudinal study in the North West of England following a cohort of 14–15-year-olds over four years, it has been noted that alcohol use is an important 'pathway' to drug use, partly, as other research confirms, because drinking brings them into social situations where drugs are on offer (Parker and Measham 1994).

One report (Beattie *et al.* 1986) estimated that about 1000 children under 15 years old in England and Wales are admitted to hospital every year with alcoholic poisoning (not just through drinking by accident). However, there is no evidence that overall alcohol consumption among the under-18s has increased over the last 15 years. What does appear to have happened is a change in drinking patterns, with both young men and women indulging more in heavy sessional or 'binge drinking'. For young people, it is more appropriate to define 'problem drinking' as binge drinking, rather than any necessarily long-term 'problem'. In a survey of drinking in Wales (Moore *et al.* 1994) binge drinking was defined as drinking half the adult weekly recommended units of alcohol per session (21 units for men and 14 units for women at this time). This type of drinking was most prevalent among young adults aged 18–24.

Although there has been a substantial amount of research on the nature, patterns and effects of alcohol consumption in the population, there are still areas for further investigation, such as the social context, value and meaning of alcohol in the lives of young men and women; and other influences, such as that of siblings' drinking attitudes and behaviour. The vast majority of UK findings on teenage drinking to date have used a cross-sectional methodology. While these kinds of studies can determine important factors, especially if repeated, longitudinal research may reveal more about patterns of imitation, maintenance, change in behaviour over time and factors associated with such changes, and the effects of these factors on drinking behaviour (Gillies 1989). Drinking is a complicated health risk for health education, as in moderation it is associated with positively enjoyable and acceptable images, and at this level it has even been claimed to be beneficial for health.

RECOMMENDATIONS FOR FURTHER RESEARCH

1. More research could explore if, how, and when families discuss drinking behaviour (Miles 1991). It would seem to be a more ambiguous health risk topic than smoking behaviour, even though there is ample evidence of its contribution to ill health and family conflict.

2. In relation to the recent interest shown into the possible 'protective factors' in smoking behaviour, some exploration should be made into how such factors could function similarly for drinking behaviour. In particular, the influence of parental attitudes and behaviour in relation to alcohol consumption merits further investigation.

3. The meaning and value of alcohol in young people's lives warrants more in-depth exploration.

4. Further research could be carried out into social and economic factors related to young people's drinking versus drug-taking behaviour which takes into account relative financial costs and perceived benefits. Alcohol costs may be more prohibitive than the cost of buying drugs.

5. The nature and effects of women's changing role in the purchase and consumption of alcohol should be examined.

6. More research could look at ethnic minority drinking patterns, especially in relation to social pressures on young people growing up.

7. A life-cycle approach to research into alcohol consumption would be useful, which would focus on the different meaning of drinking at different points in life for men and for women.

8. Research attention should look at the relationship between family structure and drinking patterns, especially for lone-parent families, and for those who are divorced/separated or widowed.

6. Smoking

Smoking has always been a concern for health education. In *The Health of the Nation: A Strategy for Health in England* (1992) the government outlined its targets for combating the harmful effects of smoking generally as being 'to reduce the prevalence of cigarette smoking in men and women aged 16 and over to no more than 20 per cent by the year 2000'. The government also hopes to reduce the consumption of cigarettes by at least 40 per cent by the year 2000, from 98 billion manufactured cigarettes in 1990, to 59 billion. Between 1972 and 1994 the number of male smokers (over 16) in Great Britain fell from 52 per cent to 28 per cent, and the proportion of female smokers fell from 41 per cent to 26 per cent (OPCS 1995a).

Young people have become a particular concern, as research has shown that a significant number are smoking regularly by the age of 15 (Diamond and Goddard 1995; Owen and Bolling 1995). This is despite the image of the smoker having become more negative over recent years. For young people especially, it is no longer seen as glamorous and grown-up, and rather more associated with being 'stupid' and 'weak'; while the non-smoker image is more positive, 'cool', 'attractive', and 'tough' (Owen and Bolling 1995). Self-image and self-esteem may still be important factors in taking up smoking (Bewley and Bland 1987; Jacobson 1986; Charlton and Blair 1989b; Owen and Bolling 1995), and the Teenage Tracking Survey (Owen and Bolling 1995) found that many young people (especially girls) saw smoking as simply 'part of growing up'.

In North America and Western Europe, one in four teenagers have become regular smokers by the age of 15 (Smith *et al.* 1992). The incidence of regular smoking among young people aged 11–15 years has increased from 10 per cent in 1990, 1992 and 1993, to 12 per cent in 1994 (Diamond and Goddard 1995), but boys are consistently found to be heavier smokers than girls. Brannen and Storey (1996) found that in the younger age groups, boys were more likely to smoke than girls. In the OPCS report, Diamond and Goddard (1995) also showed that at the age of 15, 28 per cent of young people were smoking regularly (ie at least one cigarette per week) This represented an increase in boys' and girls' smoking during 1993–1994 from 19 to 26 per cent for boys and from 26 to 30 per cent for girls. Figures on regular smoking have remained relatively consistent over the last few years but occasional smoking has risen a little.

In England, it has been suggested that up to 70 per cent of children have experimented with smoking by the age of 16 (Thomas *et al.* 1993). Survey results on young people have provided an idea of how smoking behaviour develops by age, and in a model provided in one report (Royal College of Physicians 1992) it was suggested that 'pre-contemplation' takes place at the age of 10–11; 'contemplation' at 12 years; 'initiation' at 13 years; 'experimentation' at 14 years; and regular smoking at 15 years. Children experiment with smoking at an early age, and the MORI survey (HEA 1992a) showed that 8 per cent of 9-year-old schoolchildren had tried smoking. This figure rose to 38 per cent at 13 and 61 per cent at 15 years of age. Boys seem to start experimenting with cigarettes at an earlier age than girls (Owen and Bolling 1995). This also demonstrated the importance of peer pressure in encouraging pupils to smoke, since over half had tried their first cigarette in the company of friends, and 18 per cent said they continued to smoke because their friends smoked.

Most research on young people and smoking (and substance use in general), has concentrated on the risk factors associated with smoking, but attention is now also being paid to protective factors. These include individual attributes such as activity level and sociability, intelligence and communication skills; affectional ties with the family that provide emotional support in times of stress; and external support systems, such as at school or work (Holland *et al.* 1996). It has been pointed out that factors like peer pressure can also serve to protect adolescents from taking up smoking (Urberg *et al.* 1990). Protective factors are not simply the reverse of risk factors but there is some interaction within and between them and more research should produce useful information (Arnold *et al.* 1995).

For both boys and girls in the Adolescent Health and Parenting Study (Oakley *et al.* 1992), smoking was associated with difficulties in relationships with parents, especially mothers, and with reported conflict with parents. Smoking was higher among young people of both sexes who spent a significant proportion of their leisure time outside the house. Therefore smoking behaviour is linked to social lifestyle, and to family characteristics, such as the closeness of the family, which are also factors that operate in young people's drinking behaviour.

This section examines the harmful effects of smoking, and the influence of the family on children's smoking behaviour. There are important variations in smoking behaviour by social class, family status, ethnicity and gender which need to be understood and taken into account if interventions are to be successful in reducing smoking. Particular attention is paid to gender-related factors since it is amongst young women that there appears to have been a higher take-up of smoking (Waldron 1991), and amongst women with young children that there has been a lower reduction in smoking (Graham 1992, 1993a). Smoking has been the subject of a variety of intervention studies, the limitations of which have been noted by various reviewers.

EFFECTS OF SMOKING ON HEALTH

Everybody is aware that smoking is harmful to their health. Cigarettes introduce significant amounts of chemical substances into the smoker's body. Tobacco smoke includes up to 4000 different types of toxic compounds including carcinogens, heavy metals, poisons and respiratory irritants (WHO 1985). Smoking is associated with various cancers, coronary heart disease, respiratory and other ill-health conditions. Although it was hypothesised that smoking may protect women against breast cancer through an anti-oestrogenic effect, recent research in Denmark refutes this and indicates that breast cancer will occur eight years earlier in smokers than non-smokers (Bennicke *et al.* 1995).

Pregnancy

Smoking is a major risk factor for poor outcomes in pregnancy. Many of the compounds in tobacco smoke can cross the placenta, interfering with its efficiency and causing serious, potential long-term and short-term effects on foetal development (WHO 1985). Children born to women who smoke may be premature and smaller in size and weight, and are believed to have an increased risk of sudden infant death, congenital limb abnormality, asthma, bronchitis and pneumonia, and there is concern that childhood cancers, brain dysfunction and altered CNS development may also be associated with maternal smoking (Conter *et al.* 1995; Czeizel *et al.* 1994; Burchfiel *et al.* 1986; WHO 1985; Bellinger *et al.* 1986; Bonithon-Kopp *et al.* 1986). The harmful effects on the developing foetus are made more difficult to quantify because women who have a higher health risk for other reasons, such as socio-economic factors, are also more likely to smoke. (Kleinmann and Madans 1985). This makes it important to take into account both the direct adverse effects of smoking and other factors that compound these effects.

The OPCS infant feeding survey showed that a similar proportion of women smoked in pregnancy in 1990 as they did five years earlier (White *et al.* 1992). This survey revealed significant social class differences in those giving up smoking at the onset of pregnancy. For example, 45 per cent of women with partners in partly skilled or unskilled manual occupations smoked cigarettes before their pregnancies compared with only 17 per cent in professional households. This smaller proportion of professional women were more likely than other women to give up smoking during pregnancy. A slightly higher proportion of pregnant women (27 per cent) gave up in 1990 than in 1985 (24 per cent). Women without partners showed the highest proportion of smokers (55 per cent) during this period (1985–90), while the only group not showing any change in smoking were women with partners in professional occupations who also had the lowest proportion of smokers (8 per cent). Women who had lost a partner through bereavement or estrangement, unemployed women and women who lived in deprived areas were also more likely to be smokers, and white women tended to smoke more than women from ethnic minorities (White *et al.* 1992). The latest wave of data from the National Adult Smoking Campaign Tracking Survey HEA (1995f) showed that smoking adults were more likely to be trying, or to have recently tried to give up smoking if they had children. The HEA also tracked a national campaign to reduce smoking in pregnancy, and found that pregnant smokers were more than twice as likely to have a smoking than a non-smoking partner (Campion *et al.* 1994a, 1994b).

The effects of passive smoking within the family also have to be considered. With the increase in the proportion of people, especially young children, with asthma in recent years, smoking is obviously implicated as an exacerbating factor, if not also a cause. In one family study (Holland *et al.* 1996) smoking family members rarely linked their smoking behaviour to the incidence of asthma in their children.

FAMILY FACTORS

The smoking behaviour and attitudes of members of the family living at home exert a significant influence on the experimentation, uptake and maintenance of smoking in children and adolescents.

Parental smoking behaviour

There are strong relationships between the smoking behaviour of parents and that of their children. Every OPCS survey carried out on schoolchildren supports a link between family smoking and children's smoking (Diamond and Goddard 1995). The Teenage Tracking Survey (Owen and Bolling 1995) found that pupils in families where both parents smoke are three times as likely to be regular smokers than those in families where neither parent smokes (15 per cent: 5 per cent). Newman and Ward (1989) had also reported a threefold increase in the proportion of smokers when both parents smoked compared to when neither parent smoked. Many other studies have documented the same kind of distributions (Charlton and Blair 1989b; Diamond and Goddard 1995; Brannen and Storey 1996). Green *et al.* (1991) suggested that smoking rates could be high because both generations share material and cultural factors which dispose them to smoking.

Other research has also supported parental smoking as an important factor in children smoking. A Scottish study (Mitchell and Stenning 1989; Mitchell 1990) found that 20 per cent of children who came from smoking families smoked regularly themselves, compared with seven per cent of those who came from non-smoking families. The researchers suggest that the presence of at least one smoking adult signalled that smoking was tolerated within the family and was therefore acceptable behaviour. They found that both mothers' and fathers' smoking behaviour predicted whether or not a child smoked (in two-parent families), and mothers and fathers had slightly different influences on their children. Mothers who smoked exerted a slightly stronger influence on their children than fathers who smoked, and this was particularly important for girls (Goddard 1989, 1990; Swan *et al.* 1990; MORI 1991; Cook *et al.* 1994). However, Green *et al.* (1991) argue that 'the evidence suggests that fathers have more influence than mothers on their children's smoking and heavy drinking.' It may be that as children grow older, their relationships and communication with their parents may alter in quantity and quality, allowing fathers to become more of an influence than mothers on smoking and drinking behaviours.

Exploring a different influencing aspect of parental smoking behaviour, Moreno *et al.* (1994) found that Latino parents in the South-western United States and Mexico inadvertently prompted their children to smoke by asking them to buy, or light (sometimes in their own mouths) their parents' cigarettes.

Parental attitudes to smoking

Parental approval or disapproval of smoking has long been thought to be an important influence on children's smoking behaviour irrespective of whether they themselves smoke or not, although earlier studies exploring this area yielded contradictory results (McGuffin 1982; Aaro *et al.* 1983; Sunseri *et al.* 1983). Some studies have suggested that parental attitudes towards smoking seemed to have no effect once all other factors were taken into account (Murray *et al.* 1985; Swan *et al.* 1990), while other studies have emphasised their importance. For instance, Newman and Ward (1989) reported an impressive effect of parental attitude on early adolescent smoking behaviour. They conclude that parental attitude, when expressed, appears to be important in moderating adolescent smoking behaviour, regardless of parents' smoking behaviour. They recommend that parents should be encouraged to express their opposition to risky behaviours whether or not they are smokers themselves, and that schools should recruit parents to help school-based interventions aimed at decreasing the rate of adolescent cigarette smoking.

Several other studies have supported the importance of parental attitude. In the Brigantia study (Charlton 1984b) children were shown to be seven times more likely to be smokers if they believed that their parents approved of smoking. Parental attitudes towards smoking were also found to have more influence on children's smoking status than parents' own smoking status in the Avon Study (Nelson *et al.* 1985; Eiser *et al.* 1989). This research explored the smoking and drinking behaviour of young people aged 11 to 16 years in a longitudinal study. It looked more specifically at parental opposition to smoking as a direct predictor of children's smoking intentions. The researchers found that regardless of age or sex, 'parental opposition increased in importance as a discriminator relative to peer opposition from the younger to the older age groups' whereas in terms of current smoking status, 'parental opposition appeared to be a less important discriminator relative to peer opposition for girls than for boys.' They recommended that the role of family in encouraging or discouraging smoking needs more theoretical and practical attention.

In the HEA Teenage Tracking Survey (Owen and Bolling 1995), 87 per cent pupils thought that at least one of their parents would mind if they smoked and 75 per cent thought both would mind. Teenagers in families where neither of their parents minded if they smoked were almost five times as likely to be regular smokers as those who said both their parents would mind. In an OPCS survey (Diamond and Goddard 1995), young people saw their parents as overwhelmingly against their smoking, whether or not their parents smoked themselves. In families where both parents were smokers, 80 per cent of non-smoking pupils claimed that their parents would try to stop them from smoking. Parental disapproval appears to have an effect on the smoking status of younger children but less on older children. The existence of a proportion of parents who do not mind if their children smoke suggests that there may be room for health education efforts to influence such parents to express disapproval, regardless of their own smoking status.

Siblings' smoking behaviour

Although few studies look specifically at the impact siblings may have on children's smoking behaviour and attitudes, sibling influence frequently emerges as an important factor. OPCS and HEA surveys of smoking in secondary schoolchildren have suggested that, although the smoking status of parents appeared to have an effect on 11–15-year-old children smoking, this was only appreciable if no siblings smoked (Goddard 1989, 1990; Diamond and Goddard 1995; Owen and Bolling 1995). If the effects of parental smoking behaviour are controlled, siblings' smoking behaviour is an influential factor. These surveys ask only about the smoking behaviour of older siblings and thus the MORI report (HEA 1992b) on 16–19-year-olds found the highest incidence of regular smoking (45 per cent) in this age group in families where there was an older sibling who smoked. This was also apparent, to a lesser degree, in the MORI survey (HEA 1992a) of 9–15-year-olds. Pupils in the HEA Teenage Tracking Survey (1995) with older siblings who smoked were five times more likely to be regular smokers compared with those with non-smoking older brothers or sisters (21:4 per cent).

In an earlier OPCS survey (Lader and Matheson 1990) it was suggested that if brothers and sisters do not smoke, this could actually lower the probability that children become regular smokers themselves, and this was also indicated in the later OPCS survey (Diamond and Goddard 1995). This latter survey also showed that 30 per cent of pupils who were regular smokers had smoking brothers or sisters compared with 7 per cent of pupils with no brothers or sisters who smoked. Other studies also indicated that the risk of smoking initiation increases if young people had siblings who smoked, and suggested this factor may be greater than parental smoking (Swan *et al.* 1990; Meier 1991; MORI 1991). The influence of siblings is greater in one-parent than in two-parent families. As many as 80 per cent of children in lone-parent families who lived with siblings who smoked, had at some time smoked, compared with about half the children in other lone-parent families (Lader and Matheson 1990).

Other OPCS surveys have showed that 12-year-old pupils were about three times as likely to be smokers if they had a brother or sister living at home with them who smoked than if they did not. By the age of 14 years, this effect was still apparent, although less striking (OPCS 1990b; Lader and Matheson 1990). It was suggested that the roles of siblings decline with age, when the influence of peers becomes stronger. At each age surveyed, girls seemed to be rather more susceptible to the influence of siblings than boys. A survey of adolescent health (Oakley *et al.* 1992) indicated that girls are especially influenced by same-sex sibling smoking.

Research exploring teenage smoking initiation (Friedman *et al.* 1985) found that this was not a solitary event, and although friends accounted for over half (57 per cent) of those present on these occasions, siblings made up 11 per cent. Boys experimented with cigarettes with other boys, and girls with other girls. The authors suggest that the relationship of parental smoking status to adolescent smoking status seems to reflect a different type of effect from sibling influence, since parents are seldom present at the initial smoking experiences.

Children's attitudes to smoking

A few studies have looked at children's attitudes to their parents smoking, some with a view to seeing if children may influence their parents. On the whole, little evidence has been found of such an effect, despite children's attempts. In the HEA

(1995f) teenage smoking survey, almost 7 out of 10 pupils (68 per cent) living in households where either or both parents smoked had tried to get them to give up smoking in the last six months. Mitchell and Stenning (1989) and Mitchell (1990) looked at responses by 10–11-year-olds to smoking in the family, especially maternal smoking: 72 per cent of children with smoking mothers had asked their mothers to stop smoking. If they had asked both parents to stop smoking, it was always the mother who was listed first. As far as children's own attitudes to smoking went, 82 per cent expressed unconditionally anti-smoking views, although this proportion had dropped to 50 per cent three years later. Younger children are generally much more censorious of smoking behaviour than older children (Holland *et al.* 1996; Arnold *et al.* 1995). Brannen and Storey (1996) found similar opposition and distaste voiced by 10–11-year-olds towards parental smoking.

There has been little research on the processes involved in family communication on smoking, but smoking was one of the health topics under examination in a study on communication about health in the family by Holland *et al.* (1996). It was often a source of conflict between parents and children, which was negotiated in different ways. Sometimes this involved trade-offs and compromises between parents and anti-smoking younger children, for example, one daughter accepted her mother's smoking because she was aware of the alternative irritability that ensued if her mother did not smoke. In another family the parents had offered a significant sum of money to each of their children if they refrained from smoking at least up to the age of 21.

PEER FACTORS AND GROWING UP

As children grow older, there are changes in the important influences or pressures on their attitudes and behaviour. Although there is much evidence for a significant relationship between smoking and parental behaviour and attitudes during childhood, evidence has suggested that these wane in importance as peer group influences take precedence during adolescence, especially around the age of 16 to 18. Green *et al.* (1991) found that this effect became attenuated for young people aged between 15 and 17 years, when some of the sample had left school. They further argued that health promotion programmes which encourage parents to modify smoking behaviour, will not necessarily affect young people because their smoking behaviour is subject to leaving school, employment status, youth training and so on. In the OPCS survey (Diamond and Goddard 1995), 75 per cent of regular smokers said that all or most of their friends smoked compared with 5 per cent whose friends never smoked. Some research has suggested peer factors like having a best friend or a steady boyfriend/girlfriend who smokes are important (Wang *et al.* 1995).

Although peer influence is obviously very important, consideration should be given to a longitudinal study by Chassin *et al.* (1986) who explored changes in peer and parental influence during adolescence, and also compared this approach with a cross-sectional approach. The authors suggest that these two types of studies may give different kinds of results. They were looking at: peer and parental smoking models; attitudes towards smoking; and perceptions of strictness, parental and peer supportiveness and expectations for general and academic success. They carried out two tests one year apart and found that both parental and peer influence maintained a strong effect. This contradicted the findings of many cross-sectional studies which showed that peer influence increases through adolescence and parental influence decreases. Using a cross-sectional study, Wang *et al.* (1995) also found that parental approval (but not parental smoking behaviour) remained significant for adolescents of all ages between 14 and 18.

Conrad *et al.* (1992) reviewed 27 longitudinal prospective studies carried out since 1980 to examine the predictors of onset of smoking in children. The authors found that although some predicted factors such as socio-economic status and social bonding, especially peer bonding, received support, questions were raised about others, such as the unexpected low and inconsistent support received by factors of family bonding and parental smoking and approval. They suggest that the family does not appear to play such a consistent role in predicting children's smoking behaviour than has previously been thought. However, some recent studies have confirmed the importance of family influences in smoking behaviour (Brynin and Scott 1996; Brannen and Storey 1996).

VARIATIONS IN SMOKING BEHAVIOUR

There are a number of demographic variations in smoking behaviour that relate to gender, social class, family status, and ethnicity. In their review of longitudinal studies of smoking, Conrad *et al.* (1992) noted that few studies had differentiated age, gender or ethnicity, but in those that had, there were many differences.

Gender

It is important to consider gender differences more closely. Trends in male and female smoking behaviour have been changing in the most Western countries. Waldron (1991) provides a historical overview of gender differences in smoking, and points to contributory factors such as greater equality between the sexes; increasing numbers of women in the labour force; women's higher education; and greater social acceptability of female smoking, reinforced by images of women in in the cinema and advertising. Female smoking continued to rise until the late 1960s. In 1972, 52 per cent of men and 41 per cent women in Great Britain smoked cigarettes, and the gender difference in smoking was highest in those aged over 60 years. Since then this difference has narrowed and in 1992, 29 per cent of men and 28 per cent of women were cigarette smokers (OPCS 1994b; General Household Survey 1992). Men have been more likely to have given up smoking than women and girls, whose smoking behaviour has shown a slower decline, and in some countries, female adolescents have been taking up smoking at a higher rate than male adolescents (Swan *et al.* 1989; Flay 1992; Sharpe and Oakley 1992; Thomas *et al.* 1993; Holland *et al.* 1995). Between 1990 and 1994, girls were more likely to smoke than boys, and in 1994, 10 per cent of boys and 13 per cent of girls were smokers (Diamond and Goddard 1995), but boys are consistently found to be heavier smokers than girls. Brannen and Storey (1996) found that in the younger age groups, boys were more likely to smoke than girls.

Between the ages of 11 and 20, girls and boys show different patterns of smoking. At the earlier age of 11–13 years, boys experiment with cigarettes more than girls. At this stage prevalence is less clear-cut because the incidence of regular smoking is very low and therefore gender differences are not significant. At the age of 13, the gender gap opens up and girls take the lead in smoking behaviour (Diamond and Goddard 1995). Over the next few years, smoking increases for both sexes but by the age of 16 the boys are catching up, and by 19 they have overtaken the girls (OPCS 1995a; GHS 1994). One aspect which makes the data at this age harder to compare is that up to 15/16 it usually comes from school-based studies, which probably give a higher level of anonymity than the material obtained through household census data, where children would have to admit their smoking behaviour openly. For this reason, the prevalence levels at age 16 tend to be lower in the census data than in the school studies.

Social class differences in smoking behaviour have emerged in women's smoking over the past few decades. Whereas in the late 1950s there were no significant class differences, from the 1960s smoking became a more working-class habit as the prevalence rate declined in the higher social classes. The fall in smoking has been lowest for manual workers of both sexes, who have the highest levels of smoking. By the early 1990s the proportion of smokers among women in working-class households was significantly higher than that found among women in middle- and upper-class households (OPCS 1992b).

Being a girl was one of the two factors most predictive of uptake in smoking in the Avon study, where 41 per cent of 11–13-year-old girls compared with 30 per cent of boys of the same age were still smoking two and a half years after the study began (McNeill *et al.* 1988; McNeill 1991). The other factor was prior experimentation with cigarettes. Although boys may experiment with cigarettes at an earlier age than girls, both sexes are equally likely to try smoking, and it is girls who appear more likely to carry on and overtake the boys to become confirmed smokers, at least in the mid-teens (Goddard 1989, 1990; HEA 1992a; Owen and Bolling 1995).

Family factors associated with adolescent girls' smoking
1 **Birth order** has been found to be an important influence, with eldest daughters being two and a half times more likely to smoke than eldest sons. Among younger children, daughters were twice as likely as sons to smoke. Presence of an older same-sex sibling in the household also made smoking more likely (Oakley *et al.* 1992).

2 **Perceived parental attitude** (approval or disapproval) has been suggested as having a greater influence on girls' decision to smoke than boys' (McNeill *et al.* 1988; O'Byrne 1983; Charlton 1984b; Charlton and Blair 1989b; Nutbeam 1987).

3 **Mothers' and daughters'** smoking behaviour may be related. In an Australian study of 12–16-year-old girls, mothers' smoking behaviour was found to be more important than fathers' smoking behaviour for their daughters' onset of smoking (Hover and Gaffney 1988). Other researchers have cited evidence for and against this (Swan *et al.* 1989; Oechsli and Seltzer 1984).

4 **Secret smoking**. Girls are more likely than boys to hide their smoking from their families. In one survey, 43 per cent of boys compared with 57 per cent of girls who were regular smokers said that their family did not know that they smoked (Diamond and Goddard 1995). They were more likely to keep it a secret if their parents were non-smokers (63 per cent of those with non-smoking parents compared to 43 per cent of those with smoking parents).

5 **Stress** is a familiar feature of family life that can contribute to smoking behaviour in children and young people. Daykin (1991) concentrated on girls in their late teens who smoked to break the routine of working in boring repetitive jobs, and to cope with stress and conflict at home, the pressure of household tasks, or depression. She found that their smoking was a strategy for dealing with constraints at home and at work, and argued that it is inappropriate to focus health promotion only on smoking cessation, because this ignores the meaning of smoking to the people concerned. Much work suggests that boys face the same boredom, stress, and depression as girls but may turn to sport or other physical activity as an outlet, which was less available to girls (Escobedo *et al.* 1993). Mitic *et al.* (1985) examined perceived stress in 13–19-year-olds. They defined low, medium, and high stress levels and found that non-smokers of both sexes perceived lower levels of stress than smokers. The authors point out that, because their study was cross-sectional, causal relationships cannot be assumed, but that the strongest associations with stress for boys were school work, money and parents, and for girls, these were appearance, parents and money.

Reasons why girls smoke more than boys
Figures have shown that smoking prevalence is highest among girls in Western countries (Swan *et al.* 1988). A number of factors have been suggested to account for this:

1 **Girls mature earlier** (13–14-years old) than young men and therefore they are more likely to smoke earlier, assisted by several related factors.

2 One of these is that they will be more sociable at a younger age, and that they are more likely to be going to **social environments** where people smoke, such as pubs, clubs, discos, etc.

3 The previous two factors will contribute to the finding that girls who smoke tend to have **more friends of the opposite sex** than boys do (Hover and Gaffney 1988; Piepe *et al.* 1988; Swan *et al.* 1989). Wang *et al.* (1995) has noted the important influence of the smoking status of a steady boyfriend on young women's smoking behaviour.

4 Several researchers have suggested that girls see smoking as a form of **weight control**, and this is also a reason to continue smoking (see Charlton 1984a; Charlton and Blair 1989a; Grunberg 1990; Grunberg *et al.* 1991; Ogden and Fox 1994).

5 Smoking may be used to boost **low levels of self-esteem and self-confidence**. Evidence suggests smoking is used to reinforce desired self-image (Chassin *et al.*

1991) and used as a substitute for confidence and self-esteem. One study (Hover and Gaffney 1988) suggested that girls in their study were seeking emotional and social support in cigarette smoking and that this was linked with fewer social skills.

6 Some researchers have suggested that smoking may grant girls a visible sign of **non-conformity** while for boys it is a less rebellious symbol (Piepe *et al.* 1988; Oakley *et al.* 1992).

7 Other societal reasons for girls' higher levels of smoking than boys include their experiences of adolescence, such as their different rates of **participation in sport**. Swan *et al.* (1990) found that girls were less likely to begin smoking if they took part in organised sport (but significantly more likely to begin if they were involved in organised social activities). Participation in sporting activities can operate as a 'protective factor' for both sexes, but girls are generally involved in less physical activity than boys (Escobedo *et al.* 1993).

8 It has been hypothesised that **nicotine** has differential effects for men and women. Diamond and Goddard (1995) suggest that girls' apparent dependency on smoking at lower levels of smoking behaviour may be due to physical and/or psychological dependence at a lower level of nicotine intake. There are other possible explanations, for example, girls may be more prepared than boys to admit to concern about withdrawal symptoms, or they may be more likely than boys to think that admitting to being dependent makes them feel more grown up.

9 Girls may be predisposed to smoke through greater exposure to magazine-based **cigarette advertising**. It has been shown that children's awareness of cigarette brands is a strong predictor of future smoking (Charlton and Blair 1989b), and it is clear that girls and women easily become aware of cigarette brands through their high consumption of women's magazines, where their uncritical inclusion within the magazine is a form of implicit approval (Action on Smoking and Health 1990).

All these findings raise questions as to whether a different approach to the prevention of adolescent smoking may be appropriate for girls and boys. Anti-smoking messages and intervention techniques should perhaps be tailored differently according to the gender of target groups who will not necessarily be homogeneous in terms of attitudes towards smoking.

Women and stress in the family

More women than men believe that smoking helps to control emotional states, making people calmer and more confident (Charlton and Blair 1989b). The use of cigarette smoking as a mechanism for coping with stress and other negative mood states has been suggested in research on women caring for young children in low-income families (Graham 1987b; 1989, 1993a; Wells and Batten 1990). It is women in stressful situations, struggling the hardest to bring up a family, who often find it the hardest to give up smoking, because of the deeper meaning attached to their cigarette consumption. Graham's work (1985, 1987a,1987b, 1989, 1993a) on the meaning of smoking to women in the family has shown that smoking is prevalent in less-well-off families and is associated with the caring work of women within the family. It has been shown that in very low-income families, cigarette money is often a protected area of expenditure, so that even when cuts are made in necessary items of expenditure like food and clothing, cigarette consumption is not reduced. Among women who smoke, many are likely to come from low-income households, they are more likely to be dependent on income support, to be lone parents, and to have greater responsibility than men for managing the home (Marsh and McKay 1994; Action on Smoking and Health 1993). For many of these women, smoking ceases to be a luxury. It becomes a necessity which provides a way for them to deal with their responsibilities.

Social class

Smoking is more prevalent in manual social classes, than in professional classes. The General Household Survey (OPCS 1992b) showed that only 14 per cent of male adults and 13 per cent of female adults in professional occupations smoked, compared with 42 per cent of male adults and 35 per cent of female adults in unskilled manual occupations. The decline in smoking has been highest among professionals, employers and managers, intermediate and junior non-manual workers, and skilled manual and non-account non-professionals, where it has fallen by about a third. It seems that while there are socio-economic differences associated with adult smoking status, the association with teenage smoking is less clear. For example, there was no relation found in the MORI study (HEA 1992a) of 9–15-year-olds. However, in a similar study (HEA 1992b) of a slightly older age-group (16–19 years), the socio-economic distribution of smoking status reflected that of the national adult population, with regular smoking being higher among young adults from socio-economic group DE households (35 per cent) than those from group AB households (16 per cent). In a study of 15–17-year olds, Oechsli and Seltzer (1984) found that the major family characteristics associated at birth with later teenage smoking were parental smoking habits and socio-economic status, expressed in fathers' and mothers' education. In the London-based Adolescent Health and Parenting Study, smoking was higher among young people living in rented than owner-occupier housing (Oakley *et al.* 1992).

Some studies suggest that young smokers have more conflict with their parents than non-smokers as they are perceived to be rebellious under-achievers who spend more time than the typical non-smoker involved in peer-orientated activities outside school (Nelson *et al.* 1985). Non-smokers have been found to have higher educational aspirations than smokers of either sex, and be three times less likely to be absent from school, perceiving themselves as doing well at school (Goddard 1989, 1990; Hover and Gaffney 1988; Charlton and Blair 1989a). This suggests that since smoking is more prevalent in working-class families whose children may reject and leave school at the earliest opportunity, underachievement is thus more a class effect than a characteristic of young smokers.

Family status

Some surveys have indicated that the prevalence of smoking is higher amongst children from one-parent than two-parent families. For example, Murray *et al.* (1985) and Goddard (1989, 1990) reported that a higher proportion of children who were living with a lone non-smoking parent were current or ex-smokers, compared with those children living with two non-smoking parents. The incidence of children smoking rose to 50 per cent if the lone parent was a smoker. Furthermore, the group of children most likely to start smoking were those from lone-parent families, regardless of whether the parent was a smoker. In the 1995 OPCS survey, of those pupils with lone parents who smoked, 25 per cent were regular smokers compared with 14 per cent of those with non-smoking lone parents (Diamond and Goddard 1995).

Green *et al.* (1990) examined the association between the smoking behaviours of lone mothers and their 15-year-old children. Although this research confirmed the higher level of smoking by children from single-parent families, Green *et al.* questioned the assumption of a causal link. By controlling for gender and social class they demonstrated that children in lone-parent families were no more likely to follow the example of maternal smoking behaviour than children living with two parents. The authors stress the need to look at external factors which may affect smoking behaviour, rather than assuming direct maternal influences. They also stress the need for research looking at individual parent–child dyads. In the Adolescent Health and Parenting Study (Oakley *et al.* 1992), smoking was lowest among young people living with both parents and highest among those living with lone fathers. In both these groups, girls were statistically significantly more likely to smoke than boys. Graham's work on the meaning of smoking to mothers caring for children drew attention to the situation of lone mothers (Graham, 1987a), and a more recent study has suggested that it is amongst poor families and single-parent families in particular that smoking has not significantly declined, (Marsh and McKay 1994).

Ethnicity

One area that has not received much research attention outside the United States is ethnicity and smoking (Edwards and MacMillan 1990). The evidence for ethnic difference in smoking amongst adolescents is not clear, and differing patterns of use seem to be most closely related to socio-economic status and demographic factors. While it has been the case that black adults smoked more than white adults in the United States, this trend seems to have been reversing among adolescents (Andreski and Breslau 1993), and it has been suggested that the higher smoking prevalence of white adolescents may be due to blacks starting to smoke later than white adolescents, and being less likely to give up (Escobedo *et al.* 1990). Figures in the MORI survey(HEA 1992b) of British 16–19-year-olds showed a slightly higher proportion of African–Caribbean adolescents (31 per cent) being regular smokers compared to 26 per cent white, and 6 per cent Asian. (However, the numbers of ethnic minority adolescents interviewed was small so this cannot be taken as statistically significant.) At a younger age, the MORI survey (HEA 1992a) on 5–9-year-olds suggested that it was white children (6 per cent) who were more likely to be regular smokers than African-Caribbean (2 per cent) or Asian children (2 per cent). Overall the evidence for ethnic differences in smoking among adolescents is inconclusive and, where such differences exist, they may be only indirectly related to ethnicity.

Little work has looked in more depth at family factors and communication processes related to smoking behaviour in different ethnic minority families. Smoking is frowned on in Asian families (Brannen and Storey 1994). Younger people are expected to show 'respect' for their elders by not smoking in front of them, and a study of 11–12-year-olds (Brannen *et al.* 1996) found Asian parents more pro-active and stricter about enforcing non-smoking rules within the family. The moral rather than health basis to parental anti-smoking attitudes has implications for health information and education.

INTERVENTIONS

Media

There have been a variety of different health education approaches to changing children's smoking behaviour. At a national level, people have been presented with information on the dangers of smoking to health through leaflets, articles, advertisements, comic strips, television commercials, and other media resources. Although this has had some effect in increasing knowledge, it has had a limited effect on changing behaviour. Other approaches have focused on trying to turn potential role models such as parents and peers into non-smokers; or by efforts to equip young people with the motivation and social skills to resist pressures to smoke. An HEA television campaign of 1995–6 encouraged people to give up and say 'no' to friends offering cigarettes in the pub or other social venues. Evaluation of the campaign indicated that many people had internalised the message and it affected smoking behaviour to varying degrees according to their stage in the quitting process. It seemed less successful at persuading smokers to stop, but reinforced existing intentions to give up smoking through instilling confidence and reassurance, and provided support to continue for those who had already stopped but might have considered starting again. The media have also been employed to portray the social image of smokers as unglamorous, smelly, unattractive, unsociable, weak and boring, while applying a more positive and socially desirable image to non-smokers. The effects of such projects are difficult to evaluate because of complexities and costs of testing mass media communications.

School

A significant number of intervention studies, especially in the United States, have concentrated on the school environment. Some have had a combined approach, such as involving the help of doctors (Townsend *et al.* 1991; Perry and Silvis 1987; Tuakli *et al.* 1990). The majority of school intervention studies have been undertaken in conjunction with schools' programmes of health information, and there is evidence of some success in projects carried out in Britain and other countries (Flay 1985, Flay *et al.* 1995; Vartiainen *et al.* 1986; Glynn *et al.* 1985,

Glynn *et al.* 1991; Schinke *et al.* 1986; Gillies and Wilcox 1984). However, it is not clear how long successful behavioural change will be sustained, and one long-term smoking prevention and cessation project combining television, school and family found that positive behavioural effects decayed over time.

These kinds of programmes have employed a variety of approaches including health information and general skills programmes and methods, and have targeted different age groups (Silvestri and Flay 1989). One disadvantage of trying to assess the impact of the few intervention studies carried out is the lack of adequate control groups. A review of school-based smoking intervention programmes (Oakley and Fullerton 1995) identified 74 such smoking prevention programmes published between 1970 and 1993 of which 12 were carried out in the UK. The authors found only four of these 12 studies met the minimum criteria for a methodologically adequate study. Most intervention studies of this type do not use the design of random allocation into experimental and control groups, so that evaluation of the effectiveness of the intervention is difficult to achieve. Nutbeam *et al.* (1993) carried out a study using a cluster randomised control trial of two projects taught under normal classroom conditions in which schools were allocated to one of four groups. Each received different smoking education or no intervention at all, but no significant differences were found in smoking behaviour, health knowledge, beliefs or values, leading the authors to state that school health education alone is insufficient to reduce teenage smoking. In addition, a potential limitation to schools-only intervention is the fact that children who are most vulnerable to smoking behaviour are also the least school-involved, and therefore the least likely to be effectively reached by school-oriented anti-smoking programmes (Nutbeam and Aaro 1991; Nutbeam 1995).

Family

Where the family has been involved in intervention studies, this has usually been in conjunction with a programme in schools. Studies have shown the importance of parental behaviour and attitudes in adolescent smoking prevention projects, and the need for parental support or involvement (Chassin *et al.* 1991; Mittelmark *et al.* 1988). Charlton (1986) carried out a family-linked intervention project in primary schools, based on the results of the Brigantia Smoking Survey in Northern England (Charlton 1984b). She set up a five-year controlled trial, following 9–10-year-olds until they were 14 years old. Early results of this large-scale survey showed a significant decrease in smoking among boys and their fathers, and also boys' best friends (usually also boys), but less positive results were found with girls and their mothers. Parental feedback also showed that two-thirds of smoking parents responded in asking for help in giving up smoking. Charlton concluded that this type of intervention could be effective in reducing family smoking, but that girls and their mothers were more difficult to influence. The approach used is one of self-esteem building, involving the school and family learning together. Charlton believes that 'education needs to include whole families, not just the children' (Charlton and Blair 1989b).

Reid *et al.* (1995) assessed a range of intervention programmes in an appraisal of the major options for reducing teenage smoking in Western countries, based on criteria of efficacy, cost to the health sector, replicability and impact. They concluded that the broader the approach, the greater the likelihood of success, and that teenage smoking would fall fastest in countries where funds were available for broad-based community campaigns aimed at all ages, supported by fiscal policy, restrictions on smoking at work and in school, and a ban on tobacco advertising – quite a tall order for many countries. Isolated interventions aimed specifically at young people are less likely to have lasting effects. Schools alone cannot produce such change and Reid *et al.* suggest that even the best programme for youth may only delay smoking recruitment. Mass campaigns may be more effective than schools at reaching high-risk groups.

Smoking is a complex health risk to challenge with health education interventions and initiatives, and it has been shown that combined programmes (using the school, family, media) are generally more effective than individual ones (Reid *et al.* 1995). However, bridging the gap between knowledge and behaviour in this health area can be a particularly difficult step to take and maintain, and is hampered by cigarette advertising campaigns and the availability of cigarettes to under-16s, as well as people's own resistance to giving up despite their awareness of the health risks.

OTHER HEALTH-RELATED BEHAVIOURS

There is some evidence that smoking behaviour in young people is related to other risky health behaviours, such as drinking, drug-taking and unprotected sex. Significant associations were found between drinking and smoking (Green *et al.* 1991). In the MORI survey (HEA 1992a) of young people aged 9–15 years, half (49 per cent) of regular smokers were also regular drinkers. The role of older siblings, parents and peers in influencing adolescent drug use was explored in a longitudinal study (Needle *et al.* 1986). These researchers found that, although peers were the primary source, older siblings (14–18 years old) had an important influence on their younger siblings (11–13 years old). In the Adolescent Health and Parenting study, smoking was related to both alcohol and drug use (Oakley *et al.* 1992). These relationships were stronger for girls than for boys. The MORI survey (HEA 1992b) also showed that exposure to illegal drugs was far higher among smokers than non-smokers (57 per cent compared to 6 per cent respectively had been offered illegal drugs), and experimentation with illegal drugs was similarly higher (50 per cent compared to 2 per cent respectively).

METHODOLOGICAL NOTE

When sifting through the vast amount of work carried out on smoking, it must be borne in mind that various different research methods have been used which make comparisons of findings more difficult to assess, although trends and relationships can be identified. For instance, large-scale surveys of teenage smoking have covered a broad range of ages between 11 and 18 years of age. Most of these studies have used schools or colleges where children and students are a captive population, and have tested all those present on the day of sampling. Some have used random sampling based on postal districts (Green *et al.* 1990; 1991). Surveys may be cross-sectional or longitudinal. These two different approaches may themselves furnish different kinds of results (Chassin *et al.*

1986). Sensitivity may be lost if the results are aggregated over different ages, and comparative accuracy made harder if definitions of smoking status vary between studies. For example, some research uses the categories of smoker versus non-smoker; others include ex-smokers, regular smokers and occasional smokers. The definition of a 'regular smoker' may also vary between more than one cigarette a week (OPCS and HEA studies) to more than 6 or 7 cigarettes a week (Newman and Ward 1989). Gillies (1985) has discussed these inconsistencies in the measurements used to show the prevalence of smoking in young people.

Many large-scale cross-sectional and longitudinal studies have implied causal links between various factors and smoking behaviour. The use of differing measures with variable reliability and validity has probably contributed to the contradictory nature of some findings, and future studies should try to provide more comparable data. There are clear advantages in the use of large-scale surveys, but they throw little light on the nature of the processes involved in the smoking behaviour of adults and children. In this context, qualitative studies that explore the meaning of smoking behaviour to people are important in order to illuminate the processes involved, and are especially important for the study of smoking and family communication. Although there has been some qualitative research on smoking (for instance, Friedman *et al.* 1985; Graham 1987a; 1987b; 1989; Daykin 1991; Green *et al.* 1990; 1991; Holland *et al.* 1995, 1996; HEA 1995g, 1995h, 1996), there is still room for more in-depth studies from a variety of perspectives. In contrast to the traditional focus on risk factors, the exploration of protective factors involved in adolescent smoking represents a relatively under-researched and potentially interesting approach which could also yield important information about the meaning of smoking to young people (Arnold *et al.* 1995).

In conclusion, smoking has clearly been an area that has received much attention from health research and promotion. Although there has been a significant decline in smoking in most groups, there is still some way to go. The smoking levels of young people (and girls in particular) provide continuing cause for concern. Several kinds of factors have been associated with the onset of smoking in young people, some of which are related directly or indirectly with communication and the family. These include parental and sibling attitudes, and lack of parental support during adolescence. Parental smoking behaviour does not show a clear predictive relationship with teenage smoking. Other factors include low academic achievement; rebelliousness; alienation from school; lack of skills to resist offers of cigarettes; and personal characteristics such as low self-esteem. For both boys and girls in one study (Oakley *et al.* 1992), smoking was shown to be linked to social lifestyle, and to family characteristics, such as the closeness of the family, which are factors that also operate in young people's drinking behaviour. There have been some conflicting indications with respect to family communication and smoking. Some researchers, such as Conrad *et al.* (1992), have suggested that family influences, particularly parental behaviour and approval, play a much less consistent part in predicting onset of smoking in young people than previously assumed, and that changes in parenting may be contributing to this. Other recent studies continue to emphasise the importance of family influences (Brynin and Scott 1996; Brannen and Storey 1996).

RECOMMENDATIONS FOR FURTHER RESEARCH

1. Further qualitative research could be carried out on teenage smoking, to explore the dynamics and meanings of smoking to young people, inside and outside the family.

2. Parental attitude has been shown to be a key factor in smoking outcomes in children and more research is needed to demonstrate the most effective stance that parents might take.

3. Large-scale surveys have found evidence to suggest the importance of sibling smoking behaviour, and this influence could benefit from a more in-depth exploration.

4. Research has started to explore possible 'protective factors' in young people's smoking behaviour, and these factors could benefit from further investigation.

5. The relationship between adolescent smoking behaviour and the nature of family 'culture', including aspects of closeness and conflict, could be further examined.

6. Research on the ways that patterns and meanings of smoking are different for young men and young women, could usefully contribute to targeting them separately for health messages.

7. In methodological terms, it is necessary to make studies more comparative, and pay more attention to reliability and validity. Longitudinal studies give better indications about causal relationships, but the use of randomised controlled trials can also prove to be a sound approach.

7. Sexual health

Sexual health issues have become much more prominent over the last couple of decades for several reasons, including: concerns over teenage pregnancies; the increase in HIV/AIDS; and the higher incidence of testicular cancer in young men. Sexual issues have a continuous high profile in the media, and recent national surveys have examined sexual attitudes and lifestyles in Britain (Johnson *et al.* 1994; Wellings *et al.* 1994). Sex education has also become a topic that has attained both social and political prominence, and provoked legislative changes affecting the school curriculum. However, this apparent public openness has not been transmitted to family communication about sex and sexual health, and this can clearly still be problematic between many parents and children, and also between men and women and their sexual partners.

Sex education and sexual health issues cover a wide and overlapping area, which is not merely limited to the processes of sexual intercourse and reproduction. In the process of growing up, children and teenagers have concerns around puberty and physical development, body image, emotions and emotional relationships. These broader issues have tended to be neglected and some studies have noted that the definitions of 'sex 'or 'sexual activity' are very often taken as sexual intercourse/penetrative sex by the participants (Wight 1992; Spencer *et al.* 1988; Holland *et al.* 1991), and sometimes by the researchers as well.

Ethnographic studies have mainly focused on how information about sexual health is transmitted within the family/household. New areas of interest have included 'new-middle-class households', absentee fathers, and teenage boys talking about sex (Aggleton 1987; Anderson 1989; Wight 1991). Over the last few decades, sociological studies have examined adolescent sexual behaviour, as well as family communication about sex, young women's sexuality, and young people's responsibility for health (Schofield 1965; Farrell 1978; Allen 1987; Holland *et al.* 1990a; Holland *et al.* 1990b; Dodd 1991). In psychology, studies have examined communication between spouses, peers, family members in general, and family communication about sex (Fox and Inazu 1980a; Youniss and Ketterlinus 1987; Fitzpatrick 1988a; Dorval 1990; Noller and Callan 1991; Tannen 1991).

Whatever level of communication about sex is going on within families, teenagers today are sexually active from an early age (HEA 1992b; Holland *et al.* 1990b). The Women Risk and AIDS Project (Holland *et al.* 1990b) found that 62 per cent of young women in their sample were already sexually active at the age of 16, and the average age of first intercourse was 14.5 years among working-class girls, and 16.3 years for their middle-class counterparts. The high profile given to sexual activity by society today was reflected in the finding that one in five young people agreed that their friends made them feel that sex was the only thing that mattered in a relationship (HEA 1992b). In this survey there was also some evidence of an inverse relationship between socio-economic group and being sexually active, and in terms of ethnicity, young Asians were far less likely to have had any sexual involvement than young African–Caribbeans or whites.

This chapter: sets the background to the changes in attitudes to sex education in school; looks at the ways that children and teenagers learn about 'sex' inside the family; how often and how effectively families discuss sexuality; how parents and teenagers perceive communication; and what they talk about.

SEX EDUCATION AND AIDS

The increasing incidence of HIV infection and AIDS in the 1980s sharpened the concern to communicate these and other sexual risks to the general population, and especially to the younger generation who were learning about sex and becoming sexually active. Although the early panic about HIV/AIDS has calmed down in the UK, the risk of contracting the virus has not gone away. Health campaigners remain concerned about the effectiveness of recent government targets to increase awareness about HIV. Figures on the heterosexual population show that by 1991, 24 per cent of all HIV infections resulted from heterosexual intercourse (Adler 1992). Heterosexual teenagers were seen as particularly vulnerable but in spite of their growing knowledge about the disease, evidence has shown a relatively low extent of change in behaviour in favour of using safer sex (Holland *et al.* 1990a; Wight 1991). Studies have been made of young people's beliefs and misconceptions about HIV and AIDS (Warwick *et al.* 1988b), and about their feelings of invulnerability (Abrams *et al.* 1990). There has been serious concern over this continuing gap between knowledge and behaviour, and the reasons why safer sexual practices have not been significantly taken up beyond the gay community (Weatherburn *et al.* 1992).

One important area in sexuality and health that has received relatively recent attention explores the issue of how power relations influence gender relations and structure young people's options for safer sex (Waldby *et al.* 1990; Ramazanoglu 1990). The WRAP/MRAP studies of young women's and young men's sexual attitudes and behaviour in the context of HIV/AIDS has attributed young people's difficulties with practising safer sex to gendered power relations, especially in the case of young women (Holland *et al.* 1990a; 1990b; 1991). By considering the power operating within sexual relationships it is possible to understand the 'unreality gap' between knowledge and practice. The WRAP study has explored the different meanings associated with the use and non-use of condoms, and reveals the contradictions young people have to overcome to practice safer sex. This has implications for the ways that sex education is communicated to young people, and the ways that they talk about it amongst themselves.

Another contradictory area lies in government concern for more preventative sex education in its health campaigns in view of AIDS, and in the organisation and content of school-based sex education (Thomson and Scott 1991; Whitfield 1990). Sexuality in both the AIDS awareness campaigns and at school tends to be interpreted in its narrowest sense, as reproductive sex (Prendergast and Prout 1990; Wight 1992). Discussion of the social context of relationships, the emotions involved, the conflicting pleasures and dangers associated with sexuality are generally excluded. Until quite recently sex education at school was not compulsory. Under the Education Act 1993 the government made it compulsory for secondary schools to provide sex education (DES 1993), but at the same time stipulated that education about human sexual behaviour, including education about HIV/AIDS, be removed from the National Curriculum statutory order for science. Parents were given the right to withdraw their children from all or part of the sex education offered, but not from that concerning basic reproduction which is still included under science in the National Curriculum. The governing bodies of primary schools can exercise discretion as to whether or not to provide sex education and in what form.

LEARNING AND TALKING IN THE FAMILY ABOUT SEX

Children and adolescents learn about sex in a variety of ways, from a variety of sources. As well as parents, school, peers and lovers, teenagers also learn about sex from the media, porn videos (especially boys), childhood experiences (games, abuse), and to a lesser extent from youth and health workers (Allen 1987; Wight 1992). The family tends to come fairly low on the list according to many teenagers (HEA 1992b), but it is nevertheless an important location for the provision of sex education and potential sharing of emotional or sexual anxieties.

In a survey of parents' views on sex education and its provision in schools (NFER/HEA 1994), most parents said they had discussed or intended to discuss sexual matters with their children. With very young children they would respond to questions rather than initiate discussion, and with older children they would initiate important issues themselves. Four-fifths of them expressed confidence about providing sex education for their children. However, research on sexual health reveals the lack of open family discussion about sex and shows that this is often a very difficult subject for people to talk about (Fisher 1987; Noller and Callan 1991). There is a 'general aversion to explicit conversation about sex' (Wight 1990). A study of parent–teenager communication about sex (Allen 1987) revealed that 43 per cent of teenagers had never spoken to their mothers about sexuality and 72 per cent had never spoken to their fathers. Figures from the MORI survey (HEA 1992b), showed that 33 per cent young women (16–19-years old) and 60 per cent of young men had not discussed 'topics to do with sex' with their mothers, and 82 per cent of young women and 74 per cent of young men had not discussed this subject with their fathers. In the younger age group, Brannen and Storey (1996) found that over a third of the 11–12-year-olds in their study reported that no one had spoken to them about sex.

Jaccard and Dittus (1993) suggest that few studies on parent-teenager communication about sex distinguish between sex, sexuality and birth control, and the avoidance of premarital pregnancy. They believe that researchers may fail to recognise that the term 'sexual information' has different meanings to different teenagers. One teenager might assume that it refers to birth control, whereas another might believe that it refers to a discussion on the physiology of sex. Where discussion does take place, for girls, it is often initiated with their first menstrual period, while boys rarely use their first ejaculation to initiate any such communication (Zani 1991). The most often discussed topics are menstruation, pregnancy and childbirth, whereas intercourse and birth control are rarely mentioned (Fox and Inazu 1980c; Allen 1987). Ejaculation, wet dreams and masturbation are hardly ever discussed (Warman 1986; Allen 1987), and Brannen and Storey (1996) found that over half (58 per cent) of the 11–12-year-old boys in their research said they talked to no one about puberty. In one study of family communication (Holland *et al.* 1996), three parental approaches to sex education were identified: the appropriate age, the staggered approach, and the ongoing approach. Brannen and Storey (1996) also referred to parents who waited until the 'right moment' to discuss sexual issues, and that the child's attitude and behaviour in seeking information and initiating discussion was crucial to whether and how this discussion took place.

The family clearly has an important role to play in the sexual socialisation of children. Parents are generally interested in being actively involved in children's sexual education and want to talk more about sex and human sexual relationships but do not know how to (Noller and Callan 1991). Parents' sense of uncertainty about what to tell their children and when, and their desire for guidance in relation to sex education was expressed in a research project on family communication (Holland *et al.* 1996). In a recent pilot project in Wales, discussion groups were set up to provide parents with information about sex and sex education to facilitate their involvement with their own children's learning of this subject (Health Promotion Wales 1994). However, parents would have liked more guidance on how to deal with issues such as how much to tell their children, and when to tell them, rather than to focus on sex education and attitudes to sexuality. It also highlighted some problems with recruitment in that the parents attending the groups were already motivated and came from fairly similar middle-class backgrounds, and it did not reach parents whose needs may have been greater.

The level of parental participation in the formal transmission of sex education to their children is low, although it is higher in younger age groups than during adolescence (Zani 1991; Brannen and Storey 1996). For younger children, parents are the most important source until puberty, after which friends and boyfriends/girlfriends increase in importance. In research by Brannen *et al.* (1994), significantly more 12-year-olds report talking to parents about sex than 16-year-olds, and girls talked more than boys. For teenagers, parents are not the first people they turn to for information about AIDS, nor are they cited as the most important source of information (Reader *et al.* 1988; Wight 1992; Brannen and Storey 1996). When participants in Wight's study (1992) of 14–16-year-old teenage boys in Glasgow were asked about how they had learned about sex, parents figured last in the list after friends and television. Many boys had obviously had no sex education at home; and those who did usually got brief information on condoms, pregnancy and AIDS.

The main themes researchers have examined in the home context are how often parents and young people talk about sexual issues, how much they disclose, who initiates and then dominates conversation and the link between communication, behaviour and self-confidence (Noller and Callan 1990). Adolescents who are high in self-esteem and believe they are valued by other family members are more likely to self-disclose than those who feel vulnerable and insecure (Noller and Callan 1991). Furthermore, adolescents are more self-confident about discussing sexual matters with their mothers than their fathers (Youniss and Smollar 1985). In Wight's study, nearly all the boys commented on the problem of their parents' embarrassment about sexual topics, and several other studies, such as that by Brannen and Storey (1996) have drawn attention to high levels of shyness and embarrassment on the part of both parents and children.

Frequency

In an early study, Fox and Inazu (1980a, 1980b) measured communication frequency as the number of mother–daughter discussions within the six months preceding the interview. Their findings showed that dating and boyfriends were the most discussed topics, and conception the least. They suggested that more frequent mother–daughter discussion about sexuality and contraception might allow daughters to accept their sexuality more easily as this appears to be a prelude for taking contraceptive responsibility. Discrepancies have been found between what parents believed they should talk about and what they actually intended to talk about. This is especially true for birth control. This might explain why some parents report far more discussion than their children do and how they overestimate the extent to which children find it easy to talk to them (Allen 1987).

Noller and Bagi (1985) focused on communication between parents and adolescents across 14 topics, and six 'process dimensions' – frequency, self-disclosure, initiation, recognition, domination and adolescent satisfaction. They found that frequency and disclosure varied according to gender. Young people communicated more with mothers than fathers, and mothers were more active than fathers in communicating about sexuality. The areas least discussed with the mother were sexual problems and information, and the most frequently discussed topic with the father was politics.

Most research has concentrated on how often communication occurs rather than on what is said, when, and how it is said, or the social context in which the exchange takes place, and some researchers have questioned the validity of frequency as a way of assessing the effect of communication. Fisher (1987) found that the quality of family communication seemed unrelated to the extent of family discussions. Yet there are suggestions that communication about sexual issues can lead to more responsible patterns of sexual behaviour (Fox and Inazu 1980a; Wright *et al.* 1990).

Research which stresses the context of parent–adolescent communication about sex tends to focus on issues of developmental psychology. During adolescence teenagers face pressure from parents keen to exercise their control. Young women in particular face a contradiction between their need for autonomy, their ambivalence towards the 'plurality of models of female identity' and increased parent control (Zani 1991). Parents and teenagers who acknowledge and address issues of authority and resistance are also better able to negotiate their evolving relationship even if one of the paradoxes of 'democratic parenting' is that communication leads to independence (Noller and Callan 1990).

Effectiveness

A more pertinent question than frequency is the effectiveness of open communication about sex with parents as compared with peers or lovers. Research shows that peers are often the most common source of information about sex and are models for sexual behaviour (Wight 1991; HEA 1992b). In the MORI survey, 85 per cent of the young women and 74 per cent of the young men had discussed topics to do with sex with friends of their age, and 65 per cent and 54 per cent respectively had discussed this with their boyfriends/girlfriends. (For the young men, these figures were far higher than those for discussions with their mothers.) An ethnographic study of young women's friendships suggested that they used the safety of best friendships to discuss the social relations of sex. These discussions included speculation on potential boyfriends, reviews of past experiences, and include the management strategies for sexual double standards (Hey 1996).

Parents were rated lower than friends, schools and books as sources of information in one study of family influences on sexual attitudes and knowledge (Sanders and Mullis 1988), even though they rate highest in terms of influence on their daughters' sexual opinions, beliefs and attitudes. The strengths of the family are seen as related to parental influence, parents' past reaction to sex education and their own sexual permissiveness. However, parents' disclosures to children are less well documented than children's to parents (Miller and Lane 1991). Another weakness is that parents may be ignorant of a number of sexual issues and need to be provided with more information on topics such as venereal disease, homosexuality, contraception, and guidelines for discussing sexual behaviour with their children (Allen 1987).

Adolescents also tend to experience great awkwardness in discussing sex with friends, lovers, and with social researchers (Wight 1991). Studies have found that some young teenage men engaged in very little dialogue during sex, and there were no discussions about sexual practices, pleasure or AIDS (Wight 1991; Thomson and Scott 1990). By taking account of the social context in which sex takes place, Thomson and Scott (1991) distinguish between three levels of knowledge: knowing that there is something to know about; knowing in the sense of having information; and knowing about sex from experience. These do not necessarily follow a linear pattern: one kind of knowledge might not automatically lead to another.

There is little available evidence regarding the effectiveness of parents' transmission of sex information or on parental feelings about this role. However, as mentioned above, this seems an age-dependent issue in which parents are more appropriate for younger children, and less appropriate for teenagers (Allen 1987; Brannen and Storey 1996).

DEMOGRAPHIC FACTORS

Research on family communication about sex shows that patterns of discussion are influenced by factors such as gender, class and household structure, and ethnicity.

Gender

Gender plays an important part in the ways parents perceive their children and bring them up, and how children themselves think about health and illness. With respect to sexual health and sex education within the family there is a gender difference in that it is usually mothers (rather than fathers) who act as sex educators with both their sons and daughters about general issues to do with body changes, contraception, homosexuality, HIV/AIDS, relationships, and specific aspects of women's reproductive health such as pregnancy, birth and breast cancer. Mother–daughter discussions are more common than mother–son or father–son communication (HEA 1992b). Thus daughters receive more sex education than sons, and discuss themselves more often and openly with mothers than with fathers (Allen 1987). In contrast, sons discuss themselves less openly but what they disclose they share equally with both parents (Youniss and Ketterlinus 1987).

The information that girls receive on sexual health issues takes place within a protective discourse which emphasises reproduction and the dangers of sexual activity (Thomson and Scott 1991). Boys tend to receive less formal sex education than girls (Allen 1987; Currie 1990) and this is related to an assumption of boys/men as being knowing sexual agents (Holland *et al.* 1993b). Fathers tend to leave their children's sex education and the discussion of similar 'sensitive' issues such as the body and body changes to mothers, or decide they can only deal with sons (Holland *et al.* 1996).

The MORI survey (HEA 1992b) asked 16–19-year-olds how easy they found it to discuss topics about sex with various people. Results indicated that 58 per cent of young women and 38 per cent of young men said it was easy to talk with their mothers, and only 16 per cent and 30 per cent respectively said it was easy to talk to their fathers. The gender difference was much less for discussion with friends: 84 per cent of young women and 79 per cent of young men found it easy to talk to friends of their own age, and 67 per cent:61 per cent (respectively) found it easy to talk to their boyfriend/girlfriend about sexual topics. Most boys do not talk to anyone about HIV/AIDS, except to make jokes, least of all to their parents who are too embarrassed (Wight 1991).

Young people's learning from their own sexual experience also differs according to gender, as male sexual discourse dominates both romantic ideology and young women's sexual knowledge (Holland *et al.* 1991; Thomson and Scott 1991). Brannen and Storey (1996) found that a higher proportion of boys said that they had not spoken to anyone about puberty compared with girls (58 per cent: 38 per cent). Girls had more discussions, but these were mainly about menstruation (also Zani 1991). Few adolescents talk to their parents about their first sexual experience but those who do are more likely to be female than male. In Allen's study (1987), no more than 11 per cent of teenagers said they had discussed a sexual topic other than relationships with their fathers. The first ejaculation was hardly ever a topic of conversation between fathers and sons. Male role stereotypes hinder young men from actively searching for information.

There are some other related gender differences, for instance, in the ways that boys and girls see themselves, and express themselves. In terms of body image, girls are much less happy than boys (Brannen and Storey 1996). The 11–12-year-olds in Brannen and Storey's study reflected an early concern with the idealised view of slimness, which is related to being sexually attractive. Many more girls than boys were anxious about weight, and saw themselves as being overweight (21 per cent of girls and 40 per cent of boys were happy about their weight, and almost half the girls said they would like to lose weight – this leaves a significant proportion of both sexes who were less than happy about their weight). In the area of emotions, research has shown that boys are far less likely than girls to communicate about such issues (Rogers *et al.* 1996). There was a striking difference between teenage boys and girls in this study on their willingness or ability to express emotions, or share problems with anybody, inside or outside the family.

Mothers

Mothers are more active in transmitting information to their children as they tend to be the primary carers and sex educators of their children (Fisher 1987; Mayall and Watson 1989). They also build on the continuity of open and general communication established in childhood, mainly in the mother–daughter relationship, through to adolescence when they discuss more sensitive sexual issues. Data from Fox and Inazu's early Detroit study (1980a) on the timing, content and frequency of communication about sex showed that the importance of continuity far outweighed how mothers themselves felt about sex, their attitudes to birth control and their sex role orientation in determining early sexual communication with their children. Sons and daughters have been found to communicate more with mothers than fathers and experienced more conflict with them (Noller and Bagi 1985; Noller and Callan 1991). Mothers displayed more understanding, compatibility and confidentiality than fathers did and initiated more conversations (Farrell 1978; Noller and Callan 1991).

The mother–daughter dyad is therefore an important family relationship for the direct transmission of sex education in the household (Allen 1987). Fox and Inazu (1980a) showed that mothers can play at least two roles as sex educators with their daughters – protector and guide. Thomson and Scott (1991) were concerned that discussing sex education as protection reinforced the passive model of female sexuality and neglected to balance the emphasis on contraception and danger with information on sexual pleasure and sexual identity.

Other research on the link between the mother–daughter relationship and general health issues has explored 'the cycle of deprivation hypothesis' which may also be applied to sexual health. In their study of mothers' and daughters' health care beliefs and practices, Blaxter and Paterson (1982a) considered whether daughters of socially deprived mothers reproduced their beliefs and practices. Their evidence showed that these are not transmitted in a straightforward way from one generation to the next but that resemblances depended on continuities in the socio-economic conditions in both generations.

Fathers

Communication between father and son, father and daughter and mother and son is far less well documented than that between mother and daughter (Warman 1986). Research has often appeared to concentrate on mothers, as having the primary role in the family, but anyone involved in family research will also recognise the ways that fathers tend to absent themselves from the room or house while the research is going on (Brannen *et al.* 1994; Holland *et al.* 1996). Fathers often find it harder to communicate with their children than mothers because of their absences from the home, a perceived lack of closeness with their children, and an inability to express their emotions (Dosser *et al.* 1986; Anderson 1989; Sharpe, 1994); Holland *et al.* 1996). Young people themselves report less openness and sometimes more problems in communication with fathers, who are seen by younger adolescents as recognising their views less and as initiating fewer conversations than mothers (Barnes and Olson 1985; Noller and Callan 1990). By their absence from home, fathers may offer their sons an ambivalent role model (Anderson 1989; Youniss and Ketterlinus 1987). However, it may be that as parents' employment trends alter the division of their time in paid and unpaid work, fathers will spend more time with their children (McGuire 1983; Lewis and O'Brien 1987; Mayall and Watson 1989).

Wight's study of young men aimed to explore the gap between the ideology of teenage male sexuality and young boys' sexual experiences and emotions. He was especially interested in adolescent male vulnerability and how fathers reinforced the stereotype of masculinity (Wight 1992). The study showed that the young men found it easier to talk to their fathers about sex, but in common with other research findings, they appeared to distance themselves from sex through exaggerated talk, swapping sexual insults, silence or most often through jokes (Allen 1987; Wight 1991; Holland *et al.* 1993). Wight (1992) identifies the way a young boy's sexual identity can be imposed almost entirely by other males including fathers, other relatives and peers: 'The minimal role of schools, other professionals or mothers in their developing sexuality means there is little scope for non-conventional or non-male constructions of identity.'

Fathers may express relief that their wives were 'handling the situation' when it came to discussing sex with their children (Nolin 1988), especially daughters. Father–daughter communication is often insufficient to include a discussion of the daughter's sexual attitudes. Nolin considered that fathers might feel left out of intimate family discussions or guilty for not communicating with their children. Warman (1986) in his study of father–son communication about sexuality found several reasons for fathers' passive role in family discourse. Fathers lacked role models as well as an understanding of teenage boys' sexuality and needs, so they tended to transfer this responsibility to mothers. They also experienced confusion and conflict between pressure from society to educate their sons about sexuality, and taboos around expressing emotions that stem from male gender role stereotyping (Warman 1986). Also problematic was the way fathers use their power and control to dominate family relationships and thus stifle the intimacy needed for more disclosing relationships.

Social class and household structure

Social class is also an important factor in this area (Martin 1990). There appears to be more communication and less conflict in middle-class families, whereas the least skilled, least educated families discuss topics less and provide less sex education for their children (Noller and Callan 1991; Gordon *et al.* 1990). Social class and level of education may also be relevant to HIV-related behaviour, as poverty is an important factor in any consideration of health (Wight 1990; Graham 1990).

Different household structures also affect communication patterns. It may be expected that single-parent families may find it hard to talk to children, but some research suggests that this situation makes parents and children closer. A study of 11–12-year-olds (Brannen and Storey 1996) showed that both girls and boys from lone-mother families reported talking to their mothers about sex more than those from two-parent families. Their mothers gave similar accounts, which lead the researchers to suggest that lone-mothers may be compensating for the father's absence (and perhaps attribute more interaction on his part than actually happens in two-parent families). Divorced/separated or widowed mothers may express themselves more often and more intimately to daughters than mothers in 'intact marriages' (Allen 1987; Youniss and Ketterlinus 1987). In 'new middle class families', that is, families of non-biologically related adults and children, there is often more open but impersonal debate about sexuality, and paradoxically, increased parental supervision of sexual activity (Aggleton 1987).

Ethnicity

In the MORI survey of 16–19-year-olds (HEA 1992b), only 37 per cent of young Asians were sexually active, compared with 66 per cent of white and 62 per cent of African–Caribbean. Young African–Caribbeans were more likely to express a willingness to have unprotected sex than white or Asian youth. Eighty-eight per cent of white compared to 82 per cent of African–Caribbean and 80 per cent Asian said their school had given them information about sex. However, no details were given on family discussion about sexual topics by ethnic group. Unlike their American counterparts, British researchers have generally neglected the issues of ethnicity and cultural differences relating to sexual health discourses among families (Kohli 1992). Kohli argues that there are difficulties raising the issue of HIV and AIDS among Asian communities in Britain because of the sense of 'cultural immunity' which exists, frequently fostered by leaders who consider AIDS irrelevant to their community. Brannen and Storey (1996), however, found that the 11–12-year-old Asian children in their study reported lower levels of communication about sex than white children, and black children reported even less. The researchers point to cultural taboos about sex operating to limit communication about sex, and suggest that some sex education may be passed on by older siblings or other family members who have grown up in Britain.

Anderson's ethnographic study (1989) of American, poor, inner-city black families pointed out the links between different cultural assumptions and communication patterns: 'Parents in this culture are extremely reticent about discussing sex and birth control with their children.' Another study showed that there are no significant differences in sexual attitudes except that more black women than white women anticipated support from their families rather than from social welfare agencies (Howard 1988). Noller and Callan (1991) appear to support this view from a psychological perspective, asserting that families from minority backgrounds tend to be more cohesive and place less emphasis on autonomy and individuation. They also suggested that religious families had more positive and constructive communication than families who were not perceived as being religious (Noller and Callan 1991).

Sociological studies may be more willing to include different ethnic groups in their samples. An examination of the various ethnic groups in the WRAP study (Holland 1993a) reveals a greater similarity than difference in young women's experience of sexual encounters and relationships, despite varying socio-economic class positions, cultural, religious and educational backgrounds. The similarities stem from male definitions of heterosexuality, the passive definition of female sexuality and young women's subordinate position in sexual encounters. The most significant differences were cultural: for example, Asian young women were subject to specific pressures, and double standards of sexual behaviour for men and women were particularly significant for all the ethnic minority women studied (Holland 1993a).

Age, occupational status and level of education

These factors are all of some relevance in determining family communication patterns (Zani 1991). The middle years of adolescence appear to generate more communication problems in families than the early or later years of adolescence (Noller and Callan 1991). Occupational status, education and communication are all inter-related, but no link was found between communication and parents' employment status (Wright *et al.* 1990). Education seems more closely correlated with communication than age or employment. The different educational contexts of the three groups in Zani's study (1991) – high school students, teenagers on training schemes and apprentices, and unemployed young people, showed a higher level of schooling was matched by a quantitative and qualitative increase in knowledge.

OTHER TYPES OF FAMILY COMMUNICATION

General communication and communication about sex

Some studies have looked at the correlation between general family communication and communication about sex. Although correlations cannot be taken to indicate causality, they do shed light on the link between communication and the 'sexual activity of youth' (Warren and Neer 1986). However, studies show conflicting results. Fisher (1987) studied the link between parents' reports of general family communication and sexual activity, and found that the correlation between parents' and children's sexual attitudes exists for sons rather than daughters, that the quality of general family discourse was not related to parent–child communication about sex. On the other hand, Newcomer and Udry (1985) and

Yarber and Greer (1986) have reported that sexual attitudes, communication and sexual behaviour are more closely related for daughters than sons.

Fisher's findings (1987) also failed to support the popular impression that family-based sex education is most common in 'good' parent–child relationships and point out the paradox that even in close and non-sexual relationships, sex is often very difficult to discuss. Contrary to this, research by Kotva and Schneider (1990) demonstrated a close relationship between general communication and sexual discourse. Differences between the results of this and Fisher's (1987) study may be due in part to methodological differences, and to the subjects of research. Fisher's study included male and female respondents and parents, while Kotva and Schneider's study focused on the mother–daughter dyad. Kotva and Schneider found there was more agreement between mothers and daughters on their rating of sexual communication, less on general communication and no agreement about how well they communicate during conflict. This study is also consistent with the findings of Barnes and Olson (1985), in that mothers felt they were more open and effective in communication than did daughters.

There are also conflicting results about the links between family communication and sexual behaviour (Kotva and Schneider 1990; Fisher 1987; Newcomer and Udry 1985; Fox and Inazu 1980a). A central finding of Kotva and Schneider's work was the positive link made between consistent birth control use and communication scores. Sex communication scores for both mother and daughter and the general communication scores for daughters were higher for the women who always used birth control (Kotva and Schneider 1990; Fisher 1987; Newcomer and Udry 1985). High levels of communication were not related to the probability of being sexually active, but rather to more mature and responsible behaviour by the sexually active women, an important finding in the light of AIDS, sexually transmitted diseases (STDs) and unwanted pregnancies.

Spouse communication and related communication effects

There appears to be very little reference to spouse communication about sexual health and general health issues in the available literature although general accounts of men who experience problems communicating with their wives are well documented (Fitzpatrick 1988a; Tannen 1991). Recent research which focused on spouse communication in relation to the mother's health care needs following birth, has suggested that lack of time, mothers' reluctance to talk about 'their problems' and partners' inability to communicate their own emotions while being supportive of their partners' is problematic (Mauthner 1994).

A little-researched aspect of communication is the impact of the presence of one parent (described as the 'spouse') on the other parent's interactions with the child. Few researchers have demonstrated the link between parent–child and spousal relationships, although work has been done on marital and partner communication (Fitzpatrick 1988a; 1988b; Gottman and Levenson 1988; Tannen 1991, 1995). Change in parental behaviour in the presence of the spouse depends on the quality of marital communication. Gjerde (1986) compared parent–adolescent interaction in the presence of the spouse (triad) and without the spouse present (dyad). Fathers of sons were less involved, less egalitarian, more critical and antagonistic when the mother was present than when alone with the son. Mothers' interactions were more positive, responsive, secure and consistent when the spouse was present. Therefore the presence of the spouse enhanced the mothers' interactions with their sons, but not those of the fathers in this study.

Gjerde's work (1986) focused on parents' behaviour only, and did not include young people's, which created difficulties in interpreting the results of the study. It may be that fathers' interactions changed while mothers' interactions were enhanced, because fathers were trying to present themselves as stricter than they were in practice. For mothers there was less risk of their 'positivity' (that is, their positiveness in interactions), being interpreted sexually in the presence of the spouse. More research is needed on the effect of the presence or absence of specific family members on family interaction in addition to whether adolescents behave differently in the presence of one or both parents.

Non-verbal communication

It is well known that not all communication is verbal, within or outside the family. Many aspects of behaviour can be picked up through observation rather than instruction, and some research has focused on other factors operating in the home as mediators of attitudes towards the body and sexuality. 'Much of what we learn about sex is communicated elliptically' (Thomson and Scott 1991). Indirect sources of family influence on sexual behaviour may be far more potent than the direct verbal transmission of sexual values and information.

Some researchers highlight the importance of hundreds of mundane incidents which contribute to daily living, and which transmit sexual values to children. Nolin (1988) examined direct and indirect sources of maternal influence on daughters' sexual behaviours. Indirect communication was measured through teenagers' reports about ease of family communication, family nudity, parental reaction to sex on TV, and family emotional and physical expressiveness. Results showed that daughters reported more indirect messages accepting of sexuality than sons. In addition, more than twice as many daughters as sons reported that their families were expressive and demonstrative.

In spite of the importance of body language, the predominant emphasis remains on the usefulness of verbal communication, because of its directness. It provides the most conservative and restrictive test for parental influence on children's sexual behaviour. Measures less subject to the limitations of verbal versus non-verbal communication, such as the family sexual climate, could yield even stronger evidence for parental influence.

CONTRADICTIONS

It is tempting to think that with so much discussion of sex and sexual behaviour in the public domain, especially in the media, that talking about sex would have become much easier within the private domain of the family. To some extent this has happened, for instance the parents participating in one family study spoke of how they felt that they and their children talked more about sexual topics than themselves and their own parents (Holland *et al.* 1996), and the majority of parents participating in a survey of parental views on, and school provision of, sex education (NFER/HEA 1994) felt confident about providing their children with sex education. However, family sexual discourse does not appear to be happening on a large scale. A paradox exists over communication about sex. While many parents want to be seen as active resource agents for sex education, and adolescents say that they would like to have better sex-related communication with their parents, relatively little seems to occur, and many parents would like more information or guidance (Valentich and Gripton 1989; Health Promotion Wales 1994; Holland *et al.* 1996). The parents involved in the NFER survey wanted more guidance on discussing HIV and AIDS and other STDs, contraception, homosexuality and lesbianism with their children. They also wanted to develop a partnership with the schools to facilitate communication on when and how the schools were teaching sex education topics, as well as a possible exchange of educational materials so that they could initiate or tailor their own discussions accordingly (NFER/HEA 1994). (It is characteristic of this subject and of research techniques used, that although this survey talks of 'parents', the response to their parental survey came predominantly from mothers, who are generally more accessible.)

Embarrassment seems to be one of the main obstacles parents and teenagers face when they want to discuss sexual health. A range of other factors may contribute to the lack of communication about sex, such as: the plurality of the sexual value system; changes in sexual role definitions; generational segregation; devaluation of the parental role; parents' erratic daily schedule; as well as other aspects such as lack of trust or confidence; fear of a negative reaction; ignorance; the lack of any discourse of female sexuality; and poverty (Wight 1991; Allen 1987; Anderson 1989; Thomson and Scott 1990, 1991). Parents' upbringing and their own lack of sex education coupled with inadequate knowledge or communication skills also make talking about sex a difficult experience (Allen 1987).

As researchers, educators and health policy-makers decry the absence of family sex communication it is easy to understand why family health interventions are so often looked upon as a remedy. The intervention project in Wales (Health Promotion Wales 1994) showed that, although parents' discussion groups were of some use, they neglected vital issues of what, when and how to tell children in favour of information about sex and sex education. Some studies have called for a comprehensive sex education programme which emphasises both young women's and young men's sexuality and covers AIDS, STDs, contraception and non-penetrative sex in a context of explicit school-based debate (di Clemente *et al.* 1986, 1988; Kaul and Stephens 1991; Wight 1991; Holland *et al.* 1991). Other researchers want to see sex education programmes for parents as well as joint parent–children workshops (Stenbakken 1989; Valentich and Gripton 1989; Danilewitz and Skuy 1990; Bruyn 1992). It is important that more resources go into helping parents and adolescents to open up to one another on this important topic. Methods used in the dissemination of information about health and sex for the whole family need to be examined for accessibility and understanding of the information provided.

RECOMMENDATIONS FOR FURTHER RESEARCH

1. Some investigation could be made into whether adolescents today receive conflicting messages from parents about traditional gender roles, and the potential implications for sexual health messages.

2. Further research could be carried out into parents' and children's perceptions of the importance, frequency and effectiveness of communication about sexual issues.

3. The type of communication techniques that parents use if and when they talk about sex with their children could usefully be explored, as could the nature of the sexual vocabularies used on both sides.

4. The relationship, if any, between general parent–child communication and discussion of sexual issues merits more research attention.

5. More research should be carried out into the role of fathers as sexual health educators, their own perceptions, health beliefs and what children learn from them (Warren and Neer 1986; Fisher 1987; Kotva and Schneider 1990).

6. Spouse communication about sexual and reproductive health issues is another important area that should be the focus of further research.

7. Research should look in more detail at the sexual and emotional problems of boys.

8. The issues of control, authority and independence in relation to sex education, communication about sexuality and related issues in the family is an important area for research (Noller and Callan 1991).

9. Research has shown up the problems involved in giving support or intervention to parents through providing information on when and how to communicate about sex and sexuality with their children (Health Education Wales 1994), and this warrants more study and development.

8. Diet and nutrition

The diet and nutrition targets set out in the Department of Health's *The Health of the Nation* White Paper aim to reduce fat consumption and obesity in the population by the year 2005 (DoH 1995). It is hoped to reduce the average percentage of food energy derived from fat by 12 per cent to no more than 35 per cent (DoH 1994a; HEA 1995a). Research shows that obesity has increased in both men and women over the last decade owing to the link between food intake and levels of physical activity (DoH 1995). Eating a healthy diet has been the focus of much of the HEA's prevention work (HEA 1993c; Stockley 1993). Its healthy eating message stresses the importance of enjoying food, eating a variety of foods, eating the right amount to maintain weight, eating foods rich in starch and 'fibre', avoiding sugary foods and too much fat – especially 'saturates', and eating plenty of fruit and vegetables (HEA 1995b; HEA 1991a).

Research on food and eating shows that a healthy diet is essentially linked to a range of factors, including class, income, gender and ethnicity (Dobson *et al.* 1994; Scott 1995a; HEA 1991b; Cole-Hamilton 1988; Graham 1986; Townsend and Davidson 1986). Food choice is determined by family preference, health issues and, particularly in poor families, cost (HEA 1989). Other studies examine people's changing eating habits (Murcott 1995; Martens and Warde 1995; Lilley 1995). Stockley (1993) highlights three main factors which affect food choice: knowledge and attitude about diet and healthy eating; intrinsic influences such as physiology, food aversions, habits and beliefs; and extrinsic influences such as price, accessibility, time, advertising, food labelling, culture, food scares and taste.

This section reviews research on diet and nutrition in the following areas: the links between diet and income, gender and ethnicity; children and young people; family communication and negotiation about eating; and family interventions.

DEMOGRAPHIC FACTORS

Income

Research on diet and income in Britain shows links between poor diet, deprivation and class (Craig and Dowler 1996; Dowler and Rushton 1994; Dobson *et al.* 1994; Kempson *et al.* 1994; Wilkinson 1994; Bradshaw 1993; Cohen *et al.* 1992). Few studies in the UK have examined the direct effect of the extent to which the poorest groups' choice of food is restricted by low income. This is due to the difficulties encountered in conducting this kind of research (Whitehead 1988). Assessment of all sources of income needs to be made and such statistics are not readily available. However, research shows that diets are worse in poorer households, especially those headed by lone parents who find it difficult to afford fresh fruit and vegetables: in spite of the strategies that they adopt, their nutrient intakes remain less healthy than those who are not poor (Dowler and Calvert 1995a).

A review of health research between the mid-1970s and mid-1980s examined the links between income and diet (Whitehead 1988). Differences were identified between social groups in terms of the quantity and nutritional quality of the food they ate. Comparisons were made between income groups, and it was discovered that high income groups consumed more brown bread, fresh fruit and vegetables, and less white bread, potatoes, sugar and fat than low income groups. Studies exploring the reasons for this have found lack of money to be a major factor (Dobson *et al.* 1994; HEA 1989; Burghes 1980; Lang *et al.* 1984). A study of families and single people living on income support in London, Sheffield and Liverpool asked respondents to keep food diaries before being interviewed (HEA 1989). Results showed that cost was the single most important factor when choosing food.

A study of families living on support benefit in 1980 found that some parents went without food to provide for their children, and lack of money was frequently cited as the reason for lack of fruit and vegetables in the diet (Burghes 1980). Research on people on low incomes in the North of England in 1984 shows that approximately a quarter of respondents replied that they did not have a main meal every day (Lang *et al.* 1984). A third said this was because of cost as did two-fifths of those who were unemployed. A more recent analysis of class and regional patterns in Britain showed wide differences in the quantity of food consumed, between the north and south of the country (MAFF 1994).

Some research shows that people on low incomes lack knowledge of the role of specific products in the diet, the nutritional status of fast food, and the effects of food processing on nutritional content (Dobson *et al.* 1994; HEA 1989). However, Dowler and Calvert's study (1995b) of poor lone parents' diets shows that some parents are aware of notions of healthy eating: those parents in their study who shopped around for 'fresh' or 'quality' food and said that they wanted a varied healthy diet for their family seemed to achieve a healthier diet for themselves and their families than those who did not mention these aims.

Graham's review (1984) of over 250 studies on how parents take responsibility for family health shows how various household resources such as food, income, housing, fuel and transport have the potential to influence health. The pattern of spending on these items varies between rich and poor families with poorer families spending a higher proportion of their income on basic commodities. In 1985, for instance, poor households spent 56 per cent of their income on these essential items (Department of Employment 1986).

A common finding is that food is treated as a flexible item in the household budget, unlike rent (Graham 1993b). When money is short, food spending money is cut back (Durward 1984). A number of 'desk-top calculation' studies have been carried out to estimate the cost of a 'healthy diet'. An in-depth study of women with pre-school children in Milton Keynes in 1984 found that 51 per cent of single parents and 30 per cent of low-income mothers in two-parent families were cutting down on food consumption for financial reasons (Graham 1987a). The majority of low-income women (67 per cent) found it difficult to afford what they considered to be a healthy diet for their children.

One study on pregnancy concluded that a healthy diet may be beyond the means of low-income households (Durward 1984). In 1994 for instance, one in three pregnant women was claiming benefit, an increase from one in five in 1988 (Maternity Alliance 1995). This study calls for the government's *Health of the Nation* policy to include targets for women before and during pregnancy. The British Dietetic Association (BDA) has considered the dietary problems of special groups at risk of malnutrition – children, pregnant women, minority ethnic groups, the disabled and elderly. The BDA concluded that existing benefits were inadequate for their needs (Haines and de Looy 1986).

Gender

There is a growing body of work on gender and diet. Several studies on distribution of food in families show that quantity, quality and choice of food consumed by different family members depends on gender and age throughout the occupational structure (Charles and Kerr 1987; Murcott 1983a; Murcott 1983b; Devault 1991; Keane and Willetts 1995). Studies of nutrition in families with children show that men and boys get better quality food than women and girls (Charles and Kerr 1988). Mothers are largely responsible for buying, preparing, serving and clearing away food (Holland *et al.* 1996). Research suggests that mothers think that good food is important for health and that generally they 'know' what a healthy diet is (Mayall and Watson 1989). Social expectations place responsibility for the family's health on the woman of the house and following 'expert' advice enables her to claim that she has done all that she could (Miles 1991).

There are links between gender and healthy eating. A Scottish study which analysed three age cohorts (15, 35 and 55) in 1987 in the Glasgow area found that gender, household income, class and smoking status were linked to 'healthy' eating (Anderson and Hunt 1992). Women are more than two and a half times as likely to be classified as 'healthy eaters' than men (Brannen *et al.* 1994). Brannen *et al.* found that 44 per cent of the young women but only a quarter of the young men are located in the healthiest group and that middle-class young women have the healthiest diets.

The dietary survey of British adults (Gregory *et al.* 1990) also showed that women tend to choose foods which are associated with 'healthier' diets, eating wholemeal bread, low-fat milk, salad, vegetables and fruit, and less fried fish, sausages, meat pies and chips. However, women were more likely than men to eat confectionery. People from non-manual social classes, those with higher incomes and non-smokers were twice as likely to be classified in this way compared with manual social classes, low-income households and current smokers, even though certain lifestyles, smoking and lack of physical activity, are known to cut across class.

Ethnicity

There is a paucity of information on the nutrition of Asians and African–Caribbeans in Britain (Dowler and Calvert 1995a; HEA 1991b). Studies show that British Asians are particularly at risk from coronary heart disease (CHD) (Balarajan and Raleigh 1993; Fox and Shapiro 1988). A study among South Asian families in Scotland eating 'Asian' and 'English' cuisine found significant gender differences in responsibility for healthy eating: men generally were neither aware of nor interested in health and diet information (Landman and Wyke 1995).

Few studies have examined nutrition among African–Caribbeans (Scott 1995a). One exception includes research on lay beliefs about food among West Indians with diabetes which shows close links between their cultural beliefs about food and the body and their questioning of professionals' advice about diet (Scott 1995b). Another is an anthropological study of cultural beliefs that shape food choice carried out in south-east London (Keane and Willetts 1995). Keane and Willetts found that West Indian food culture was associated with a positive cultural identity by black Britons. Brannen *et al.* (1994) found that Asian young men were significantly more likely to be in the healthiest diet group than white and young black men. And Dowler and Calvert (1995a) in their study of lone parents found that those who shop for and eat meals that are typical of black British or African–Caribbean families do better nutritionally than those eating meals typical of white families.

A briefing paper produced by the HEA for health professionals in 1991 suggests that dietary intakes of Asian women might be inadequate, but also indicates that research results have not been consistent (HEA 1991b). In the past, rickets and osteomalacia, caused by a deficiency of vitamin D, have been serious problems for Asian people (Qureshi 1985; Grimsley and Bhat 1988). A report by the Committee on Medical Aspects of Food Policy (COMA) in 1980, suggested that while rickets appeared to be declining, osteomalacia has increased slightly (DHSS 1980). Vitamin D has since been added to chapatti flour which is used to make bread in Asian families. There have been no studies identified to show the results of this action.

CHILDREN AND YOUNG PEOPLE

The childhood years and family life are thought to be key stages for promoting healthy eating, but there are few data on parents' influences on their children's eating habits (Wardle 1995). New data provides information on very young children's diets (Gregory *et al.* 1995). Research has examined children's eating patterns at home and at school and their preferences for particular foods and eating patterns such as 'grazing and snacking' (Charles and Kerr 1988; Turner *et al.* 1995; Morrison 1995; Rousseau 1983; James 1982; Coles and Turner 1995). Other research documents the links between deprivation and children's diets (Middleton *et al.* 1994; Kumar 1993; Wilkinson 1994).

Charles and Kerr (1988) interviewed women about the effect of children and partners on food purchasing, preparation and consumption. Studies on children and food have shown that food is a highly charged symbol of relations in families, used as a weapon by both children and adults (James 1982). Children control their eating patterns and choose food to assert their independence; conflict about eating and food may be seen between grandmothers, mothers and daughters (Kitzinger and Kitzinger 1989).

A study by Rousseau (1983) challenged conventional assumptions about children's preference for crisps and sweets. Rousseau argued these snacks were popular because they met children's needs to control their eating, to eat in small quantities, at any time and anywhere. They also like to manipulate food directly in their hands, crunching and chewing as part of the process of socialising by sharing food. Another study found that children also eat certain foods, for example sweets, as a way of resisting and transgressing adult rules (James 1982). Focusing on the social relations of 'food' consumption, and in particular on children's resistance to food, James made connections between food preferences, practices and children's material world. A recent study documents children's social experiences of eating at school compared with eating at home (Turner *et al.* 1995).

There is little reliable data on the diets of young people (DoH 1994b) although the next national dietary survey will be on children. Recent work by Aggleton (1996) on young people and health promotion suggests links between young people's diets and risk factors for coronary heart disease (HEA 1993c). Their diets are typically high in fat, and iron and calcium deficiencies have been reported in young women (DoH 1989; Nelson 1994).

Social pressures that equate slimness with beauty can lead to the onset of eating disorders such as anorexia nervosa and bulimia, especially in young women (Hempel 1994; Lee 1995). Although women suffer more than men from eating disorders, young men are also affected (Royal College of Psychiatrists 1993; Siegel *et al.* 1995; Illman 1996). Changes in weight in young people may initially be observed in the family: recent empirical work on family communication about food reveals links between awareness of body image and food consumption in young girls (Holland *et al.* 1996; Brannen *et al.* 1994). While a child with an eating disorder can represent a strain for the household, in some cases it is mothers rather than fathers who pressure their daughters to lose weight (Hempel 1994; Kanakis and Thelen 1995).

Research shows links between psychological vulnerabilities – needs for autonomy/control, concerns about sexuality and depression – and eating disorders among adolescents (Striegel-Moore *et al.* 1986; Beumont *et al.* 1981). French *et al.* (1994), who found that excessive involvement in sport and avoidance of certain high-fat foods may place young people at risk for developing eating disorders also suggest that exercise could be a protective factor by increasing self-esteem, feelings of autonomy, control and social support. A review of eating disorders highlights the need to develop self-esteem and healthy attitudes among children and young people about their body image, and to improve the sociocultural influences that promote eating disorders (Fisher *et al.* 1995).

101

FAMILY COMMUNICATION AND NEGOTIATION

Several studies carried out as part of the ESRC's Research Programme on The Nation's Diet and the HEA's Family Health Research Programme have explored eating patterns in the family and the way responsibility for the provision of food is managed (Gregory 1995; Anderson *et al.* 1995; Holland *et al.* 1996; Prout 1996). Gregory's work (1995) documents the gender division of labour in the family for responsibility for health and nutrition and for the provision of meals, whereas Anderson *et al.* (1995) focus on the influence on eating patterns and food choice associated with the transition from single to married and cohabitation status.

Prout (1996) proposed two models as a result of his analysis of family beliefs about health including diet. The first emphasises individual choice and includes families who prioritise individual health behaviour and encourage children to take responsibility for their own choices, regarding eating for example. In the second model which emphasises 'control', parents stress conformity to received values and beliefs and decide on children's diets. Kenyson (1994) in a study of poor families and their attitudes to budgeting also distinguishes between 'controllers' who sacrifice food in order to keep out of debt and 'jugglers' who do not skimp on food.

Holland *et al.* (1996), who examined the way families talk and negotiate about health including food, found that a number of elements contribute to both a healthy diet and family cohesiveness. These include: knowledge about food that is 'good' and 'bad' for you, enjoyment of cooking a range of cuisines, both parents being able to cook, preparing a single meal for the whole family and eating together as a family. Eating patterns varied among families, and mealtimes could be either filled with tension or occasions for talking. Brannen *et al.* (1994) report on the links between household tension and eating disorders.

INTERVENTIONS

Reviews of interventions concerned with nutrition in a range of settings are provided by both Raats and Sparks (1995) and Aggleton (1996). Few interventions have specifically targeted the family. Family-based studies include a study by Nader *et al.* (1983) of the effects of eight, weekly, evening meetings on the consumption of food high in sodium and saturated fat. Relative to control-group families, those participating in the intervention reported significant reductions in five high-salt categories and three saturated-fat categories of food.

Several family interventions have relied on individual dietary counselling (Knutsen and Knutsen 1991; Witschi *et al.* 1978). In Knutsen and Knutsen's Norwegian study following a doctor and dietitian's visits to families with one member at risk of cardiovascular disease, changes in dietary habits were seen in the intervention group relative to controls. Similar changes occurred in a US study where dietitians visited families (Witschi *et al.* 1978). One drawback to this type of intervention is the cost (Aggleton 1996).

Other family interventions targeting children have resulted in behaviour changes in both children and parents regarding healthy eating (Perry *et al.* 1988; Puska *et al.* 1983, 1982; Farquhar *et al.* 1990). The Heart Health Programme in Minnesota reported changes in knowledge and behaviour about diet among young people but not their parents (King *et al.* 1988). A Finnish intervention led to changes in behaviour in both young people and their parents (Puska *et al.* 1983, 1982). Studies on cardiovascular disease and on obesity show that family involvement provides a good basis for health education messages as an alternative to one-to-one approaches (Nicklas *et al.* 1988; Cade and O'Connell 1991). Research into obesity indicates that the family may be one of the most important influences on the behaviour of an obese person.

RECOMMENDATIONS FOR FURTHER RESEARCH

1. Further exploration could be carried out into the meanings of food in the context of family communication and conflict (Prout 1996; Kitzinger and Kitzinger 1989).

2. Possible links between family cohesiveness and the patterns and organisation of food buying, cooking, and eating warrant investigation.

3. More research could be carried out on the relationship between diet and parenting styles (Prout 1996).

4. The health beliefs, diets, and practices of young people, and their risk-taking behaviour around food choice, preparation and consumption could benefit from more study.

5. There is scope for more research on how parents' eating patterns, diets, etc. influence children's eating behaviours, or vice versa, and (in the light of increasing easy-cook and instant meals, and microwave cooking) on the extent to which parents (usually mothers) teach or provide a direct or indirect model for their children in choosing, preparing, and cooking food.

9. Physical activity

Although research has been carried out to assess levels of physical activity among men and women, boys and girls, not much work has been done within families Some study has been made of the relationship between children's physical activity, family influences and psychological motivation (Lewko and Greendorfer 1988; Biddle and Armstrong 1992; Biddle *et al.* 1992), and physical activity has been touched on within projects focusing on other family health interactions (Prout 1996). Other research has examined the effects of promotional material placed in schools, the community, the workplace and medical settings on awareness of physical exercise and behaviour (Biddle and Mutrie 1991).

LEVELS OF PHYSICAL ACTIVITY

The HEA has carried out a number of research projects on physical activity, one of the most detailed of which was the Allied Dunbar National Fitness Survey (Allied Dunbar/HEA 1992). This study assessed people's levels of participation in sport and active recreation, physical activity at work, in housework, DIY, gardening, walking, cycling and climbing stairs. Lifestyle factors such as smoking, alcohol consumption and diet were taken into account, as well as current and past health status. Measures were also taken of psychological well-being, social support and stress, and knowledge of, and attitudes to, health and fitness. At a physical fitness level, each participant's body dimensions, fitness, joint flexibility, blood pressure and strength were noted. The results showed that the majority of men (75 per cent) and women (83 per cent) were not exercising enough. This also has implications for the increasing proportions of both sexes who are overweight or obese, the effects of which become more dangerous to health with age. It appeared that taking regular exercise in youth increased the likelihood of taking exercise later in life. The suggestion that adult physical activity levels may have their origins in childhood and adolescence has been supported by other research (Engstrom 1986; Kuh and Cooper 1992; Raitakari *et al.* 1994).

A study of primary health care schemes promoting physical activity in England (University of Exeter/HEA 1994) showed that most were managed at leisure centres, but a third were held in health centres. In the majority of these schemes, the main participants were middle-aged women. In an effort to promote physical activity in England, the HEA organised an international symposium in which experts discussed strategies and made key recommendations for the amount and type of exercise that individuals should be taking (Killoran *et al.* 1995).

DEMOGRAPHIC FACTORS

Social class

As with so many health-related issues, it seems that there is a strong social-class difference, with professional groups exercising far more than manual occupational groups. One study suggests exercise as one health behaviour (like diet) that may be 'traded-off' against social or economic factors (Prout 1996). The General Household Survey figures (OPCS 1992b) have also revealed a class gradient which interacts with gender. Among women, vigorous physical activity declines with decreasing social class, while it increases for men in the lower social groupings. However, if more moderate levels of physical activity are involved, such as heavy housework or walking, the social class gradient is not so steep. There is a positive link between a 'healthy' diet and physical activity, but a more complex and usually negative relationship between a 'healthy' family diet and social class (see also Chapter 8 above), since for many families, access to good food and sports facilities depends on their resources and where they live (Townsend and Davidson 1986).

Gender

Although there are no available long-term trend figures on physical activity, information from sources such as the General Household Survey (OPCS 1992b) and the Allied Dunbar National Fitness Survey (Allied Dunbar/HEA 1992) show that men tend to be more active than women. The latter survey showed that people had a tendency to overestimate their level of fitness. Men tended to see the benefits of exercise lying in its enjoyment, while women looked to improve their physical appearance. This gender difference was endorsed in a qualitative research study subsequently commissioned by the HEA (1993a) which aimed to explore the factors which people find encouraging or inhibiting in relation to taking regular exercise. It showed that age and gender were important factors and different messages should be aimed at different target groups, and, for instance, older respondents placed more emphasis on mental agility and independence.

In the context of gender and sport, one qualitative study (Rogers *et al.* 1996) found a belief in families that sport is good for male children, and that it was spoken of frequently by men in terms of mental health as a stress-reducing activity. These researchers also found football and sport in general to be part of a 'male emotional agenda', so perhaps the role of football as a form of facilitating (and 'safe') communication between men at work, and fathers and sons in the family, deserves more attention. Apart from activities like walking and bicycling, not many such activities involve the whole family in exercise together. Both sexes can play sports such as tennis and badminton, but other types of physical exercise and sporting activities tend to separate the genders – men play team sports like football and rugby, and women take part as individuals in exercise classes such as yoga, keep fit and aerobics.

In the past, it has been the fitness and physical activity levels of adult men and women that have been of main concern, with schools being relied upon to provide a reasonable level of physical exercise for their pupils. The MORI survey into lifestyle characteristics of 9–15-year-olds (HEA 1992a) showed that, on the assumption that a school lesson lasted approximately 45 minutes, then teenagers were getting an average of 4.7 hours exercise a week inside and outside school. Boys had more exercise than girls (5.2:4.2 hours per week). Both sexes showed an increase in the amount of exercise they took until the age of 12/13, after which there was a decline. These findings were supported in research by Armstrong *et al.* (1990) who found surprisingly low levels of physical activity in 11–15-year-olds; boys were more active than the girls, whose activity levels deteriorated as they moved through secondary school. In research by Brannen and Storey (1996) it was also found that boys were more physically active than girls, with respect to activities outside school and going to local sports centres.

It has been suggested that the origins of teenage girls' low activity patterns may lie in parental attitudes (Armstrong 1995). Boys get more parental reinforcement for exercise than girls, and the sorts of games boys play and levels of skills required may be more challenging (Gottlieb and Chen 1985). Parents should be encouraged to provide more positive role models for children's activity behaviour. Related to this is research by Biddle *et al.* (1992) which has suggested that for girls to participate more in sport and exercise, they need more positive perceptions of themselves in both physical and general terms, to combat negative stereotypes associated with gender roles and physical activity.

Ethnicity

There are some significant differences in physical activity and ethnicity. The MORI survey showed that African–Caribbean boys showed the strongest orientation to exercise with an average weekly exercise rate of 5.5 hours. Children from lower socio-economic groups (D/E), and those from families of Asian origin did less exercise on average (4.4 and 3.7 hours respectively). Asian girls were the least likely to do much exercise (3 hours average per week) (HEA 1992a), and this is a reflection of cultural restrictions on girls' activities outside the home.

FAMILY COMMUNICATION

It has been suggested that parental attitudes towards physical activity have a significant effect on children's intentions to exercise (Sallis and Nader 1988), and family involvement in vigorous activity is effective in promoting children's involvement in physical activity. The HEA (1993a) study looked at families at different life-stages, and found that at the younger life-stage (25–34 years) neither mothers, nor to some extent fathers, had sufficient time or money for physical activities. It observed that at this time of life, men and women could 'put off' the need to take exercise until the signs of middle age appear when there is a stronger need to be physically active. At the older family life-stage (35–54 years) some men and women found the need for exercise more pressing, and some joined in sport and activities with their older, less dependent children. However, in terms of parental influence on the health of their children, this study concluded that 'parents rarely felt it was important to educate, motivate or set an example to their children with respect to physical activity.' It could also be said that such pressure is equally absent from the other direction, that is, children do not tend to nag parents about physical activity in the ways they do about parental behaviour around smoking and alcohol consumption. Therefore, although positive parental attitudes and behaviour around physical activity may be important, social circumstances may dictate that they are not realised.

However, other changes in the lifestyles of young people inside and outside school may be starting to affect this aspect of their health status. Some researchers have argued that the contemporary culture of television, video and computer games has had detrimental affects on the physical activity of children (Dietz and Gortmaker 1985), but this has been challenged by others (Robinson *et al.* 1993). Children's lives may now also be more restricted through parental fears for their safety outside the home, and this could mean that they are involved in less physical activity than children in the past. For these and other reasons, such as increasing levels of obesity, physical activity is something that will increasingly have to be included in family health communication and research. More investigation could be made not only of these changes in children's relationship to sport and other outside physical activities, but also the role of sport in mental health, and related gender differences.

RECOMMENDATIONS FOR FURTHER RESEARCH

1. There is a need for research on what type of physical activity children choose to engage in, and especially the influence that parents have on the level and type of activity adopted by their children. The influence of age, gender, and social class should be considered (Biddle and Armstrong 1992).

2. More research is required on the role of men's involvement and watching sport (usually football, but also other forms of sport) in helping to promote positive mental health (Rogers *et al.* 1996).

3. Sport also appears to provide a 'safe' way for men and boys to communicate in the family, and this deserves more exploration (Rogers *et al.* 1996).

4. The nature of gender differences in physical activity merit more attention, which could perhaps contribute to increasing the activity levels of girls and women.

5. It is perhaps worth looking at how parents and children express less concern for each other's health in terms of their need for physical activity compared to issues like smoking, and possible ways to raise both children's and parents' awareness of the need for the other to take exercise.

10. Parenthood education

Parenthood education covers: the antenatal period which includes preparation during pregnancy for coping with advancing pregnancy and approaching childbirth, and generally for caring for a new baby; the provision of information before, during and after childbirth; and the development of parenting skills or 'parentcraft' in the postnatal period (Belski and Kelly 1994). Much of the available literature is on access to and attendance of antenatal classes with less research on education within antenatal care or in the early postnatal period (Combes and Schonveld 1992).

PROVISION

Combes and Schonveld reviewed parent education over the last decade and conducted a qualitative study on first-time parents' needs and their experiences of parent education. They found a discrepancy between needs and provision. For example, many parents did not receive any parenthood education as many pregnant women do not attend antenatal classes. Men's needs for parenthood preparation were largely ignored and there were few postnatal groups for men, or which accommodated men. This relative neglect of men's education for parenting is echoed in an earlier review of parenthood education in secondary schools (Prendergast and Prout 1987) and since then there have been some attempts to develop parenting programmes in schools (Pugh 1994). Other studies have also analysed the need for more parenthood education at school which goes beyond the biology of reproduction (Whitfield 1990; Prendergast and Prout 1990). It has been suggested that education for parenthood programmes should be compulsory at school as this could be a vehicle to enhance family relationships, child development and general coping strategies (Elkes and Crocitto 1987). Such programmes could include the practical issues of daily life and parent education classes for mothers and fathers. Elkes and Crocitto stressed the need to focus on teaching the dynamics of relationships (personal, interpersonal, familial) to adolescents, parents or primary caretakers.

Furthermore, parent education has focused more on medical and physical health issues rather than on the social or emotional aspects. For instance, while some health professionals have tended to view motherhood as a physical process in a woman's life cycle, women place more emphasis on social and psychological aspects of their new role (Laryea 1991; Gjerdingen and Chaloner 1994). More recent research has concentrated on parenting education that includes raising confidence in parenting (Pugh *et al.* 1994) and also benefiting children (Hartley-Brewer 1994).

VULNERABLE PARENTS

Some studies have looked at parenting skills in families with problems like learning difficulties (Angeli *et al*. 1994; Booth and Booth 1994). Another vulnerable group are teenage parents, particularly teenage mothers, and there has been quite a substantial interest and research in this area (Sharpe 1987; Hudson and Ineichen 1991; Phoenix 1991; Francome and Walsh 1995; Jacobson *et al*. 1995). Teenage motherhood is highest in the lowest social classes (OPCS 1993) and the highest conception rates in under-16s occur in London, and in the North of England, in inner cities and deprived areas with high rates of unemployment. While there is always discussion of the need for primary prevention in the form of sex education, contraceptive advice and counselling, some studies have argued that it is not teenage pregnancy per se that is a risk but society's attitudes to it (Hardy and Zabin 1991; Phoenix 1991; Jacobson *et al*. 1995). Hardy and Zabin (1991) point to the lack of access to qualified prenatal care and essential support among adolescents as a major problem, and Jacobson *et al*. suggest exploring the attitudes of teenagers and their families before treating pregnancy as a problem. These authors call for health professionals to become more aware of the specific needs of teenage health, and to consider teenage pregnancy from a clinical, individual and contextual perspective. Other work has looked at ways of building up confidence and competence in teenage parents (Butler *et al*. 1993).

ANTENATAL AND POSTNATAL EDUCATION

More research has been done on antenatal care than on postnatal care (Martin 1990; Lester and Farrow 1988; Mauthner 1994). In an investigation of the sources which influenced women's attendance at antenatal booking clinics, Lester and Farrow (1988) identified books, the media, health service literature, friends and relatives as being of importance. They found that late attenders were less likely to be influenced by personal contact with a partner, relative, friend or health professional than early attenders. There is concern about this under-utilisation of maternity services (Combes and Schonveld 1992). In Britain, it appears that health services cater more to the needs of the provider than those of the consumer. This is not the case in some countries. For example, in France and Finland, financial incentives have been successfully introduced in order to increase postnatal attendance rates (Townsend and Davidson 1986). Martin (1990) examined antenatal care and health care professionals as a source of information for mothers. She found that mothers dissatisfied with information they received antenatally from their doctor were much less likely to be able to discuss issues with health professionals than women who saw the same doctor or midwife throughout, as continuity of care may be associated with improved information giving. Martin concluded by emphasising the importance of continuity of care for communication satisfaction between mothers and health professionals.

Mauthner's research (1994) on postnatal depression examined postnatal care of mothers and various information sources. Results have shown that there is little parentcraft education or education on postnatal care during antenatal classes, the main focus of information provision being on pregnancy and childbirth. After childbirth there was little information on parenting issues or on the mother's health needs. Furthermore, there was little discussion with health professionals, friends or family about postnatal health issues, and little spouse communication between partners. A study which focused on postnatal care found that low self-esteem after childbirth and inability to cope with baby care such as feeding, for example, was associated with conflicting advice given to new mothers by health professionals during the postnatal period (Ball 1991). Some research has suggested, however, that there may be a change in the division of domestic labour and a decline in emotional and practical support received by new mothers in their first post partum year from husbands, relatives and friends (Gjerdingen and Chaloner 1994), especially if they have normal births and do not return to work.

DEMOGRAPHIC FACTORS

The role of fathers has changed over the past few decades, as men have become more involved in the development and care of their children, and as men as parents have begun to be the focus of research (Lewis and O'Brien 1987; Fulop 1992; O'Brien and Jones 1994; Sharpe 1994; Baker and Lane 1994; Dearden *et al.* 1995; Burgess 1996). This has not been reflected, however, in the provision of parenthood education, which is still geared towards mothers.

In terms of social-class differences, working-class women in the study by Martin (1990) demonstrated that they clearly identified what their needs were and were less satisfied than middle-class women about the communication they had with health care professionals during pregnancy, labour and delivery. There is not much work specifically on the situation and needs of different ethnic groups, although a recent study aimed to explore the support needs of black parents (Evans and Grant 1995). One intervention study in Ireland (Johnson *et al.* 1993) used a randomised control trial to see whether non-professional mothers could deliver a child development programme to disadvantaged mothers and babies who came from the same community. The intervention group received monthly visits from the 'community mother' volunteer. At the end of the study, both mothers and children in the intervention group showed positive gains. For instance, children were more likely to be immunised, read to, and play more cognitive games; and their mothers had a better diet, and were less likely to feel tired or miserable or show negative feelings.

It has been argued that parenthood education should include non-sexist and non-violent child-rearing techniques (Kitzinger and Kitzinger 1989). Research has shown that non-sexist child rearing is difficult to achieve in practice (Statham 1986). The Family Planning Association has produced a number of booklets which have been aimed at helping parents talk with their children (FPA 1992). In the absence of a national family policy, some researchers have stressed the need for a child-rearing and education framework that covers the teaching and development of parenting skills (Goldman and Goldman 1988). But although maternity and parenting information is useful and wanted by parents, care should be taken in the way it is delivered in order to support and maintain self-esteem. It is too easy for health professionals to define what they think parents should be doing for their children without recognising parental needs (Edwards 1995; Rogers *et al.* 1996).

RECOMMENDATIONS FOR FURTHER RESEARCH

1. Research on parenting needs to look at both communication between parents about parenting, and also to see how parents' own needs in this area are matched by those of health professionals. A related factor is parents' preferences for the ways that this information could be passed on, with the aim of improving the transmission of parenting information within and from outside the family.

2. Men as fathers need targeting to develop their parenting skills. This also means exploring ways of raising the awareness of those fathers who do not see this knowledge as relevant to them.

3. Research programmes are needed for teaching parenthood to both boys and girls in school (Whitfield 1990; Prendergast and Prout 1990; Pugh 1994) relating it to home and family life.

4. Research on social and emotional aspects of parenting is needed, including possible ways of building up confidence and competence in parents of all ages, who may have different social and emotional needs, as well as those involving practical and medical skills (eg possibly different needs evoked by the particular situations of teenage, and middle aged/older, mothers and fathers).

5. More research is required on the parenting support needs in families from different ethnic backgrounds.

6. Research could pay more attention to postnatal health issues, which appear to be neglected in favour of antenatal health concerns.

11. Childhood accidents

The family home is not necessarily a physically safe place for children: home accidents account for 23 per cent of all accidental deaths nationally, and this proportion is higher in children under five. Accidents of all kinds are the most important cause of death amongst all children aged 1 to 14, followed by respiratory disease, neoplasms, congenital abnormalities and infections (Townsend and Davidson 1986; Roberts 1991; OPCS 1994a; Popay and Young 1993). This mainly involves motor-vehicle accidents, with child pedestrians. Deaths from fires, drowning and falls are also significant. Non-fatal accidents give a different picture, most (43 per cent) being due to falls (Popay and Young 1993). Accidental injury has been identified as a key area for improvements by *The Health of the Nation* strategy document. Its target is for mortality due to childhood accidents to be reduced from 6.7 per 100,000 head of population in 1990 to 4.5 per 100,000 by the year 2005.

DEMOGRAPHIC FACTORS

Social class, gender, large family size, unemployment and single parenthood are factors associated with children's accidents (Wadsworth *et al.* 1987). Material and cultural factors including environmental hazards and dangerous behaviours such as negligence, adventure or irresponsibility influence the incidence of childhood accidents (Townsend and Davidson 1986). Townsend and Davidson argue that differences in parents' material resources affect the levels of care and protection they can give to their children. Accidental death in childhood has the steepest social class gradient of all causes of death; for instance, children from families in social class V are three times more likely to die accidentally than those in social class I households (Popay and Young 1993). This is reflected in the geographical pattern in that for children under 15, mortality rates from accidents are highest in the North and West of England, and generally lower in the South. Less data are available for non-fatal accidents, but figures for hospital admissions for accidents are high for areas with higher material disadvantage and linked to factors like parental unemployment, overcrowding and shared accommodation. Other contributing factors are parents' level of education, experience of life events, family structure, and aspects of children's behaviour. Children of parents in occupational classes IV and V have less opportunity to play safely than other children. Furnishings, including forms of heating in the home, are likely to be less safe, as are other domestic appliances.

Material differences also mean that some children are more likely to be left to their own devices after school and during holidays. Among child pedestrians the risk of death from being hit by a car is 5 to 7 times greater for children in social class V compared with those from social class I. The risk from accidental death caused by fires, falls and drowning is even greater between the classes, with social class V having the greatest risk. Popay and Young (1993) note that some approaches to accident prevention have actually served to widen such social inequalities through being taken up more easily by better-off families. Some parents lack the means to provide their children with a safe environment.

One extensive review (Graham 1984) showed that a lower rate of accidents exists in one-parent families than one would expect, given the inverse relationship between number of childhood accidents and social class. The author has suggested that this is the result of less divided attention given by lone parents to their children, but no detailed research has been carried out on this subject.

Social or behavioural factors?

Childhood accidents provide good examples of what some researchers believe is an artificial distinction between the cultural/behavioural and material/structuralist approach, since behaviour cannot be separated from its social context (Blane 1985; Blaxter 1983). The observation that children from manual social groups have more accidents than other children may be explained using the behavioural/cultural view as due to reckless, risk-taking behaviour and inadequate parental care. The materialist view would highlight the cost of safety equipment and devices, unsafe play areas, the lack of fenced-off gardens and the greater difficulty of supervising playing children from high-rise housing. From this perspective, the environment dictates the behaviour of both parent and child.

However, these two explanations are not seen to be mutually exclusive (Whitehead 1988). It appears that planning deficiencies, car drivers' carelessness and poor kitchen and balcony designs have not been adequately considered by decision-makers and environmental designers (Sinnott and Jackson 1990; Ranson 1987). Stone (1993) believes that environmental engineering is more important than health education. For instance, housing families with small children in ground-floor or first-floor flats lowers the risk of falls (Littlewood 1987). This evidence suggests that the best way to increase the safety of children's environment is to take account of both the behavioural and the material perspectives.

Recommendations made by Townsend and Davidson (1986) in the Black report for healthy environments included preventative measures aimed at planners, architects and engineers in order to improve children's physical environment. Townsend and Davidson also recommended routine collection and reporting of children's accidents, including the class and age of victims, where the accident happened (road, home, school) and any building design features involved. In 1982 the only national source of information was the Hospital In-Patient Enquiry (HIPE). Accidents which do not require hospital in-patient admission are less well recorded.

FAMILY COMMUNICATION

In research on family communication about health (Holland *et al.* 1996), differences were suggested between fathers' and mothers' concerns and safety consciousness. It seemed that mothers were generally more aware of the need to monitor day-to-day safety measures at home than fathers, even though it may be the fathers who purchase and install some of the more formal safety measures, such as stair-gates, and socket protectors. Families also took different approaches to accidents at home: some anticipated them and tried to guard against them, while others just respond to a situation as it arises. In terms of safety outside the home, the high-profile media reporting of child abduction and street crime statistics has led to families, especially in inner-city areas, not allowing children to play outside on their own. Holland *et al.* point out that this in its turn may lead to other health hazards in the form of increased anxiety on the part of parents, particularly mothers, who worry when their children go out to play, yet are subject to greater personal stress if they choose to confine their small children 'safely' indoors instead.

A study by Woods *et al.* (1994) examined parents' perceptions of the age at which a variety of activities were considered to be safe in the areas of the home, road, and leisure safety, and assessed parental and child safety practice appropriate to the age of their children. The authors found certain inconsistencies between parental perception and behaviour. These inconsistencies were greatest with regard to leaving children alone in the bath, not using stair-gates or providing cycle helmets, and allowing children to play with small toys. But they also noted that most parents adopted safe behaviour most of the time, and were aware of the age when children could do certain activities safely. The most hazardous places for children's accidents in the home are the kitchen and the living room (Bande-Knops 1987), followed by the bathroom (Gray 1987). Injuries in these areas include falls, burns and scalds, suffocation, poisoning and drowning (Towner *et al.* 1993).

INTERVENTIONS

A Health Education Authority review (Towner *et al.* 1993) examined health promotion interventions aimed at preventing childhood accidents among children aged 0–14 years in the home, at leisure times, for example in playgrounds, swimming areas and so on, and on the roads. The numbers of children under the age of one who have accidental injuries are small. This review found few evaluated studies on accidental injury, and only a limited number of interventions available. Furthermore, some injury types were more researched (for example, cycle helmets and car safety restraints for children) than others (such as sports and leisure injuries). Single-measure interventions, such as window-bars in the home and car child-safety restraints, were particularly effective, because they had a single focus. The success of campaigns was increased by improving availability and reducing the costs of the measures. Some injury types, such as scalds and other home injuries, had no single-measure strategies available and health promotion campaigns have met with limited success (Towner *et al.* 1993). Community-wide programmes were found to have positive results but took longer to be effective, as alliances needed to develop between individuals, policy-makers and the communities. The reviewers stressed that as 'education' was the key to creating an environment of protection that would reduce injury and be acceptable to the public, it should be directed to policy-makers, individuals and groups (Towner *et al.* 1993).

A selection of interventions in childhood accident prevention carried out in various countries have been reviewed by Popay and Young (1993). Some used a health planning model of community initiatives and some involved community participation initiatives. They found the evidence on effectiveness to be contradictory and probably reflecting the great diversity in initiatives. For example, they suggest that general campaigns aimed at improving safety in the home are less effective than more targeted initiatives aimed at certain at-risk groups or those that involved constructive follow-up sessions.

In one initiative, researchers worked alongside a parents' action campaign to improve child safety in Glasgow, which integrated the views of parents, children and workers in the area (Roberts 1991, 1992; Roberts *et al.* 1991). The aim of this study was to understand how parents, mothers in particular, maintained children's safety in practice in order to produce a basis for safety at home, at play and 'in transit' in the community. Roberts (1991) was particularly critical of the dominant behavioural approach including the urban myths of parents as inadequate safety-keepers (ill-informed, incompetent and ill-equipped) and the suggestion that mothers' and children's poor performance can be modified by exhortation and health education.

Another initiative in the North of England involved a local scheme on a council estate which aimed to sell safety equipment at cost price and raise parents' awareness of safety issues. The aim was to empower them to take control of ensuring the safety of children on the estate through providing access to equipment that not many of them would otherwise be able to obtain or afford. The scheme appears to have achieved some success (Crew and Fletcher 1995).

There has been quite a wealth of work done on childhood accidents, inside and outside the home, and on research into children's health and safety (Roberts 1991, 1992; Mayall and Watson 1989). Many studies have focused on mothers' attitudes and behaviour, some have looked at the nature of the environment, and others have taken children's characteristics (clumsiness, over-activity) into account. Some interventions have tried to increase parental awareness of safety issues through the community, but relatively little work has looked at communication processes about this subject within the family.

RECOMMENDATIONS FOR FURTHER RESEARCH

1. Further studies could look at children's own perceptions of risk and risky behaviour in relation to accidents and safety, and the nature of their lifestyles in this respect and how these develop and change.

2. More research could develop ways of raising parental awareness and empowerment on safety issues, and examine underlying factors behind parents' differing approaches to home safety (for instance, pro-active or reactive).

12. Immunisation

The goals set out in the WHO 'Health for all by the year 2000' included a commitment to eliminate indigenous measles, neonatal tetanus and diphtheria, and eradicate poliomyelitis and congenital rubella in the European region. The government White Paper, *The Health of the Nation,* set immunisation targets in Britain of 95 per cent by 1995. By the end of 1993, there was a 93 per cent uptake for diphtheria, tetanus and poliomyelitis by British children before their first birthday, with a 91 per cent and 92 per cent uptake of whooping cough and measles, mumps and rubella (MMR) immunisation (HPSSSE 1993; Communicable Disease Report 1994). Research on bacterial meningitis initially showed a lack of knowledge about this disease or about the existence of Hib (*Haemophilus influenzae* type b) immunisation (Braun *et al.* 1992). In 1992 the vaccine to provide protection against Hib, the most common cause of bacterial meningitis in the under fives, was publicly launched (McGuire 1992). A subsequent survey commissioned by the Health Education Authority found a significant increase in the levels of awareness of Hib immunisation among mothers (from 6 per cent before to 73 per cent afterwards) (HEA 1992c; 1993e).

Recently, a mass immunisation programme against polio took place in India when about 75 million children were vaccinated in one day. Immunisation against disease has certainly been effective in preventing childhood disease in certain countries (Romanus *et al.* 1987). However, trends in the success of immunisation have to be examined critically. Although statistics from the Department of Health in Britain show the uptake of all childhood immunisation has shown a steady rise from the 1980s to the 1990s, it must be kept in mind that a proportion of this may be due to substantial improvements in record keeping. There are also regional or district variations in immunisation which tend to be concealed by national figures, especially in the case of measles and pertussis, and there are also variations between and within regions for different vaccines. Comparing the graphs of disease incidence between some countries which have and have not had a routine immunisation programme can show a similar but limited downward profile, suggesting that other factors, for example, improvements in material and social conditions such as nutrition, sanitation, clean water, and general standards of living have played a part in the movement to eradicate disease.

Research in immunisation has tended to concentrate on mapping the success of immunisation campaigns through collection of figures on immunisation status, or looking at possible reasons for parents' not immunising their children

NON-IMMUNISATION

While a substantial majority of families do have their children immunised against many childhood diseases, and conform to mass immunisation programmes, a minority do not. Those who do not comply do this for various reasons. Four specific factors related to the low uptake of immunisation are explored in a review by Egan *et al.* (1992) commissioned by the HEA. These are: socio-economic factors; groups with unstable residency; organisation of health practices; and parents' health beliefs, knowledge and motivation.

Socio-economic factors

Studies on the uptake of childhood immunisation have highlighted the importance of social factors (Barlow and Walker 1990; Bennett and Smith 1992; Pearson *et al.* 1993; Graham 1989; Whitehead 1988). With respect to socio-economic factors, parents with large families may simply find it hard to organise immunisation, and their concerns with socio-economic survival may over-ride concerns with immunisation. In an overview of the social science literature on communicable diseases, Jones and Moon (1992) quote earlier work of Stewart (1977,1979) on a whooping cough outbreak in Glasgow, which found that social class was three times as important as immunisation status in predicting infection levels. A study which compared parents from a 'deprived' area with matched controls from a 'more endowed' area found poorer immunisation rates in the deprived group (Marsh and Channing 1986). However, there have been noticeable improvements in the provision of immunisation services for different communities, for example, by providing mobile clinics in Southwark to increase immunisation rates in areas with low take-up rates (Whitehead 1988). Jarman developed a measure consisting of a combination of factors contributing to deprivation called the 'Jarman Index' which was applied in various studies of immunisation uptake (1983, 1988, 1991).

Groups with unstable residency

Immunisation programmes may bypass certain sorts of families whose housing is not stable due to social circumstances, such as the homeless and those on benefit in bed and breakfast accommodation and other hostels (Parsons 1991), and travellers (Gordon *et al.*1991; Zarb and Steele 1993). Recent arrivals in this country, such as immigrants and refugees are also among those who tend to become 'lost' to the medical authorities.

Organisation of health practices

Egan *et al.* (1992) described the ways health practices were organised and the level of knowledge, attitudes, beliefs and training of the health professionals involved, and the positive and negative effects of these on immunisation levels. In an HEA evaluation of low uptake immunisation projects carried out by Zarb and Steele (1993), a retrospective study was made of the records of a six-month cohort of children, and staff were interviewed in a number of practices in Birmingham about their low immunisation uptake. The authors highlighted certain deficiencies in record-keeping systems including a lack of accurate and up-to-date information on immunisation status. This affected the following-up of defaulters. They also found some poor liaison between GPs, health visitors, child health and community clinics, and drew attention to the difficulties of following up mobile families.

Parents' health beliefs, knowledge and motivation

In an investigation of the effects of a health education campaign on perceptions of childhood immunisation, McGuire (1990) discovered that mothers appreciated that it was their responsibility to have their children immunised, but believed that ultimately, it was the health professionals' responsibility to give them accurate information so that they could make informed choices. However, this view does not take into account the unequal power balance that may characterise relationships between doctor and client, in terms of parental education levels and social class, and a lay view of doctors as 'knowing best'.

In terms of parental beliefs and attitudes, the assumptions made by health professionals may be at odds with those held by parents themselves about why parents do not immunise. Health professionals tend to see this as parental reluctance, apathy and fear, whereas parents often specify inappropriate advice or inertia on the part of the health authorities (Egan *et al.* 1992). According to the GPs interviewed in the study by Zarb and Steele (1993), the basic problem with non-immunisation is not parental apathy but lack of awareness. They suggest there should be a raising of consciousness about the negative consequences of non-immunisation.

The information needs of a range of parents of 5–15-year-olds living in North-West England (Bolton) about immunisation in general, and measles in particular, was investigated in advance of a forthcoming measles mass vaccination programme (Woodhouse and Nicholson 1994). The researchers used small groups or depth interviews with mothers and health professionals and found that knowledge of diseases varied significantly between older and younger mothers. Older mothers, who may have had some childhood diseases themselves and have had information passed down to them, knew more than younger mothers, who had minimal knowledge nor experience of many of these diseases. They all, however, placed illnesses in a consistent hierarchy, with meningitis at the top, then polio, TB, diphtheria and tetanus, through whooping cough, rubella and mumps, down to measles, chicken pox and flu. There was little real awareness of the extent of risk posed by measles. They found a need for increased access to information, and in terms of measles, a need to change parents' conception so that they may be 'jolted' out of complacency.

It is the first-born children who are most likely to be immunised. This is perhaps because at this stage parents are more open to advice from professionals on the most protective treatment for their child. With subsequent children, parents may become more confident about deciding for themselves about the issue (and choosing not to), or other more material/socio-economic factors may intervene. Amongst mothers of older children there were some who were more anxious and questioning of an immunisation programme designed to be given to their younger children, due to reaction to vaccines by an earlier child, and/or adverse media coverage of vaccine effects (Woodhouse and Nicholson 1994).

Some health professionals appear to hold certain negative assumptions about the awareness of and attitudes towards immunisation held by parents from some of the minority ethnic groups. Such beliefs should be challenged (Bhopal and Samim 1988; Atun and Jenkins 1992). Asian mothers were particularly appreciative of immunisation in one study (Woodhouse and Nicholson 1994), and research on the orthodox Jewish community in North East London showed no lower levels in take-up of immunisation in this group compared to others in the local population (Cunninghame *et al.* 1994).

NON-COMPLIANCE

As well as those social groups who are less likely to take up immunisation, such as the homeless, another group of non-compliers has been identified (Egan *et al.* 1992) and consists of middle-class, well-educated parents possibly under the influence of homeopathic ideas.

These parents may choose not to immunise their children, rather than this situation arising out of their ignorance about the subject. They may have very strong views on immunisation derived from friends and/or media information. The research by Zarb and Steele (1993) focused attention on the fact that, unlike previous generations, the vast majority of the present generation of parents of under-fives have no knowledge or experience of diphtheria or whooping cough, etc. They have, however been exposed to media coverage and peer influence about the possible side effects of immunisation vaccines. There is evidence that some children are not immunised because of their parents' concern about the safety of vaccines (Barlow and Walker 1990).

There are other dilemmas involved in the issue of parental choice about immunisation, which may affect the relationship between families and their doctor. For example, parents who actively choose not to immunise their children may be seen by their doctors as 'troublesome'. Furthermore, the new target payment system for doctors which came into operation in 1990, by which GP's payments depend on immunisation take-up, makes it even more likely that active non-compliance may be unpopular with doctors.

A group of such parents who did not comply with the British childhood immunisation programme was researched by Rogers and Pilgrim (1993) using depth interviews with parents and health professionals. They examined the process of becoming a non-complier, the role of homeopathy, and concerns about side effects from vaccination. The researchers note that little work has been done on this area partly because these parents tend to be dismissed as irrational and driven by neurotic anxiety. Where they have been included, their concerns have been dubbed as 'mythical contra-indications' (Klein *et al.* 1989) or 'parentally concerned contra-indications' (Barlow and Walker 1990). Questioning the assumption that parents who were actively against immunisation were merely a vocal middle-class minority (suggested to be about 5 per cent) Rogers and Pilgrim noted that most, but not all, non-immunising parents in their sample were middle-class.

Another study on non-compliance was carried out by Forrest (1995) who interviewed mothers about their health beliefs and reasons for refusing vaccination. She found this to be an articulate group of parents holding holistic beliefs about preventative health care. Their objections to vaccination focused on the effectiveness of the vaccine and the possibility of it causing damage, and concerns about its long-term effects on health. They also felt there was a lack of information available and lack of informed debate about the subject. These parents felt under pressure from family and health professionals to immunise their children, and this propelled them away from compliance and more towards seeking advice and support from alternative sources, rather than their GP. The author emphasised the need for informed, open and honest debate about the issues, and different health education literature that discussed the problems as well as the benefits of vaccination.

Few studies have tried to measure the differences between parents who do and do not vaccinate their children on the basis of perceived benefits and risks of vaccination. In this respect, Bennett and Smith (1992) found significant differences in levels of parental concern about the risk of children developing permanent health problems as a result of pertussis immunisation. Parents who chose not to have their children immunised reported a higher perceived risk of their child developing pertussis if vaccinated, as well as a lower risk of the disease if not vaccinated. Similar concerns were found for the MMR vaccine but less risk was attributed to measles, tetanus, polio and diphtheria. This research found more concern over long-term health problems resulting from immunisation. What it did not explore was the nature of the influences on parents to weigh up costs and benefits as they did.

Bennett and Smith (1992) have suggested that health education programmes must be able to reach families in order to raise their awareness. To do this, the way that information is given must be considered carefully so as to be informative, fairly argued but not coercive. In this respect, most of the health professionals sampled in a Fife study were unimpressed with the education material on the measles, mumps and rubella vaccine, which had been prepared for parents, considering the 'propaganda' surrounding the leaflets to be 'one-sided' (Walker 1990). It was found that parents who did not have their babies immunised were unhappy about adverse publicity about particular conditions, and some had previous experiences and a family history of specific illnesses which contra-indicated immunisation (Barlow and Walker 1990). Another qualitative study of infant immunisation in two health authorities (New and Senior 1991) found that parents' decisions were influenced by personal experiences such as the child's reaction to first injection, and type of health advice given. Some parents felt that if the baby was damaged in any way through vaccination it would be their fault.

Some parents are also influenced by alternative literature on immunisation, such as the newsletter 'The Informed Parent', and the literature produced by WTDDTY ('What the Doctors don't tell you'). The homeopathic practitioner's position on immunisation, which is laid out by Richard Moskowitz (1984, 1992) and Trevor Gunn (1992), forms an important aspect of this literature, and contributes to the general belief systems operating in this area. This presents a strong contrast with the views of the Council of the Faculty of Homeopathy which favours routine immunisation.

The types of studies done on immunisation have varied in focus and approach. Some have acquired quantitative information, giving figures on take-up of immunisation, while others have taken a qualitative approach, using depth interviews with parents and health professionals (Rogers and Pilgrim 1993; Woodhouse and Nicholson 1994). This has been particularly relevant in looking at those parents who do not have their children immunised, through ignorance, apathy or conscious decision. Both approaches are important to provide an overall picture of immunisation uptake and information about the nature of and reasoning behind non-immunisation. Whilst mass immunisation campaigns have undeniably been effective in the reduction of childhood disease, a number of commentators argue that literature on immunisation needs to present a more balanced, less coercive picture if it is to persuade those with unresolved doubts or fears about immunisation.

RECOMMENDATIONS FOR FURTHER RESEARCH

Most research has concentrated on mapping the success of immunisation campaigns through collecting data on immunisation status, or looking at possible reasons for parents not immunising their children.

1. It would be useful to have more research on the nature of and reasoning behind non-take-up of immunisation. Egan *et al.* (1992) have suggested a need for large-scale trials to investigate the effects of an adapted health education programme on those parents who are well-educated in the arguments against mass immunisation.

2. Research could also provide complementary data on the attitudes and beliefs of GPs and other health professionals in relation to active non-compliance by parents.

3. Further studies could be carried out on the effectiveness of health education on immunisation in high-risk groups, such as families on low incomes, and those in unstable accommodation, with a view to find ways to facilitate getting information about and access to immunisation for children of such families who may also find this practically difficult.

13. Men's health

Although some diseases, such as prostatism, are obviously unique to men, the main differences in mortality and morbidity relate to variations in exposure to risk factors. . . . Despite an apparent indifference, if not resistance, to health promotion messages among men, it must be brought home to them that many of the risk factors to their health – such as smoking, physical inactivity, poor diet, excess alcohol consumption, unsafe sexual practices and risky behaviour likely to lead to accidents – are preventable. Thus the scope for men to improve their health, and to prolong active, healthy life, is considerable (Calman, 1993).

Men's health is a neglected area of research, which reflects the way men themselves tend to neglect their health (HEA 1995e). In one study of the family (Holland et al. 1996) it was clear that fathers were less aware of the state of individual family member's health than mothers, and in common with men in general, they were less concerned with their own health and less willing to go and see the doctor. Yet men are actually at risk from a large range of illnesses and their life expectancy is well known as being lower than women's (Calman 1993). The male gender role has been shown to have a negative effect on their health and mortality (Skelton 1988; Wingard 1984); they have different perceptions from women of their own and other peoples' health (Saltonstall 1993); they do not use the health services in the same way as women, and they delay medical intervention; and many men find it hard to ask for help or do not see a need for it until too late (Blaxter 1990).

Studies specifically relating to men and health behaviour have tended to focus on young men, especially in relation to sexuality, sexual health and risk-taking (Holland et al. 1993; Wight, 1993) and youth cultural forms (Baldings 1993). Sexual health in particular has received more attention in recent years (Davidson and Lloyd 1994) through the risks of HIV infection. Older men tend to appear in discussions of health statistics, which show that men die younger than women, particularly from heart disease and cancer. Characteristics of the male lifestyle, seen typically as competitive, violent, aggressive, and involving higher alcohol consumption, has been linked to this earlier mortality. This makes men more likely to expose themselves to health risks involving, for instance, alcohol, drugs, accidents, and violent incidents or crimes (OPCS 1991a).

Family health research traditionally looks to women, in their caring role as wives/partners and mothers, as being responsible for monitoring health, giving health advice, filtering health messages, and taking or pressurising family members to consult a doctor. Men are seen as being generally more fit and healthy than women (whose more frequent visits to doctors are partly due to children's health and women's own reproductive health). Their key concern is to be fit, though good health may be welcomed as a spin-off from this. They appear less open to health messages, and in some situations they may resist changing their own health behaviour, such as in the case of using condoms for safer sex. The linking social and psychological concept which underlies men's health experience and behaviour is that of masculinity. Although the study of masculinity is increasing, men's health has not been a concern in much of this work. Some work has been done on mental health, and psychoanalytic interpretations of masculinity (Breen 1993; Frosh 1994; Rogers *et al.* 1996).

The increasing public discussion of sexuality and women's expectations from men (as found in women's magazines) may have affected men's awareness of their bodies and (sexual) health. Relatively new magazines such as Men's Health, and XL are attempting to motivate men to seek health through exercise and diet, although encouragement, it seems, is offered mainly through the enticement of acquiring greater sexual drive.

MORBIDITY AND MORTALITY

It is a well known fact that men die earlier than women. Throughout this century there has been at least five years difference, and the life expectancy of women between 1985 and 1990 was almost 6 years more than men (78.1: 72.4 years)(OHE 1992). The death rate over the period 1989–91 for adult men is always higher than for women of the same age (Craig 1995).

The most common causes of male death are circulatory diseases and cancer (70 per cent of all male deaths in England in 1992). The most common cause of death for women is some form of cancer (50 per cent). Circulatory diseases accounted for 38.6 per cent of male deaths, most of which was accounted for by coronary heart disease (CHD) (Calman 1993). Major factors contributing to CHD in men include age, lower social class, and living in the north of England.

In 1990, cancer accounted for the deaths of 31 per cent of men between the ages of 15 and 64. Although 31 per cent of these were from lung cancer, 11 per cent died from prostate cancer. Although testicular cancer accounts for only a relatively small proportion of cancers, concern has been rising as the incidence of testicular cancer has doubled since the 1970s (Carroll 1994). This form of cancer tends to affect younger men (mainly 20–34 years) and has a high level of recovery. Efforts are being made to make men (young men in particular), more aware of testicular health and the techniques of self-examination (Paolozzi 1994; Hamilton 1995; HEA 1995e). A significant (50 per cent) drop in the sperm count over the last 50 years has also caused some medical concern, which some scientists have blamed on environmental factors, such as exposure to oestrogen through pesticides and chemicals (Sharpe and Skakkeback 1993). This was also supported in a recent report which showed similar evidence of deteriorating semen quality in the UK (Irvine *et al.* 1996).

Young men are seen as a high-risk group, and indeed, the difference in the death rate for young women and young men of the same age rises sharply from age 15 to 24 years. This difference is attributed to the high level of deaths from injury (sports and motor accidents), poisoning, drugs and suicide amongst young men (OPCS 1992a). Between 1989 and 1991, the mortality rates for men aged 17–26 years were two and a half times as much as those for women of the same age

(Craig 1995). In 1991, 42 per cent of all deaths of young men within this age range were due to accidents, most of which are road traffic accidents (OPCS 1991a).

Another increasing concern is the rising suicide rate for both women and men, but particularly young men, whose rates are four times those of women (Charlton *et al.* 1993). It is men from the highest and lowest social class levels who are most likely to commit suicide (class I and V), as well as: men who are unemployed; single, divorced and widowed men; men with AIDS; men in prison; and those abusing alcohol or drugs.

There is disagreement in the literature on whether men have higher morbidity rates than women, although the current consensus suggests a 'hidden morbidity' – that there are higher levels of morbidity amongst males which go unreported (Robertson 1995; Waddell and Floate 1986; Blaxter 1990, Macintyre 1993).

SOCIAL AND PSYCHOLOGICAL FACTORS

Certain changes in demographic factors such as family structure have indirectly affected men's health. Women have traditionally been used as the way of targeting men for health education messages, and also helping to influence their diet and use of medical services. However, with the increasing incidence of divorce and family breakdown, this approach may become increasingly ineffective.

Marriage

Marriage (or its equivalent) has been identified as a protective factor for men's health, as is a good social support network (Welin *et al.* 1992). Research by Gove (1973) showed unmarried men, particularly those who are divorced or separated, have higher mortality and morbidity rates; and widowed and divorced or separated men, are more likely than their peers to smoke and drink to excess (OPCS 1986). Rushing *et al.* (1992) suggest that marriage and employment together help to protect men's health. Since women are generally the gatekeepers for health and health information for their partners and children, it is therefore single men who are more at risk, unless living at home with their mother, since they are not attached to a woman (Holland *et al.* 1996).

Employment and social class

Regular employment also serves to protect men's health, and unemployment has been shown to have serious affects on men's self-image, self-esteem and in turn, their health (Moser *et al.* 1986a, 1986b; Lewis 1988; Stafford *et al.* 1990; Aggleton *et al.* 1995). Becoming unemployed leads to material changes in family life, leading to a poorer diet and inadequate provision of other basic needs. Longstanding illness is significantly higher among unemployed men compared to those in work, and studies have also shown a deterioration in men's mental health through unemployment (Stafford *et al.* 1990).

Unemployment has traditionally predominated among lower social-class groups, although an increasing number of job cuts have been made in middle-class occupations over the last decade. Fear of redundancy is a constant worry for many men, especially those with young families. Variations in people's state of health by social class are well established and a positive linear relationship between health status and social class has been demonstrated (Harding 1995; Townsend *et al.* 1988; Davey Smith and Eggar 1993; Arber and Ginn 1993). For working-class men, their greater representation in the more hazardous occupations of manual work, and as operatives, contributes to this relationship, and the more dangerous sporting activities such as rugby football and boxing may also be implicated.

Male role and masculinity

The male gender role and concepts of masculinity in relation to health also have an impact on men's health, and may lead men to ignore their health needs. Differences have been suggested in how men and women may perceive and evaluate symptoms, what they do about them, and how doctors perceive and react to their symptoms (Macintyre 1993; Verbrugge 1985). Men are perceived by both sexes as being healthier, and they tend to stress health as being associated with fitness, strength, energy and being physically active and in control, while women place more emphasis on not being ill or seeing a doctor (Saltonstall 1993; Blaxter 1990). The author of one study on male body image and health beliefs (Watson 1993) suggested that a significant factor in men may be that they do not have physical markers relating to their bodies over the course of their lives, such as women have through menstruation and menopause. Other aspects may contribute instead, such as a movement from participation in some kind of sport or exercise, to observation of it.

A qualitative study of men's awareness of men's cancers (HEA 1995e) confirmed that men are far more reluctant than women to monitor their health and seek help at an early stage. They tend to become interested in health issues when something affects them personally, such as illness in the family or in friends. The report suggested that young men in particular feel it is not macho to pay too much attention to their health, and also find it embarrassing to talk about any type of personal problems with friends. parents or health professionals, although this may be helped by developing a close relationship. Many men remain ignorant about their bodies for much of their lives, although they may get some information from women's magazines (and now men's health magazines). Their findings also indicated a widespread feeling amongst men that serious health problems affect only the over-50s and therefore check-ups are relatively unnecessary before this age. However, on the positive side, it was found that once men were made aware that they were at risk from testicular cancer from their teenage years onwards, and that this can be easily monitored and rectified, they felt that it was very important that men's awareness on this issue should be raised.

Men generally place a lower priority on health needs than women and put work and other demands before going to the doctor. Women visited the doctor twice a much as men in 1990, although this proportion is somewhat inflated by women's concerns with family planning, pregnancy, and children (OPCS 1991b). Men were also more reluctant to have regular dental check-ups. Conforming with a 'macho' image tends to make men feel they need to be in control and self-sufficient which means not asking for help (Blaxter 1990). This starts at an early age, and helps to confirm an association between being feminine and being concerned with health (Baldings 1993).

SEXUAL AND REPRODUCTIVE HEALTH

Research relating to sexual health has shown that young men's concern with developing masculine sexuality makes them initially more concerned with conforming to the expectations of their peers, and their own sexual performance, than using condoms or other methods for safe sex (Holland *et al.* 1993). One survey showed that 77 per cent of young men aged 16 had used condoms in their last sexual encounter, but for 19-year-olds, this figure dropped to 47 per cent (HEA 1993b). Their sexual health also involves other anxieties that they may have related to penis size, shape, and performance, and emotional aspects of sexual relationships, all of which are subjects that are not easily discussed inside or outside the family. Brannen and Storey (1996) in their study of 10–11-year-olds found that boys reported less sexual health communication than girls. More than half the boys had not talked with anyone about puberty. Fathers reported much less discussion about sex with their children than mothers. But it is not just young men who are at risk from unsafe sexual practices; all men could put themselves at risk, and widowed and divorced/separated men are five times more likely to report unsafe sex than married men (Wellings *et al.* 1994).

Concern with men's sexual health has also provided a spur to efforts to make men more aware of their general reproductive health. As mentioned above, there has been increasing concern with prostate and testicular cancers in men, which has led to more publicity and the creation of some Well Men Clinics. Research has shown the potential for health education in this area: one campaign (Hamilton 1995) which targeted men at a large rugby match with information, created a great deal of interest in the nature and treatment of testicular cancer. The widespread concern over the increasing incidence of HIV/AIDS since the mid-1980s has also generated a number of research studies which highlight the need for more comprehensive and targeted sex education for boys and girls (Thomson and Scott 1991; Holland *et al.* 1990b; Wight 1993; Brannen and Storey 1996), and the need for a more open and enlightened approach to methods for ensuring safer sex.

FATHERS AND HEALTH

As with men's health in general, there is a need for more research on fathers and health. Research on family and health communication (Holland *et al.* 1996) showed that fathers were less aware of the state of individual family members' health than mothers, and in common with men in general, they were less concerned with their own health and less willing to go and see the doctor. Both men and women have traditionally accepted that family health matters are more the responsibility of the mother.

Communication

It is commonly assumed that women are more willing to talk about personal and family issues than men. This is reflected in men's comparative reluctance to talk to researchers, and in their communication style within the family itself. Women are usually more practised and articulate in the expression of emotions and feelings, and more willing and interested to explore the nature of relationships. Reflecting a traditional belief in the 'natural' order of things, several mothers in one family study (Holland *et al.* 1996) considered that 'with mothers it is inbuilt in you somewhere' when it comes to things like communicating with your children. This relative lack of ease shown by men in talking about personal issues radically affects the kinds of conversations that children, especially daughters, tend to have with their fathers (Sharpe 1994). Aspects of girls growing up, such as starting periods, sex education, boyfriends and other such issues are more readily approached with mothers than with fathers (see Chapter 7 above). Boys growing up are also faced with physical changes and personal and emotional concerns, but they are generally more reluctant to talk about these issues, especially with parents, and feel that they should deal with them alone (Brannen and Storey 1996; Rogers *et al.* 1996). In these and other studies, men and boys appear to find family communication and self-expression harder than women and girls do, and prefer to talk about other topics. In the research by Rogers *et al.*, football and sport featured significantly on the 'male emotional agenda'. With gendered belief systems remaining relatively intact, it is quite difficult to get fathers to take a more substantial part in looking after both their own health and that of other members of their families, and to get mothers to relinquish their side of this division.

Food

The role of many men within the family is as food consumer rather than initiator of menus, diets or culinary concoctions (see also Chapter 8 above). As the arbiters of food buying, and the greater consumers of all the health and food information fed through magazines and television programmes, women are more concerned with weight and diet. Men are not traditionally thought to be as oppressed by body image as women, although it has been suggested that a significant proportion (about a third) of men are 'dissatisfied' with their bodies, and it appears that some boys, like many girls, are becoming obsessed with trying to achieve an idealised body image (Illman 1996). The Eating Disorders Association for Anorexia and Bulimia has reported that more than one in ten of their reported cases are male, and there may be many more who are undiagnosed (Royal College of Psychiatrists 1993; Siegel *et al.* 1995).

Despite women's increased working role and ideas about domestic equality, research has confirmed that food-buying and preparation in the family is still mainly in the hands of wives/partners (Gillon *et al.* 1993). Gillon *et al.*'s study also raised an interesting contradiction between women's role in monitoring family health and in improving or maintaining the family diet, versus meeting the food preferences of her husband/partner which may be for less healthy 'male' foods such as red meat. Therefore if women are coming up against resistance from male partners, these men too need to be worked with if dietary patterns are to be changed. This is one way that men can influence health through their power relations in the family (Charles and Kerr 1988).

Stress and mental illness

Both men and women suffer from stress and mental illness, and some studies have addressed the issue of men and stress (Matthews 1988). Rogers *et al.* (1996) noted the different ways in which men and women experience conflict and how this is expressed and communicated within the family. Men did not communicate their worries as much as women, who were anxious that their male partners and sons were 'bottling things up'. Fathers are generally less likely to admit to the stresses they may be under, or those that other members of the family may be experiencing. Another gender difference appears to lie in evidence that mothers are affected by sources of stress emanating from both within and outside the family while fathers are more affected by sources of stress from outside the family, such as from work pressures (Holland *et al.* 1996). The current instability in most areas of employment makes redundancy an ever-present fear and source of stress for many men, and even more so if they have a family with small children to support, while the experience of unemployment, as mentioned above, has adverse affects on psychological health (Lewis 1988). This is rendered more complex by the possibility that men are stressed by family issues but are more likely to express work-related anxieties as these are more 'acceptable' for men.

There is an absence of research data in many areas of men's health. Raising men's consciousness about their own (and their family's) health, increasing facilities such as Well Men clinics, carrying out more research and targeted health education could go a long way in improving not only men's health but the consequent well-being of their families. This is, unfortunately, not a straightforward process because men's apparent resistance to health messages is also tangled up with social psychological aspects of masculinity and certain 'macho' aspects of the male lifestyle which are difficult to challenge and change.

RECOMMENDATIONS FOR FURTHER RESEARCH

1. More study should be made of men's image of health and fitness, and their body image. This would look at the processes by which the male role and masculinity hinders men's monitoring of their own health, and at ways of raising their consciousness in this area.

2. Boys' physical image is also an area needing research, especially as reports suggest that one in ten sufferers of anorexia nervosa are male. It is possible that boys are beginning to feel similar pressures to girls about conforming to some idealised physical body image.

3. It would be useful to look further at the poor communication between men and boys in families (Rogers *et al.* 1996; Brannen and Storey 1996).

4. In the light of the relatively high incidence of suicide in young men, more research should be carried out on the situation of young men and their

experiences of stress, psychological problems, and mental illness, related especially to factors such as family and school pressures, and identity loss through unemployment.

5. Further work should be done on the protective role that being in a relationship/marriage has for men's health, and the converse of this, which lies in the health risks to men of being single, divorced/separated, or widowed.

6. The effects of stress, from inside or outside the family on fatherhood, could receive more research attention.

7. Much attention has been paid to teenage motherhood, and it would also be useful to look at aspects of teenage fatherhood in relation to certain health issues.

8. More research is needed on cultural factors: the relationship between health beliefs and behaviours and aspects of masculinity and the male role in different ethnic groups.

9. There appear to be areas of relative ignorance for both sexes on the health issues of the other. Research could look at ways of promoting health information that would increase women's understanding of boys' and men's specific health problems, and men's understanding of girls' and women's specific health problems.

1 These are: Brannen and Storey 1996; Holland *et al.* 1996; Prout 1996; Rogers *et al.* 1996; Beattie *et al.* (forthcoming) 1996; Brynin and Scott (forthcoming) 1996. Summaries of the first four of these studies can be found in Hogg *et al.* (1996)

References

Aaro, L.E., Bruland, E., Hauknes, A. and Lochsen, P.M. (1983) Smoking among Norwegian schoolchildren 1975–1980 – III The effect of anti-smoking campaigns, *Scandinavian Journal of Psychology* 23: 277–283.

Aaro, L.E., Wold, B., Lannas, L. and Rimpela, M. (1986) Health behaviour in school children: a W.H.O. cross-national survey, *Health Promotion* 1(1): 17–33.

Abdulrahim, D., White, D., Phillips, K., Boyd, G., Nicholson, J. and Elliott, J. (1994) *Ethnicity and Drug Use: Towards the Design of Community Interventions,* Vol. 1 *Executive Summary and Recommendations,* AIDS Research Unit, University of East London, London.

Abraham, C., Sheeran, P., Abrams, D., Spears, R. and Marks, D. (1991) Young people learning about AIDS: a study of beliefs and information sources, *Health Education Research: Theory and Practice,* January, 6(1): 19–29.

Abrams, D. *et al.* (1990) *AIDS Invulnerability: Relationships, Sexual Behaviour and Attitudes Among 16–19 year olds.* In Aggleton, P., Davies, P. and Hart, G. (eds) AIDS: *Individual, Cultural and Policy Dimensions,* Falmer Press, Lewes.

Action on Smoking and Health (1990) Working Group in Women and Smoking, *Smoke Still Gets in Her Eyes,* Action on Smoking and Health, London.

Action on Smoking and Health (1993) Working Group in Women and Smoking, *Her Share of Misfortune: Women, Smoking and Low Income,* Action on Smoking and Health, London.

Adler, M. (1992) Education, sexual health and the hidden agenda, letter to *The Guardian,* 15 April.

Aggleton, P. (1987) *Rebels Without a Cause: Middle Class Youth and the Transition From School to Work,* Falmer Press, Lewes.

Aggleton. P. (1996) *Young People and Health Promotion,* HEA, London.

Aggleton, P. *et al.* (1995) *Young Men Speaking Out,* Report prepared for the HEA by the Health and Education Research Unit, Institute of Education, University of London.

Ahmad, W. and Chaplin, J. (1994) Ethnicity, health and health care: some recent publications, *Critical Public Health* 5(4): 48–52.

Ajzen, I. and Fishbein, M. (1980) *Understanding Attitudes and Predicting Social Behaviour,* Prentice Hall, Englewood Cliffs.

Alcohol Concern (1991) *Warning. Alcohol can Damage Your Health,* Alcohol Concern, London.

Alderson, P. and Mayall, B. (1994) *Children's Decisions in Health Care and Research,* Consent Series Conference, No. 5, Social Science Research Unit, Institute of Education, London.

Allen, C.E. (1994) Families in poverty, *Nursing Clinics of North America,* 29(3), 377–393.

Allen, I. (1987) *Education in Sex and Personal Relationships,* Policy Studies Institute Report No. 665, London.

Allied Dunbar and HEA (1992) *Allied Dunbar National Fitness Survey: a Report on Activity Patterns and Fitness Levels Commissioned by the Sports Council and Health Education: Main Findings,* HEA/Sports Council, London.

Amin, K. (1992) *Poverty in Black and White: Deprivation and Ethnic Minorities,* Runnymede Trust, London.

Amos, A. (1993) In her own best interests? Women and health education: a review of the last fifty years, *Health Education Journal* 52(3): 141–150.

Anderson, A., Marshall, D. and Kemmer, D. (1995) The marriage menu – food and diet in transition, Paper presented at *The Nation's Diet Conference,* ESRC, 14 November.

Anderson, A.S. and Hunt, K. (1992) Who are the 'healthy eaters'? Eating patterns and health promotion in the west of Scotland, *Health Education Journal* 51(1): 3–10.

Anderson, E. (1989) Sex codes and family life among poor inner-city youths, *The Annals of the American Academy of Political and Social Science*, January, 501: 59–78.

Andreski, P. and Breslau, N. (1993) Smoking and nicotine dependence among young adults: differences between blacks and whites, *Drug and Alcohol Dependency* 32: 119–125.

Angeli, N. *et al.* (1994) Facilitating parenting skills in vulnerable families, *Health Visitor* 64(7): 130–132.

Arber, S. (1991) Class, paid employment and family roles, making sense of structural disadvantage, gender and health status, *Social Science and Medicine* 32: 425–436.

Arber, S., Gilbert, N. and Dale, A. (1985) Paid employment and women's health: a benefit or a source of role strain? *Sociology of Health and Illness* 7: 375–400.

Arber, S. and Ginn, J. (1993) Gender and inequalities in health in later life, *Social Science and Medicine* 36(1): 33–46.

Arksey, H. (1994) Expert and lay participation in the construction of medical knowledge, *Sociology of Health and Illness* 16(4): 448–468.

Armstrong, N. (1995) *The Challenge of Promoting Physical Activity*, Conference: The Health of the Next Generation, Royal Society of Health, London.

Armstrong, N., *et al.* (1990) Patterns of physical activity among 11 to 16 year-old British children, *British Medical Journal*, 301: 203–205

Arnold, S. *et al.* (1995) *Risk and Protective Factors in Adolescent Smoking*, Unpublished paper, SSRU, Institute of Education, London.

Atun, R. and Jenkins, S. (1992) Health needs of the Turkish community in Hackney: a study of child health clinic attenders, *Maternal and Child Health*, 17(5): 134–142.

Backett, K. (1990) Image and reality: health enhancing behaviour in middle-class families, *Health Education Journal* 49: 61–63.

Backett, K. and Alexander, H. (1991) Talking to young children about health: methods and findings, *Health Education Journal* 50(1): 34–38.

Backett, K. *et al.* (1994) Lay evaluation of health and healthy lifestyles: evidence from three studies, *British Journal of General Practice* 44: 277–80.

Baer, P.E. (1987) Stress, coping, family conflict and adolescent alcohol use, *Journal of Behavioural Medicine* 10(5): 449–466

Bagnall, G. (1991) *Educating Young Drinkers*, Routledge, London.

Baily, S. (1990) Women with alcohol problems: a psycho-social perspective, *Drug and Alcohol Review* 9: 125–131.

Baker, S. and Lane, M. (1994) The good father: how is the role of fathers in child care changing? *Child Health* 2(1): 28–30.

Bakx, K. (1991) The 'eclipse' of folk medicine in Western society, *Sociology of Health and Illness* 13(1): 20–38.

Balarajan, R. (1991) Ethnic differences in mortality from ischaemic heart disease and cerebrovascular disease in England and Wales, *British Medical Journal* 302: 560–564.

Balarajan, R. and Raleigh, V.S. (1993) *Ethnicity and Health: A Guide for the NHS*, HMSO, London.

Baldings, J. (1993) *Young People in 1992*, Schools Health Education Unit, University of Exeter, Exeter.

Ball, J. A. (1991) *Post–natal Care and Adjustment to Motherhood*. In Robinson, S. and Thomson, A.M. (eds) *Midwives, Research and Childbirth*, Vol. 1., Chapman and Hall, Bury St. Edmunds.

Bande-Knops, J. (1987) *Accident Study in Children 0–4 years*. In Berfenstam, R., Jackson, H. and Eriksson, B. (eds) *The Healthy Community: Child Safety as Part of Health Promotion Activities*, Folksam, Stockholm.

Barlow, H. and Walker, D. (1990) Immunisation in Fife Part II – Failure to immunise against whooping cough – reasons given by parents, *Health Education Journal* 49(3): 103–105.

Barnes, G. G. (1990) Making family therapy work: research findings and family therapy practice, *Journal of Family Therapy* 12(1): 17–29.

Barnes, H.L. and Olson, D.H. (1985) Parent–adolescent communication and the circumplex world, *Child Development* 56: 437–447.

Bartley, M., Popay, J. and Plewis, I. (1992) Domestic conditions, paid employment and women's experience of ill-health, *Sociology of Health and Illness* 14(3): 313–343.

Bartley, M., Power, C., Blane, D., Davey Smith, G. and Shipley, M. (1994) Birthweight and later socio-economic disadvantage: evidence from the 1958 British cohort study, *British Medical Journal* 309: 1475–1478.

Basen–Engquist, K. (1994) Evaluation of a theory-based HIV prevention intervention for college students, *AIDS Education and Prevention*, 6(5): 412–424.

Bean, P. *et al.* (1988) Knowledge of drugs and consumption of alcohol among Nottingham 15 year-olds, *Health Education Journal* 47(2/3): 79–82.

Beattie, A. *et al.* (1982) *Adolescent Health Perceptions Project*, Final Report, Department of Health and Welfare, Institute of Education, London University, London.

Beattie, A. J. *et al.* (1996) *Family Health and Housing Poverty*, HEA, London.

Beattie, J.O. *et al.* (1986) Children intoxicated by alcohol in Nottingham and Glasgow 1973–1984, *British Medical Journal* 292: 519–521.

Bechhofer, F. (1989) Individuals, politics and society: a dilemma for public health research. In Martin, C. and McQueen, D. (eds) *Readings for a New Public Health,* Edinburgh University Press, Edinburgh.

Becker, M.H. (ed) (1974) *The Health Belief Model and Personal Health Behaviour*, Slack, Thorofare, New Jersey.

Bell, C. and Roberts, H. (eds) (1984) *Social Researching: Politics, Problems, Practice*, Routledge, London.

Bellinger, D., Leviton, A., Needleman, H.L., Waternaux, C. and Rabinowitz, M. (1986) Low-level lead exposure and infant development in the first year, *Neurobehavioural Toxicology and Teratology* 8(2): 151–161.

Belski, J. and Kelly, J. (1994) *The Transition to Parenthood: How a First Child Changes a Marriage: Based on a Landmark Study*, Vermilion, London.

Bendelow, G. and Oakley, A. (1993) *Beliefs About Cancer in Children and Young People*, Social Science Research Unit/Women's Worldwide Cancer Control Campaign, Institute of Education, London.

Bennett, P. and Smith, C. (1992) Parents' attitudinal and social influences on childhood vaccination, *Health Education Research* 7(3): 341–348.

Bennett, P. *et al.* (1991) Patterns of drinking in Wales, *Alcohol and Alcoholism* 36(3): 367–374.

Bennicke, K. *et al.* (1995) Cigarette smoking and breast cancer, *British Medical Journal*, June 3: 310, 1431–1433.

Bertalanffy, L. von (1969) *General Systems Theory: Essays in its Foundation and Development*, Brazilier, New York.

Beumont, P.J.V., Abraham, S.F. and Simson, K.G. (1981) The psychosexual histories of adolescent girls and young women with anorexia nervosa, *Psychological Medicine* 11: 131–40.

Bewley, B.R. and Bland M. (1987) The child's image of a young smoker, *Health Education Journal* 98(37): 236–241.

Bewley, B.R. *et al.* (1984) Adolescent patterns in an inner London general practice: their attitudes to illness and health care, *Journal of the Royal College of General Practitioners* 34(267): 543–546.

Bhopal, R.S., Phillimore, P. and Kohli, H.S. (1991) Inappropriate use of the term 'Asian': an obstacle to ethnicity and health research, *Journal of Public Health Medicine* 13(4): 244–246.

Bhopal, R.S., and Samim, A.K. (1988) Immunisation among Glasgow Asian children: paradoxical benefit of communication barriers?, *Community Medicine* 10: 215–220.

Biddle, S. and Armstrong, N. (1992) Children's physical activity: an exploratory study of psychological correlates, *Social Science and Medicine*, 34(3): 325–331.

Biddle, S., Mitchell J. and Armstrong, N. (1992) The assessment of physical activity in children: a comparison of continuous heart rate monitoring, self-report and interview recall techniques, *British Journal of Physical Education Research Supplement* 10: 4–8.

Biddle, S. and Mutrie, N. (1991) *Psychology of Physical Activity and Exercise: a Health-Related Perspective*, Springer-Verlag, London.

Birenbaum, L.K. (1990) Family coping with childhood cancer – Special issue: Research form the annual meeting of the National Hospice Organisation, *Hospice Journal* 6(3): 17–33.

Blane, D. (1985) An assessment of the Black Report's explanation of health inequalities, *Sociology of Health and Illness* 7: 423-445.

Blaxter, M. (1983) Health services as a defence against the consequences of poverty in industrialised societies, *Social Science and Medicine* 17: 1139–1148.

Blaxter, M. (1987) Alcohol consumption. In Cox, B. D. *et al.* (eds) *The Health and Lifestyle Survey*, Health Promotion Research Trust, London.

Blaxter, M. (1990) *Health and Lifestyles*, Tavistock/Routledge, London.

Blaxter, M. and Patterson, E. (1982) *Mothers and Daughters: A Three Generational Study of Health Attitudes and Behaviour*, Heinemann, London.

BMA (1992) Alternative therapies. In Saks, M. (ed.) *Alternative Medicine in Britain*, Clarendon, Oxford.

Bonithon-Kopp, C., Huel, G., Moreau, T. and Wending, R. (1986) Pre-natal exposure to lead and cadmium and psychomotor development of the child at 6 years, *Neurobehavioural Toxicology and Teratology* 8(3): 307–310.

Booth, T. and Booth, W. (1994) *Parenting Under Pressure: Mothers and Fathers with Learning Difficulties*, Open University Press.

Bowie, C. and Ford, N. (1989) Sexual behaviour of young people and the risk of HIV infection, *Journal of Epidemiology and Community Health* 43(1): 61–65.

Boyle, M., Pitts, M., Phillips, K., White, D.G., Clifford, B. and Woolett, E.A. (1989) Exploring young people's knowledge of and attitudes to AIDS: the value of focussed group discussions, *Health Education Journal* 48: 21–23.

Bradby, H. (1995) Ethnicity: not a black and white issue: a research note, *Sociology of Health and Illness* 17(3): 405–417.

Bradshaw, J. (1993) *Household Budgets and Living Standards*, Rowntree/University of York, York.

Bradstock, K., *et al.* (1988) Alcohol use and health behaviour lifestyles among US women: the behaviour risk factor surveys, *Addictive Behaviours* 13(1): 61–71.

Brannen, J. (1988) Research note: the study of sensitive subjects, *Sociological Review* 36(3): 552–562.

Brannen, J., Dodd, K. and Oakley, A. (1991) Getting involved: the effects of research on participants, Paper presented at the *BSA Conference on Health and Society*.

Brannen, J., Dodd, D., Oakley, A. and Storey, P. (1994) *Young People, Health and Family Life*, Open University Press, Milton Keynes.

Brannen, J. and O'Brien, M. (1995a) *Childhood and Parenthood: Proceedings of the Intenational Sociological Association Committee for Family Research Conference 1994*, Institute of Education, London.

Brannen, J. and O'Brien, M. (1995b) *Children and the Sociological Gaze: Paradigms and Paradoxes*, *Sociology* 29(4): 729–737.

Brannen, J. and O'Brien, M. (eds) (1996) *Children in Families: Research and Policy*, Falmer Press, London.

Brannen, J. and Storey, P. (1996) *Child Health in the Social Context: Parental Employment and the Start of Secondary School*, HEA, London.

Brannen, J. *et al.* (1995) Young people and their contribution to household work, *Sociology* 29(2): 317–338.

Braun, M. *et al.* (1992) Immunisation: What do parents and health visitors in Barnet know about meningitis and Haemophilus influenzae type b?, *Health Education Journal*, 51(4): 178–188.

Breen, D. (1993) *The Gender Conundrum*, Routledge, London.

Breeze, E. (1985) *Women and Drinking*, OPCS, HMSO, London.

Bribace, R. and Walsh, M.E. (1980) Development of children's concepts of illness, *Paediatrics* 66: 912–917.

Briscoe, M. E. (1989) Sex differences in mental health, *Update*, November: 834–839.

British Market Research Bureau (1989) *The Up-Take of Pre-School Immunisation in England: Report on a National Study of Variation in Immunisation Uptake between District Health Authorities*, BMRB, London.

Brown, G. (1990) Popular epidemiology: community response to toxic waste induced disease. In Konrad, P. and Kern, R. (eds) *The Sociology of Health and Illness: Critical Perspectives*, St Martin's Press, New York.

Bruyn, M. de (1992) Women and AIDS in developing countries, *Social Science and Medicine*, 34(3): 249–262.

Brynin, M. and Scott, J. (1996) *Young People, Health and the Family: Results from the British Household Panel Study*, HEA, London.

Burchfiel, C.M., Higgins, M.W., Keller, J.B., Howatt, W.F., Butler, W.J. and Higging, I.T.T. (1986) Passive smoking and pulmonary function in Tecumseh, Michigan, *American Review of Respiratory Diseases* 133(6): 966-973.

Burgess, A. (1996) *Fatherhood Reclaimed*, Vermillion, London.

Burghes, L. (1980) Living from hand to mouth: a study of 65 families living on supplementary benefit, *Child Poverty Action Group*, Family Services Unit.

Burghes, L. (1994) What happens to the children of single parents? *British Medical Journal* 308: 1114–1115.

Burr, W.R., Hill, R., Nye, F.I. and Reiss, I.L. (eds) (1979) *Contemporary Theories About the Family*, vol.1: *Research Based Theories*, The Free Press, New York.

Bury, A. (1993) Researching children: the same or different? Paper presented at the *BSA Conference 'Research Imaginations', Essex University*, Colchester 5–8 April.

Butler, C. *et al.* (1993) An intervention programme to build competencies in adolescent parents, *Journal of Primary Prevention* 13(3): 183–198.

Butler, S. and Wintram, C. (1991) *Feminist Groupwork*, Sage, London.

Cade, J. and O'Connell, S. (1991) Management of weight problems and obesity: knowledge, attitudes and current practice of general practitioners, *British Journal of General Practice*, April: 147–150.

Callan, V.J. (1985) *Choices About Children*, Longman Cheshire, Melbourne.

Callan, V.J. and Noller, P. (1986) Perceptions of communicative relationships in families with adolescents, *Journal of Marriage and the Family* 48: 813–820.

Callan, V.J. and Noller, P. (1987) *Marriage and the Family*, Methuen, Australia.

Calman, K.C. (1993) *On the State of the Public Health 1992*, HMSO, London.

Calnan, M.W. and Johnson, B.M. (1983) Influencing health behaviour: how significant is the general practitioner? *Health Education Journal* 42: 39–45.

Cameron, D. and Jones, I.G. (1984) Social class analysis – an embarrassment to epidemiology, *Community Medicine* 6: 37–46.

Campbell, M.J., Browne, D. and Waters, W.E. (1985) Can general practitioners influence exercise habits? Controlled trial, *British Medical Journal* 290: 1044–1046.

Campion, P. *et al.* (1994a) Evaluation of a mass media campaign on smoking and pregnancy, *Addiction* 89(10): 1245-1254.

Campion, P. *et al.* (1994b) Smoking before, during and after pregnancy in England, *Health Education Journal* 53 (2): 163–173.

Cancer Research Campaign (1991) *Factsheet 16: Testicular Cancer*, Cancer Research Campaign, London.

Cancer Research Campaign (1994) *Factsheet 20: Prostate Cancer*, Cancer Research Campaign, London.

Carroll, S. (1994) *The Which? Guide to Men's Health*, Which? Books, Consumers Association.

Charles, N. and Kerr, M. (1985) Attitudes towards the feeding and nutrition of young children, *Research Report No. 4*, HEC.

Charles, N. and Kerr, M. (1987) Just the way it is: gender and age differences in family food consumption. In Brannen, J. and Wilson, G. (eds) *Give and Take in Families: Studies in Resource Distribution*, Allen and Unwin, London.

Charles, N. and Kerr, M. (1988) *Women, Food and Families*, Manchester University Press, Manchester.

Charlton, A. (1984a) Smoking and weight control in teenagers, *Public Health* 98: 277–281.

Charlton, A. (1984b) The Brigantia smoking survey: a general review, *Public Education About Cancer*, V.I.C.C. Technical Report Series 77: 92–102.

Charlton, A. (1986) Evaluation of a family-linked smoking programme in primary schools, *Health Education Journal* 45(3): 140–144.

Charlton, A. and Blair, V. (1989a) Absence from school related to children's and parental smoking habits, *British Medical Journal* 298, 90–92.

Charlton, A. and Blair, V. (1989b) Predicting the onset of smoking in boys and girls, *Social Science and Medicine* 29(7): 813–818.

Charlton, J. *et al.* (1993) Suicide deaths in England and Wales: trends in factors associated with suicide deaths, *Population Trends* 71, Spring.

Chassin, L., Presson, C.C., Montello, D., Sherman, S.J. and McGrew, J. (1986) Changes in peer and parental influence during adolescence: longitudinal versus cross-sectional perspectives on smoking initiation, *Developing Psychology* 22(3): 327–334.

Chassin, L., Presson, C.C., Sherman, S.J. and Edwards, D.A. (1991) Four pathways to young-adult smoking status: adolescent social-psychological antecedents in a Midwestern community sample, *Health Psychology* 10(6): 409–418.

Chaturvedi, N. and McKeigue, P.M. (1994) Methods for epidemiological surveys of ethnic minority groups, *Journal of Epidemiology and Community Health* 48(2): 107–111.

Chew, R. (1986) *Health Expenditure in the UK*, Office of Health Economics, London.

Coggans, N. and McKellar, S. (1994) Drug use among peers: peer pressure or peer preference, *Drugs: Education, Prevention and Policy* 1(1): 15–26.

Cohen, R., Coxall, J., Craig, G. and Sadiq-Sangster, A. (1992) *Hardship Britain: Being Poor in the 90s*, Child Poverty Action Group, London.

Cole-Hamilton, I. (1988) *Review of Food Patterns Amongst Lower Income Groups in the UK*, A Report to the HEA, HEA, London.

Coles, A. and Turner, S. (1995) *Diet and Health in School Age Children*, A Briefing Paper Prepared for the Health Education Authority, HEA, London.

Collins, R.L. *et al.* (eds) (1990) *Alcohol and the Family Research and Clinical Perspectives*, Guilford Press, New York.

Combes, G. and Schonveld, A. (1992) *Life Will Never Be The Same Again: A Review of Antenatal and Postnatal Health Education*, HEA, London.

Communicable Disease Report (1994) 4(2). CDSC/PHIS, 4 Feburary.

Conrad, K.M. *et al.* (1992) Why children start smoking cigarettes: predictors of onset, *British Journal of Addiction* 87: 1711–1724.

Conter, V. *et al.* (1995) Weight growth in infants born to mothers who smoked during pregnancy, *British Medical Journal* 25: 768–771.

Conway, J. (ed) (1988) *Prescription for Poor Health – the Health Crisis for Homeless Families*, London Food Commission, Maternity Alliance, SHAC and Shelter, London.

Cook, D.G., Whincup, P.H., Jarvis, M.J., Strachan, D.P., Papacosta, O. and Bryant, A. (1994) Passive exposure to tobacco smoke in children aged 5–7 years: individual, family and community factors, *British Medical Journal* 308: 384–390.

Corea, G. (1988) *The Mother Machine: Reproductive Technologies from Artificial Insemination to Artificial Wombs*, The Women's Press, London.

Cornwell, J. (1984) *Hard-Earned Lives: Accounts of Health and Illness from East London*, Tavistock, London.

Cornwell, J. and Gordon, P. (eds) (1984) *An Experiment in Advocacy – The Hackney Multi Ethnic Women's Health Project*, King's Fund Centre, London.

Corrigan, E. M. (1987) Women's combined use of alcohol and other mind-altering drugs. In Burden, D. S. and Gottlieb, N. (eds) *The Woman Client*, Tavistock, New York.

Corti, B. *et al.* (1989) *Women, Drugs and Alcohol: Risk factors and Health Beliefs*, National Centre for Research into the Prevention of Drug Abuse, Western Australia.

Coxon, A. (1989) Who's doing what and to whom... *The Times Higher Education Supplement*, 17 November.

Craig, G. and Dowler, E. (1996) Let them eat cake: poverty, hunger and the UK state. In Riches, G. (ed) *First World Hunger: Food Security and Welfare Politics*, Macmillan, Basingstoke.

Craig, J. (1995) Males and females – some vital differences, *Population Trends* 80: 26–30.

Crew, K. and Fletcher, J. (1995) Empowering parents to prevent childhood accidents, *Health Visitor* 68(7): 291.

Cunninghame C.J., Charlton C.P.J. and Jenkins, S.M. (1994) Immunisation uptake and parental perceptions in a strictly orthodox Jewish community in North-East London, *Journal of Public Health Medicine* 16(3): 314–317.

Currer, C. (1986) Concepts of mental well- and ill-being: the case of Pathan mothers in Britain. In Currer, C. and Stacey, M. (eds) *Concepts of Health, Illness and Disease: a Comparative Perspective*, Berg, Leamington Spa.

Currie, C. (1990) Young people in independent schools, sexual behaviour and AIDS. In Aggleton, P., Davies, P. and Hart, G. (eds) *AIDS: Individual, Cultural and Policy Dimensions*, Falmer Press, Lewes.

Czeizel, A.E., Kodaj, I. and Widukind, L. (1994) Smoking during pregnancy and congenital limb deficience, *British Medical Journal* 308: 1473–1477.

Danilewitz, D. and Skuy, M. (1990) A psychoeducational profile of the unmarried mother, *International Journal of Adolescence and Youth* 2(3): 175–184.

Davey Smith, G., Bartley, M. and Blane, D. (1990) The Black report on socio-economic inequalities in health 10 years on, *British Medical Journal* 301: 373–377.

Davey Smith, G. and Eggar, M. (1993) Socio-economic differentials in wealth and health: widening inequalities in health, *British Medical Journal* 307: 1085–1086.

Davey Smith G. *et al.* (1994) Explanations for socio-economic differentials in mortality, *European Journal of Public Health* 4(2): 131–144.

Davidson N. and Lloyd T. (1994) *Working with Heterosexual Men in Sexual Health*, HEA, London.

Davies, J.B. (1992) Peer group influence and youthful alcohol consumption: an opinion. In *Addictions Forum Conference Report – Alcohol and Young People: Learning To Cope*, 7 October.

Davison, C., Davey Smith, G. and Frankel, S. (1991) Lay epidemiology and the prevention paradox: the implications of coronary candidacy for health education, *Sociology of Health and Illness* 13(1): 1–19.

Daykin, N.B. (1991) Young women and smoking: sociological perspectives explored. Paper presented at the *BSA Conference on Health and Society*.

Dearden, K.A. *et al.* (1995) The antecedants of teen fatherhood: a retrospective case-control study of Great Britain youth, *American Journal of Public Health* 85(4): 551–554.

Department of Employment (1986) *Family Expenditure Survey: Report for 1985*, HMSO, London.

Department of Transport (1994) *Road Accidents: Great Britain 1993*, HMSO, London.

Devault, M.L. (1991) *Feeding the Family*, Chicago University Press, Chicago.

DoH (1989) *The Diets of British Schoolchildren*, Report on Health and Social Subjects, HMSO, London.

DoH (1994a) *Eat Well! An Action Plan from the Nutrition Task Force to Achieve the Health of the Nation Targets on Diet and Nutrition*, Department of Health, London.

DoH (1994b) *On the State of the Public Health: The Annual Report of the Chief Medical Officer of the Department of Health for the Year 1993*, HMSO, London.

DoH (1995) *The Health of the Nation – Variations in Health: What Can the Department of Health and the NHS Do?* A Report Produced by the Variations Sub-Group of the Chief Medical Officer's Health of the Nation Working Group, October.

D'Houtaud, A. and Field, M. (1986) New research on the image of health. In Currer, C. and Stacey, M. (eds) *Concepts of Health, Illness and Disease: a Comparative Perspective*, Berg, Leamington Spa.

DHSS (1980) *Rickets and Osteomalacia*, Report of the Working Party on Fortification of Food with Vitamin D, Committee on Medical Aspects of Food Policy (COMA), HMSO, London.

DHSS (1987) *Asian Mother and Baby Campaign*: A report by the Director, DHSS, London.

DHSS (1992) *The Health of the Nation: A Strategy for England*, Cmd.1986, HMSO, London.

Diamond, L. D. *et al.* (1988) The incidence of drug and solvent misuse amoung Southern English normal comprehensive schoolchildren, *Public Health* 102: 107–114

Diamond, A. and Goddard, E. (1995) *Smoking Among Secondary School Children in 1994*, OPCS, London.

Dickinson, R. and Bhatt, A. (1994) Ethnicity, health and control: results from an exploratory study of ethnic minority communities' attitudes to health, *Health Education Journal* 53(4): 421–429.

Dickson-Markman, F. and Markman, H.J. (1988) The effects of others on marriage: do they help or hurt? In Noller, P. and Fitzpatrick, M.A. (eds) *Perspectives on Marital Interaction*, Multilingual Matters, Cleveland and Philadelphia.

di Clemente, R.J., Boyer, C.B. and Morales, E.S. (1988) Minorities and AIDS: knowledge, attitudes and misconceptions among black and Latino adolescents, *American Journal of Public Health* 78(1): 55–57.

di Clemente, R.J., Zorn, J. and Temeshok, L. (1986) Adolescents and AIDS: a survey of knowledge, attitudes and beliefs about AIDS in San Francisco, *American Journal of Public Health* 76(12): 1443–1445.

Dietz, W.H. and Gortmaker, S.L. (1985) Do we fatten our children at the television set? Obesity and television viewing in children and adolescents, *Paediatrics* 75: 807–812.

Dinkmeyer, D. and McKay, G. (1976) *Systematic Training for Effective Parenting: Parents' Handbook*, American Guidance Services Inc., Circle Pines, Minn.

Dobkin, P.L. *et al.* (1994) Is having an alcoholic father hazardous for children's health?, *Addiction* 89(12): 1619–1628.

Dobson, B., Beardsworth, A., Keil, T. and Walker, R. (1994) Eating on a low income, Findings, *Social Policy Research* 66.

Dodd, K. (1991) Interviewing adolescent subjects: negotiating access. In Brannen, J., Dodd, K. and Oakley, A. *Getting Involved: the Effects of Research on Participants*, Paper presented at the *BSA Conference on Health and Society*.

Doherty, W.J. and Campbell, T.L. (1988) *Families and Health*, Family Studies Text Series 10, Sage, London.

Donovan, C. and McEwan, R. (1995) A review of the literature examining the relationship between alcohol use and HIV-related sexual risk-taking in young people, *Addiction* 90: 319–328

Donovan, J.L. (1986) *We Don't Buy Sickness, It Just Comes*, Gower, Aldershot.

Donovan, J.L. and Blake, D.R. (1992) Patient non compliance: deviance or reasoned decision making, *Social Science and Medicine* 34(5): 507–13.

Dorval, B. (ed) (1990) *Conversational Coherence and its Development*, Ablex, Norwood, NJ.

Dosser, D.A. Jr., Balswick, J.O. and Halverson, C.F. Jr. (1986) Male inexpressiveness and relationships, *Journal of Social Personal Relationships* 3: 241–258.

Douglas, J. (1992) Black women's health matters. In Roberts, H. (ed) *Women's Health Matters*, Routledge, London.

Dowler, E. and Calvert, C. (1995a) Diets of Lone–Parent Families, Findings, *Social Policy Research* 71.

Dowler, E. and Calvert, C. (1995b) Looking for 'fresh' food: diet and lone parents, Symposium on 'Psycho-social influences on food choice: implications for dietary change', *Proceedings of the Nutrition Society* 54: 759–769.

Dowler, E. and Rushton, C. (1994) Eating on a low income, Findings, *Social Policy Research* 66.

Doyal, L. (1985) Women, health and the sexual division of labour: A case study of the women's health movement in Britain, *Critical Social Policy*, 7, 21–32.

Doyal, L. (1995) *What Makes Women Sick? Gender and the Political Economy of Health*, Macmillan Basingstoke.

Dufour, M.C. *et al.* (1994) Knowledge of FAS and the risks of heavy drinking during pregnancy, *Alcohol Health and Research World* 18(1): 86–92.

Durward, L. (1984) *Poverty in Pregnancy*, Maternity Alliance, London.

Eadie, D.R. and Leathar, D.S. (1988) *Concepts of Fitness and Health: an Exploratory Study*, Scottish Sports Council, Edinburgh.

Eames, M. *et al.* (1993) Social deprivation and premature mortality: regional comparisons across England, *British Medical Journal* 307: 1097–1102

Easterbrooks, M.A. and Emde, R.N. (1988) Marital and parent-child relationships: the role of affect in the family system. In Hinde, R.A. and Hinde, J.S. (eds) *Relationships Within Families: Mutual Influences*, Oxford University Press, Oxford.

Edwards, G. *et al.* (1994) *Alcohol Policy and the Public Good*, Oxford University Press, Oxford.

Edwards, J. (1995) Parenting skills: Views of community health and social service providers about the needs of their clients, *Journal of Social Policy* 24(2): 237–259

Edwards, N.C. and MacMillan, K. (1990) Tobacco use and ethnicity: the existing data gap, *Canadian Journal of Public Health* 81(1).

Edwards, R. (1993) *Mature Women Students: Separating or Connecting Family and Education*, Taylor and Francis, London.

Egan, S., Logan, S. and Bedford, H. (1992) *Factors Associated with Low Uptake of Immunisation: The Role of Health Education Initiatives*, HEA, London.

Eiser, J.R., Morgan, M., Gammage, P. and Gray, E. (1989) Adolescent smoking: attitudes, norms and parental influence, *British Journal of Social Psychology* 28: 193–202.

Elkes, B.H. and Crocitto, J.A. (1987) Self-concept of pregnant adolescents: a case study, *Journal of Humanistic Education and Development* 25(3): 122–135.

Engfer, A. (1988) The interrelatedness of marriage and the mother–child relationship. In Hinde, R.A. and Hinde, J.S. (eds) *Relationships Within Families: Mutual Influences*, Oxford University Press, Oxford.

Engstrom, L.M. (1986) The process of socialisation into keep-fit activities, *Scandinavian Journal of Sports Science* 8: 89–97.

Escobedo, L.G. *et al.* (1990) Socio-demographic characteristic of cigarette smoking initiation in the United States, *Journal of the American Medical Association* 261: 49–55

Escobedo, L.G. *et al.* (1993) Sport participation, age at smoking initiation, and the risk of smoking among US high school students, *Journal of the American Medical Association* 269: 1391–1395

Eshuys, J., Guest, V., Lawrence, J., Jackson, C. and Bunnage, D. (1990) *Fundamentals of Health and Physical Education*, Heinemann, Oxford.

Ettorre, E. (1992) *Women and Substance Use*, Women in Society, Macmillan, Basingstoke.

Ettorre, E. (1994) What can she depend on? Substance use and women's health. In Wilkinson, S. and Kitzinger, C. (eds) *Women and Health: Feminist Perspectives*, Taylor and Francis, London.

Ettorre, E. and Riska, E. (1993) Psychotropics, sociology and women: are the 'halcyon days' of the 'maelstream' over? *Sociology of Health and Illness* 15(4): 503–524.

Evans, G. and Grant, L. (1995) *A Project to Research the Specific Support Needs of Black Parents*, Moyenda Project Report 1991–1994, Exploring Parenthood, London.

Family Planning Association (1992) *Growing Up*, FPA, London.

Farquhar, C. (1990) *What do primary children know about AIDS? A Report of a Feasibility Study Exploring Children's Knowledge and Beliefs about AIDS*, Working Paper No. 1, Thomas Coram Research Unit, 27–28 Woburn Square, London.

Farquhar, J.W., Fortmann, S.P., Flora, J., Taylor, B., Haskell, W.L., Williams, P.T., Maccoby, N. and Woods, P.D. (1990) The Stanford 5 Community Project, *Journal of the American Medical Association* 264(3): 359–365.

Farrell, C. (1978) *My Mother Said... The Way Young People Learned About Sex and Birth Control*, Routledge, London.

Ferris, P.A. and Marshall, C.A. (1987) A model project for families of the chronically mentally ill, *Social Work* 32(2): 110–114.

Field, J., Johnson, A., Wadsworth, J. and Wellings, K. (1991) The National Survey of Sexual Attitudes and Lifestyles. In Wellings, K. (ed) *MRC AIDS Behavioural Forum: Register of Research*, Academic Department of Public Health, St. Mary's Hospital Medical School, London, November.

Fillmore, K.M. (1987) Women's drinking across the adult life course as compared to men's, *British Journal of Addiction* 82: 801–811.

Finch, J. (1984) 'It's great to have someone to talk to': the ethics and politics of interviewing women. In Bell, C. and Roberts, H. (eds) *Social Researching: Politics, Problems, Practice*, Routledge, London.

Finch, J. and Mason, J. (1993) *Negotiating Family Responsibilities*, Routledge, London.

Fisher, M. *et al.* (1995) Eating disorders in adolescents: a background paper, *Journal of Adolescent Health* 16: 420–437.

Fisher, T. (1987) Family communication and the sexual behaviour and attitudes of college students, *Journal of Youth and Adolescence* 16(5): 481–495.

Fitzpatrick, M.A. (1988a) *Between Husbands and Wives: Communication in Marriage*, Sage, New York.

Fitzpatrick, M.A. (1988b) Negotiation, problem solving and conflict in various types of marriages. In Noller, P. and Fitzpatrick, M.A. (eds) *Perspectives on Marital Interaction*, Multilingual Matters, Cleveland and Philadelphia.

Fitzpatrick, M.A. (1990) Ageing, health and family communication: a theoretical perspective. In Giles, H., Coupland, N. and Wiemann, J.M. (eds) *Communication, Health and the Elderly*, Fulbright Papers, vol. 8, Manchester University Press, Manchester.

Fitzpatrick, M.A. and Badzinski, D. (1985) All in the family: communication in kin relationships. In Knapp, M.L. and Miller, G.R. (eds) *Handbook of Interpersonal Communication*, Sage, Beverly Hills.

Flay, B.R. (1985) Psychosocial approaches to smoking prevention: a review of findings, *Health Psychology* 4(5): 449–488.

Flay, B.R. (1992) Youth tobacco use: risk, patterns and control. In Slade, J. and Orleans, C.T. (eds) *Nicotine Addiction: Principles and Management*, Oxford University Press, Oxford.

Flay, B.R. *et al.* (1995)The television, school and family smoking prevention and cessation project, *Preventive Medicine* 24(1): 29–40

Ford, N. (1991) *The Socio-Sexual Lifestyles of Young People in South West England*, SWRHA/Institute of Population Studies, Exeter.

Ford, N. and Morgan, K. (1989) Heterosexual lifestyles of young people in an English city, *Journal of Population and Social Studies* 1(2): 167–185.

Forna, M. (1992) When being in a minority can be a major problem, *The Guardian*, 5 May.

Forrest, J. (1995) *Who calls the shots: An analysis of lay beliefs about childhood vaccination*, South Bank University: School of Education, Politics and Social Science, London.

Fox, G.L. and Inazu, J.K. (1980a) Patterns and outcomes of mother–daughter communication about sexuality, *Journal of Social Issues* 36(1): 7–29.

Fox, G.L. and Inazu, J.K. (1980b) Maternal influence on the sexual behaviour of teenage daughters: direct and indirect sources, *Journal of Family Issues* 1: 81–102.

Fox, G.L. and Inazu, J.K. (1980c) Mother–daughter communication patterns about sexuality, *Family Relations: A Journal of Applied Family and Child Studies* 29: 347–352.

Fox, J. *et al.* (1985) Social class mortality differentials: artifact, selection or life circumstances? *Journal of Epidemiology and Community Health* 39(1): 1–8.

Fox, K. and Shapiro, L. (1988) Heart disease in Asians in Britain: commoner than in Europeans, but why? *British Medical Journal* 297: 311–312.

Fox, S. *et al.* (1987) Perception of risks of smoking and heavy drinking during pregnancy: 1985 NHIS findings, *Public Health Reports* 102(1): 73–79

Foxcroft, D.R. and Lowe, G. (1991) Adolescent drinking behaviour and family socialisation factors: a meta analysis, *Journal of Adolescence* 14: 255–273.

Foxcroft, D.R., Lowe, G. and May, C. (1994) Adolescent alcohol use and family influences: attributive statements by teenage drinkers, *Drugs: Education, Prevention and Policy* 1(1): 63–69.

Francome, C. and Walsh, J. (1995) *Young Teenage Pregnancy*, Middlesex University, London.

French, S.A., Perry, C.L., Leon, G.R. and Fulkerson, J.A. (1994) Food preferences, eating patterns, and physical activity among adolescents: correlates of eating disorders symptoms, *Journal of Adolescent Health* 15: 286–294.

Friedman, L.S., Lichstenstein, E. and Biglan, A. (1985) Smoking onset among teens: an empirical analysis of initial situations, *Addictive Behaviour* 10: 1–13.

Frosh, S. (1994) *Sexual Difference: Masculinity and Psychoanalysis*, Routledge, London.

Fulop, N.J. (1992) *Gender, Parenthood and Health: A Study of Mother's and Father's Experiences of Health and Illness*, Unpublished PhD thesis, Institute of Education, University of London.

Furman, W. and Buhrmester, D. (1985) Children's perceptions of the personal relationships in their social networks, *Developmental Psychology* 21: 1016–24.

Garbarino, J., Sebes, J. and Schellenbach, C. (1984) Families at risk for destructive parent–child relations in adolescence, *Child Development* 55: 174–183.

Garcia, J. *et al.* (1994) *Improving Infant Health: The Effectiveness of Health Promotion Activities to Reduce Stillbirth, Infant Mortality and Morbidity: A Literature Review*, HEA, London.

Gelles, R.J. (1994) *Contemporary Families: A Sociological View*, Sage, London.

Gilgun, J.F., Daly, K. and Handel, G. (1992) *Qualitative Methods in Family Research*, Sage, London.

Gillies, P. (1985) Accuracy in the measurement of the prevalence of smoking in young people, *Health Education Journal* 44(1): 36–38.

Gillies, P. (1989) Health behaviour and health promotion in youth. In Martin, C. and McQueen, D. (eds) *Reading for a New Public Health*, Edinburgh University Press, Edinburgh.

Gillies, P. and Wilcox, B. (1984) Reducing the risk of smoking amongst the young, *Public Health* 98: 49–54.

Gillon, E. *et al.* (1993) Researching the dietary beliefs and practices of men, *British Food Journal* 95(6): 8–12

Gilvarry, C.M. (1993) *Is there Really a Problem?* NACOA Quantification Study, National Association for the Children of Alcoholics, Bristol.

Gjerde, P.F. (1986) The interpersonal structure of family interaction settings: parent–adolescent relations in dyads and triads, *Developmental Psychology* 22(3): 297–304.

Gjerdingen, D.K. and Chaloner, K. (1994) Mothers' experience with household roles and social support during the first post partum year, *Women and Health* 21(4): 57–74.

Glynn, K. (1991) Tobacco use reduction among high-risk youth: recommendations of a National Cancer Institute Advisory Panel, *Preventive Medicine* 20: 279–291.

Glynn, K., Leventhal, H. and Hirschman, R. (1985) A cognitive developmental approach to smoking prevention, N.I.D.A. *Research Monograph* 63: 130–152.

Goddard, E. (1989) *Smoking among Secondary School Children in 1988*, HMSO, London.

Goddard, E. (1990) *Why Children Start Smoking*, HMSO, London.

Goddard, E. (1992) Young people's drinking, *Proceedings from the Alcohol and Young People Conference*, Addictions Forum, Alcohol Research Group, October.

Goddard, E. and Iken, C. (1988) *Drinking in England and Wales in 1987*, OPCS, HMSO, London.

Gofton, L. (1990) On the town: drink and the new lawlessness, *Youth and Policy* 29: 33–39.

Goldblatt, P. (1989) Mortality by social class, 1971–85, *Population Trends* 56: 6–15.

Goldman, R. and Goldman, J. (1988) *Show Me Yours: What Children Think About Sex*, Penguin, Harmondsworth.

Gordon, B.N., Schroeder, C.S. and Abrams, J.M. (1990) Age and social class differences in children's knowledge of sexuality, *Journal of Clinical Child Psychology* 19(1): 33–43.

Gordon, M. *et al.* (1991) The health of travellers' children in Northern Ireland, *Public Health* 105: 387–391.

Gordon, S.B. and Davidson, N. (1981) Behavioural parent training. In Gurman, A. and Kniskern, D.P. (eds) *Handbook of Family Therapy*, Brunner/Mazel, New York.

Gottlieb, N.H. and Chen, M.S. (1985) Sociocultural correlates of childhood sporting activities: their implications for heart health, *Social Science and Medicine* 21: 533–539.

Gottman, J.M. and Levenson R.W. (1988) The social psychology of marriage. In Noller, P. and Fitzpatrick, M.A. (eds) *Perspectives on Marital Interaction*, Multilingual Matters, Clevedon and Philadelphia.

Gove, W. (1973) Sex, marital status and mortality, *American Journal of Sociology* 79 (1): 45–67.

Graham, H. (1984) *Women, Health and the Family*, Wheatsheaf, Brighton.

Graham, H. (1985) *Caring for the Family*, Open University, HEC, Buckingham.

Graham, H. (1986) *Caring for the Family*, Research Report No.1, Health Education Council.

Graham, H. (1987a) Being poor: perceptions and coping strategies of lone mothers. In Brannen, J. and Wilson, G. (eds) *Give and Take in Families: Studies in Resource Distribution*, Allen and Unwin, London.

Graham, H. (1987b) Women's smoking and family health, *Social Science and Medicine* 25(1): 47–56.

Graham, H. (1988) Health promotion and women's smoking, *Health Promotional International 3*, 371–382.

Graham, H. (1989) Women and smoking in the United Kingdom: implications for health promotion, *Health Promotion* 3(4): 371–382.

Graham, H. (1990) Behaving well: women's health behaviour in context. In Roberts, H. (ed) *Women's Health Counts*, Routledge, London.

Graham, H. (1992) *Smoking Among Working Class Mothers with Children*, Report to the Department of Health, London.

Graham, H. (1993a) *When Life's a Drag: Women, Smoking and Disadvantage,* Department of Health, London.

Graham, H. (1993b) *Hardship and Health in Women's Lives*, Harvester, Wheatsheaf.

Graham, H. and Oakley, A.(1985) *Health and Welfare*, Macmillan, Basingstoke.

Graham, P. (1989) Social class, social disadvantage and child health, *Children and Society* 2: 9–19.

Gray, G. (1987) Burn-injured children, *Nursing Times* 83(21): 49–51.

Green, G., Macintyre, S., West, P. and Ecob, R. (1990) Do children of lone parents smoke more because their mothers do? *British Journal of Addiction* 85: 1497–1500.

Green, G., Macintyre, S., West, P. and Ecob, R. (1991) Like parent like child? Associations between drinking and smoking behaviour of parents and their children, *British Journal of Addiction* 86: 745–758.

Green, J.M. and France-Dawson, M. (1993) Women's experiences of routine screening during pregnancy: the sickle cell study. In *Targeting Health Promotion: Reaching Those in Need – Proceedings of a Symposium* pp. 4–23, Health Promotion Research Trust, Cambridge.

Gregory, S. (1995) Roles and responsibilities for food within families, Paper presented at *The Nation's Diet Conference*, ESRC, 14 November.

Gregory, J., Collins, D.L., Davies, P.S.W., Hughes, J.M. and Clarke, P.C. (1995) *National Diet and Nutrition Survey: Children aged 1.5 to 4.5*, HMSO, London.

Gregory, J., Foster, K., Tyler, H. and Wiseman, M. (1990) *The Dietary and Nutritional Survey of Bristish Adults*, HMSO, London.

Griffiths, V. (1990) Using drama to get at gender. In Stanley, L. (ed) *Feminist Praxis: Research, Theory and Epistemology in Feminist Sociology*, Routledge, London.

Grimsley, M. and Bhat, A. (1988) Health. In Bhat, A., Carr–Hill, R. and Ohri, S. (eds) *Britain's Black Population: A New Perspective*, Gower, Aldershot.

Grunberg, N. E. (1990) The inverse relationship between tobacco use and body weight. In Kozlowski, L. T. *et al.* (eds) *Research Advances in Alcohol and Drug Problems*, Plenum Press, New York.

Grunberg, N. E. *et al.* (1991) Gender differences in tobacco use, *Health Psychology* 10: K13–155.

Gudykunst, W.B., Chua, E. and Ting-Toomey, S. (1988) *Culture and Interpersonal Communication*, Sage, New York.

Gunn, T. (1992) *Mass Immunisation: A Point in Question*, Cutting Edge Publications, Spark Bridge.

Haines, F.A. and de Looy, A.E. (1986) *Can I Afford the Diet? The Effect of Low Income on People's Eating Habits, with Particular Reference to Groups at Risk*, British Dietetic Association, Birmingham.

Hamilton, L. (1995) *Raising Awareness about Testicular Cancer*, Paper given at the conference, Promoting Men's Sexual Health, Conference Report 30–36, Health Promotion Wales.

Hanson, S.M. (1986) Healthy single parent families. Special issue: The single parent family, *Family Relations Journal of Applied Family and Child Studies* 35(1): 125–132.

Harding, G. (1989) Adolescence and health: a literature review. In Smith, M. and Harding, G., *Health Education and Young People: AIDS and Other Health Related Knowledge*, TCRU Occasional Paper, Institute of Education, London University.

Harding, S. (1995) Social class differences in mortality of men: recent evidence from the OPCS longitudinal study, *Population Trends* 80: 31–37.

Harding, T. (1988a) *Asian Women's Group Easton: Evaluation Report*, Bristol and Weston Health Authority.

Harding, T. (1988b) *Health Links Scheme: Evaluation Report*, Bristol and Weston Health Authority.

Harding, T. (1989) *KHASS Asian Opportunity Group: Evaluation Report*, Bristol and Weston Health Authority.

Hardy, J.B. and Zabin, L.S. (1991) *Adolescent Pregnancy in an Urban Environment: Issues, Programmes and Evaluations*, Urban Institute Press, Washington DC.

Hartley-Brewer, E. (1994) *Positive Parenting: Raising Children With Self Esteem*, Cedar, London.

Hawkes, S.R. (1993) Fetal alcohol syndrome: implications for health education, *Journal of Health Education* 24(1), 22–26.

HEA (1989) *Diet, Nutrition and 'Healthy Eating' in Low Income Groups*, HEA, London.

HEA (1990) *Beliefs about Alcohol*, Research Report Series, HEA, London.

HEA (1991a) *Healthy Eating Factsheets*, HEA, London.

HEA (1991b) *Nutrition in Minority Ethnic Groups: Asians and Afro-Caribbeans in the United Kingdom – A Briefing Paper Prepared for Health Professionals by the the HEA*, HEA, London.

HEA (1992a) *Tomorrow's Young Adults: 9–15 year olds Look at Alcohol, Drugs, Exercise and Smoking*, MORI/HEA, London.

HEA (1992b) *Today's Young Adults: 16–19 year olds Look at Diet, Alcohol, Smoking, Drugs, and Sexual Behaviour*, MORI/HEA, London.

HEA (1992c) Management Summary 1991. *Immunisation TV, Poster and Press Campaign Evaluation*, Unpublished data, HEA, London.

HEA (1993a) *Physical Activity: Strategic Research Report*, November, HEA, London.

HEA (1993b) *Talking About It: Young People, Sexual Behaviour and HIV*, HEA, London.

HEA (1993c) *Health Update 1: Coronary Heart Disease*, HEA, London.

HEA (1993d) *Health Update 3: Alcohol*, HEA, London.

HEA (1993e) Management Summary, *Advertising Monitor – Immunisation Module*, Unpublished data, HEA, London.

HEA (1994a) *Black and Minority Ethnic Groups in England, Health and Lifestyles*, HEA, London.

HEA (1994b) *Toward Better Health Service Provision for Black and Minority Ethnic Groups*, HEA, London.

HEA (1995a) *Introducing the National Food Guide: The Balance of Good Health*, HEA, London.

HEA (1995b) *Enjoy Healthy Eating: The Balance of Good Health*, HEA, London.

HEA (1995c) *Toward Better Health Service Provision for Black and Minority Ethnic Groups*, HEA, London.

HEA (1995d) *A Survey of the UK Population. Part 1. Health and Lifestyles*, HEA, London.

HEA (1995e) *Awareness of Men's Cancers*, Report prepared for HEA, HEA, London.

HEA (1995f) *National Adult Smoking Campaign Tracking Survey*, HEA, London.

HEA (1995g) *Smoking Research with Partners of Pregnant Women*, Unpublished, HEA, London.

HEA (1995h) *Communication Strategy for Young Pregnant Women who Smoke*, Unpublished, HEA, London.

HEA (1995i) *Young People and Alcohol*, Unpublished report, HEA, London.

HEA (1996) *Smoking, Health and Contemporary Culture*, Unpublished, HEA, London.

Health Promotion Wales (1994), *Sex Education for Parents: Evaluation of a Pilot Project in South Wales*, Technical Report No. 9, Health Promotion Wales.

HEC (1987) *Health Education Council's Guide to Health Education for Young People*, London.

Heller, J. *et al.* (1988) Alcohol in pregnancy: Patterns and association with socio-economic, psychological and behavioural factors, *British Journal of Addiction* 85: 1177–1185.

Helman, C. (1981) Disease versus illness in general practice, *Journal of the Royal College of General Practice* 31, 548–552.

Helman, C. (1986) Feed a cold, starve a fever: folk models of infection in an English surburban community and their relation to medical treament. In Currer, C. and Stacey, M. (eds) *Concepts of Health, Illness and Disease: a Comparative Perspective*, Berg, Leamington Spa.

Hempel, S. (1994) Eating disorders: facts pack, *Community Outlook* 4(7): 33–34.

Herzlich, C. and Pierret, J. (1986) Illness: from causes to meaning. In Currer, C. and Stacey, M. (eds) *Concepts of Health, Illness and Disease: a Comparative Perspective*, Berg, Leamington Spa.

Hey, V. (1996) *'The Company she Keeps': An Ethnographic Study of Girls' Friendships*, Open University Press, Milton Keynes.

Hey, V., Holland, J. and Mauthner, M. (1993) Behind closed doors: researching the family, paper given at the *BSA Conference on the Research Imagination*, Essex University, Colchester, 6 April.

Hillier, S.M (1986) Women as patients and providers. In Patrick, D. and Scambler, G. (eds) *Sociology as Applied to Medicine*, Balliere, Eastbourne.

Hinde, R.A. and Hinde, J.S. (eds) (1988) *Relationships Within Families: Mutual Influences*, Oxford University Press, Oxford.

HMSO (1991) *Key Area Handbook on Accidents*, HMSO, London.

Hoare, T., Thomas, C., Biggs, A., Booth, M., Bradley, S. and Friedman, E. (1994) Can the uptake of breast screening by Asian women be increased? A randomised controlled trial of a linkworker intervention, *Journal of Public Health Medicine* 16(2): 179–185.

Hogg, C. *et al.* (1996) *Health Promotion and the Family: Messages from Four Research Studies*, HEA, London.

Holland, J. (1992) *Interviewing Young People about Sensitive Subjects*, Paper presented at the Institute of Education, London University, April.

Holland, J. (1993) *Sexuality and Ethnicity: Variations in Young Women's Sexual Knowledge and Practice*, WRAP (Women Risk and AIDS Project) Paper 8, Tufnell Press, London.

Holland, J., Mauthner, M., and Sharpe, S. (1996) *Family Matters: Communicating Health Messages in the Family*, HEA, London.

Holland, J. and Ramazanoglu, C. (1994) Coming to conclusions: power and interpretation in researching young women's sexuality. In Maynard, M. and Purvid, J. (eds) *Researching Women's Lives From a Feminist Perspective*, Taylor and Francis, London.

Holland, J., Ramazanoglu, C. and Scott, S. (1990a) *Sex, Risk and Danger: AIDS Education Policy and Young Women's Sexuality*, WRAP (Women Risk and AIDS Project) Paper 1, Tufnell Press, London.

Holland, J., Ramazanoglu, C., Scott, S., Sharpe, S. and Thomson, R. (1990b) *'Don't Die of Ignorance' – 'I Nearly Died of Embarrassment': Condoms in Context*, WRAP Paper 2, Tufnell Press, London.

Holland, J., Ramazanoglu, C., Scott, S., Sharpe, S. and Thomson, R. (1991) *Pressure, Resistance, Empowerment: Young Women and the Negotiation of Safer Sex*, WRAP Paper 6, Tufnell Press, London.

Holland, J., Ramazanoglu, C. and Sharpe, S. (1993) *Wimp or Gladiator: Contradictions in Acquiring Masculine Sexuality*, WRAP/MRAP Paper 9, Tufnell Press, London.

Holland, J. *et al.* (1995) *Protective Factors in Adolescent Smoking: a Literature Review*, Report for the Department of Health, SSRU, Institute of Education, London University.

Hover, S.J. and Gaffney, L.R. (1988) Factors associated with smoking behaviour in adolescent girls, *Addictive Behaviour* 13: 139–145.

Howard, J.A. (1988) A structural approach to sexual attitudes: interracial patterns in adolescents' judgments about sexual intimacy, *Sociological Perspectives* 31(1): 88–121.

Hudson, F. and Ineichen, B. (1991) *Taking it Lying Down*, Macmillan, London.

Ihlen, B.M. *et al.* (1993) Reduced alcohol use in pregnancy and changed attitudes of the population, *Addiction* 88: 389–394.

Illman, J. (1996) Boys trapped by the beauty myth, *The Guardian*, February 6.

Ineichen, B. (1986) Compulsory admission to pyschiatric hospital under the 1959 Mental Health Act: the experience of ethnic minorities, *New Community* XIII, 1, Spring–Summer.

The Informed Parent (1994) *The Bulletin of the 'Informed Parent Group'*, Issue 7, April.

Irvine, S. *et al.* (1996) Evidence of deteriorating semen quality in the UK: birth cohort study of 577 men in Scotland over 11 years, *British Medical Journal* 312: 467–470

Isohanni, M. *et al.* (1994) Teenage alcohol drinking and non-standard family background, *Social Science and Medicine* 38(11): 1565–1574.

Jaccard, J. and Dittus, P. (1993) Parent–Adolescent communication about pre-marital pregnancy, *Families in Society: The Journal of Contemporary Human Services*: 329–343.

Jacobson, B. (1986) *Beating the Ladykillers: Women and Smoking*, Pluto, London.

Jacobson, L.D. *et al.* (1995) Teenage pregnancy in the United Kingdom in the 1990s: the implications for primary care, *Family Practice* 12(2): 232–236.

James, A. (1982) Confections, concoctions and conceptions. In Waites, B., Bennett, T. and Martin, G. (eds) *Popular Culture: Past and Present*, Croom Helm, Beckingham, Kent.

Jansen, M.T., *et al.* (1989) Meeting psychosocial and developmental needs of children during prolonged intensive care unit hospitalisation, *Children's Health Care* 18(2): 91–95.

Jarman, B. (1983) Identification of underprivileged areas, *British Medical Journal* 286: 1705–1708.

Jarman, B. (1991) Jarman Index, *British Medical Journal* 302.

Jarman, B. *et al.* (1988) Uptake of immunisation in district health authorities in England, *British Medical Journal* 296: 1775–1778.

Jemmott, L.S. and Jemmott, J.B. (1992) Increasing condom use intentions among sexually active black adolescent women, *Nursing Research* 41: 273–279.

Jennings, A.J. and Sheldon, M.G. (1985) Review of the health of children in one-parent families, *Journal of the Royal College of General Practitioners* 35: 478–483.

Johnson, A. *et al.* (1994) *Sexual Attitudes and Lifestyles*, Blackwell Scientific Publications, London.

Johnson, Z. *et al.* (1993) Community mothers' programme: randomised controlled trial of non-professional intervention in parenting, *British Medical Journal* May 29: 1449–1452.

Jones, K. and Moon, G. (1992) *Health, Disease and Society: An Introduction to Medical Geography*, Routledge, London.

Jung, J. (1995) Parent–child closeness affects that similarity of drinking levels between parent and their college-age children, *Addictive Behaviours* 20(1): 61–67.

Kalnins, I. *et al.* (1992) Children, empowerment and health promotion: some new directions in research and practice, *Health Promotion International* 7(1): 53–59.

Kanakis, D.M. and Thelen, M.H. (1995) Parental variables associated with bulimia nervosa, *Addicitive Behaviors* 20(4): 491–500.

Kantor, D. and Lehr, W. (1975) *Inside the Family*, Jossey–Bass, San Francisco.

Kaul, R. and Stephens, J. (1991) AIDS: knowledge, attitudes and reported sexual behaviour among students in West Glamorgan, *Health Education Journal*, 50(3) 128–130.

Keane, A. and Willetts, A. (1995) *Concepts of Healthy Eating: An Anthropological Investigation in South East London*, Goldsmiths College, University of London.

Kempson, E. *et al.* (1994) *Hard Times: How Poor Families Make Ends Meet on a Budget*, Policy Studies Institute, London.

Killoran, A. *et al.* (1995) *Moving On: International Perspectives on Promoting Physical Activity*, HEA, London.

King, A. *et al.* (1988) Promoting dietary change in adolescents: a school-based approach for modifying and maintaining healthful behaviour, *American Journal of Preventive Medicine* 4: 68–74.

Kippax, S., Crawford, J., Waldby, C. and Benton, P. (1990) Women negotiating heterosex: implications for AIDS prevention, *Women's Studies International Forum* 13(6): 533–542.

Kitzinger, S. and Kitzinger, C. (1989) *Talking With Children About Things That Matter*, Pandora, London.

Klein, N. *et al.* (1989) Parents' beliefs about vaccination: the continuing propagation of false contra-indications, *British Medical Journal* 292: 1687.

Kleinman, A. (1986) Concepts and a model for the comparison of medical systems as cultural systems. In Currer, C. and Stacey, M. (eds) *Concepts of Health, Illness and Disease: a Comparative Perspective*, Berg, Leamington Spa.

Kleinmann, J.C. and Madans, J.H. (1985) The effects of maternal smoking, physical stature and educational attainment on the incidence on low birthweight, *American Journal of Epidemiology* 121(6): 843–854.

Klesse, R. and Sontag, U. (1989) Health behaviours and lifestyles of young mothers. In Martin, C. and McQueen, D. (eds) *Readings for a New Public Health*, Edinburgh University Press, Edinburgh.

Knight, L. (1982) Protect their minds too, *Mind Out* 12–14.

Knutsen, S. and Knutsen, R. (1991) The Tromsø Survey: the family intervention study, *Preventive Medicine* 20: 197–212.

Kogevinas, M. (1990) *The Longitudinal Study: Socio-Demographic Differences in Cancer Survivors 1971–83*, OPCS Series LS No.5, HMSO, London.

Kohli, S. (1992) Defying the deadly myth of the white man's disease, *The Guardian*, 15 April.

Kokotailo, P. K. *et al.* (1992) Cigarette, alcohol and other drug use by school-age pregnant adolescents: prevalence, detection and associated risk factors, Pediatrics 90 (3): 328–334.

Kotva, H.J. and Schneider, H.G. (1990) Those 'talks' – general and sexual communication between mothers and daughters, *Journal of Social Behaviour and Personality* 5(6): 603–613.

Kreppner, K. (1988) Changes in dyadic relationships within a family after the arrival of a second child. In Hinde, R.A. and Hinde, J.S. (eds) *Relationships Within Families: Mutual Influences*, Oxford University Press, Oxford.

Krueger, R.A. (1994) *Focus Groups: a Practical Guide for Applied Research*, Sage, London.

Kuh, D.J.L. and Cooper, C. (1992) Physical activity at 36 years: patterns and childhood predictors in a longitudinal study, *Journal of Epidemiological and Community Health* 46: 114–119.

Kumar, V. (1993) *Poverty and Inequality in the UK: the Effects on Children*, National Children's Bureau, London.

Lader, D. and Matheson, J. (1990) *Smoking in Secondary School Children*, HMSO, London.

Landman, J. and Wyke, S. (1995) *Healthy Eating and South Asian Families in Scotland*, Report of a Research Project under the Special Projects Programme, Department of General Practice, University of Edinburgh.

Lang, T. *et al.* (1984) *Jam Tomorrow*, Food Policy Unit, Manchester Polytechnic, Manchester.

Laryea, M. (1991) *Midwives' and Mother's Perceptions of Motherhood*. In Robinson, S. and Thomson, A.M. (eds) *Midwives, Research and Childbirth*, Vol. 1., Chapman and Hall, Bury St. Edmunds.

Latham, T. (1981) Facing sexual issues with the family, *Journal of Family Therapy* (UK), 3(2): 153–165.

Lee, S. (1995) Reconsidering the status of anorexia nervosa as a western culture-bound syndrome, *Social Science and Medicine* 42(1): 21–34.

Leon, D. and Wilkinson, R. (1989) Inequalities in prognosis; socioeconomic differences in cancer and heart disease survival. In Fox, J. (ed) *Health Inequalities in European Countries,* Gower, Aldershot.

Leonard, D. and Delphy, C. (1992) *Familiar Exploitation: a New Analysis of Marriage in Western Societies*, Polity Press, Cambridge.

Lester, C. and Farrow, S. (1988) Consumer opinion of when to attend for hospital antenatal care, *Health Education Journal* 47(1): 29–31.

Lewis, G. (1986) Concepts of health and illness in a Sepik society. In Currer, C. and Stacey, M. (eds) *Concepts of Health, Illness and Disease: a Comparative Perspective*, Berg, Leamington Spa.

Lewis, T. (1988) Unemployment and men's health, *Nursing* 3(26): 969–971, 974.

Lewis, C. and O'Brien, M. (1987) *Fatherhood Reassessed*, Sage, London.

Lewko, J.H. and Greendorfer, S.L. (1988) Family influences in sport socialisation of children and adolescents. In Smoll, F.L., Magill, R.A. and Ash, M.J. (eds) *Children in Sport,* Human Kinetics, Champaign, Illinois.

Lilley, J. (1995) Food choice in later life, Paper presented at *The Nation's Diet Conference*, ESRC, 14 November.

Lisansky Gomberg, E. (1994) Risk factors for drinking over a woman's life span, *Alcohol Health and Research World* 18(3): 220–227.

Littlewood, J. (1987) Housing conditions as a factor in children's accidents. In Berfenstam, R., Jackson, H., and Eriksson, B. (eds) *The Healthy Community: Child Safety as Part of Health Promotion Activities*, Folksam, Stockholm.

Littlewood, R. and Cross, S. (1980) Ethnic minorities and psychiatric services, *Sociology of Health and Illness* 2(2): 194–201.

Littlewood, R. and Lipsedge, M. (1982) *Aliens and Alienists: Ethnic Minorities and Psychiatry*, Penguin Books, Harmondsworth.

Loveland-Cherry, C.J. (1984) Family system patterns of cohesiveness and autonomy: relationship to family members' health behaviours, *Nursing Research* 33: 51–52.

Lowe, G., Foxcroft, D.R. and Sibley, D. (1993) *Adolescent Drinking and Family Life*, Harwood Academic, Reading.

Macfarlane, A., McPherson, A., McPherson, K. and Ahmed, L. (1987) *Teenagers and their health*, Unpublished report, Oxford.

MacIntyre, S. (1986) The patterning of health by social position in contemporary Britain: directions for sociological research, *Social Science and Medicine* 234: 393–415.

MacIntyre, S. (1986b) Understanding the social patterning of health: the role of social sciences, *Journal of Public Health Medicine* 16(1): 53–59.

MacIntyre, S. (1994) Gender differences in the perceptions of common cold symptoms, *Social Science and Medicine* 36(1): 15–20.

MAFF (1994) *The Dietary and Nutritional Survey of British Adults – Further Analysis*, HMSO, London.

Macran, S., Clarke, L., Sloggett, A. and Bethune, A. (1994) Women's socio-economic status and self–assessed health: identifying some disadvantaged groups, *Sociology of Health and Illness* 16(2): 182–208.

Mandelbaum, D.G. (1982) The study of life history. In Burgess, R.G. (ed) *Field Research: a Sourcebook and Field Manual*, Allen and Unwin, London.

Manning, T.M. (1991) Perceived family environment as a predictor of drug and alcohol usage among offspring, *Journal of Health Education* 22(3): 144–149, 165.

Mares, P., Henley, A. and Baxter, C. (1985) *Health care in Multi-Racial Britain*, Health Education Council/National Extension College, London.

Marmot, M.G. (1994) Social differences in health within and between countries, *Daedalus* 123: 197–216.

Marmot, M.G., Adelstein, A.M. and Busulu, L. (1984) Lessons from the study of immigrant mortality, *Lancet*: 1455–1457.

Marmot, M.G., Adelstein, A.M. and Busulu, L. (1983) Immigrant mortality in England and Wales 1970–1978, *Population Trends* 33: 14–17.

Marmot, M.G. and McDowell, M.E. (1986) Mortality decline and widening social inequalities, *Lancet* 274–276.

Marmot, M.G. *et al.* (1993) Health inequalities among British civil servants: The Whitehall II Study, *Lancet* 337(1): 397–393.

Marsh, A. and McKay, S. (1994) *Poor Smokers*, Policy Studies Institute, London.

Marsh, G.N. and Channing, D.M. (1986) Deprivation and health in one general practice, *British Medical Journal* 292: 1173–1176.

Martens, L. and Warde, A. (1995) On the future of eating out, Paper presented at *The Nation's Diet Conference*, ESRC, 14 November.

Martin, C. (1990) How do you count maternal satisfaction? A user-commissioned survey of maternity services. In Roberts, H. (ed) *Women's Health Counts*, Routledge, London.

Martin, C. and McQueen, D. (1989) Framework for a new public health. In Martin, C. and McQueen, D. (eds) *Readings for a New Public Health*, Edinburgh University Press, Edinburgh.

Martin, G. and Posner, S.F. (1995) The role of gender and acculturation in determining the consumption of alcoholic beverages among Mexican Americans and Central Americans in the United States, *The International Journal of the Addictions* 30(7): 794–797.

Masis, K. B. and May, P. A. (1991) A comprehensive local program for the prevention of fetal alcohol syndrome, *Public Health Reports* 106 (5): 484–489.

Maternity Alliance (1995) *Poor Expectations: Poverty and Undernourishment in Pregnancy*, Summary, Maternity Alliance and National Children's Home Action for Children, London.

Matthews, S.J. (1988) Men and stress, *Nursing* 3(26): 972–974.

Mauthner, M. (1992) *Families and Sexual Health: A Literature Review*, SSRU/HEA, London, April.

Mauthner, M. (forthcoming) Methodological aspects of collecting data from children: lessons from three research projects, *Children and Society*.

Mauthner, N.S. (1994) *Post-Natal Depression: A Relational Perspective*, Unpublished PhD thesis, University of Cambridge, Cambridge.

May, C. (1992) A burning issue? Adolescent alcohol use in Britain 1970–1991, *Alcohol and Alcoholism* 50: 195–199.

Mayall, B. (1994) *Negotiating Health: Childen at Home and Primary School*, Cassell, London.

Mayall, B. (1995) *Children's Childhoods: Observed and Experienced*, Falmer Press, London.

Mayall, B. and Watson, M. (1989) *Family Policy Review*, study commissioned by the HEA, Thomas Coram Research Unit, London.

McAllister, G. and Bowling, A. (1993) Attitudes to mammography among women in ethnic minority groups in three areas in England, *Health Education Journal* 52/4, 217–220.

McAvoy, B. and Raza, R. (1991) Can health education increase the uptake of cervical smear testing among Asian women, *British Medical Journal* 302: 833–836.

McDonald, G.W. (1980) Family power: the assessment of a decade of theory and research, 1970–1979, *Journal of Marriage and the Family* 42: 841–854.

McEwan, R. *et al.* (1992) Sex and the risk of HIV infection: the role of alcohol, *British Journal of Addiction* 87(4): 577–584.

McGuffin, S. (1982) Smoking – the knowledge and behaviour of schoolchildren in Northern Ireland, *Health Education Journal* 41: 53–59.

McGuire, C. (1990) Accounting for public perceptions in the development of a childhood immunisation campaign, *Health Education Journal* 49(3): 105–107.

McGuire, C. (1992) The *Haemophilus influenzae* type B (Hib) vaccine: a pre-launch qualitative study of parental perceptions, *Health Education Journal* 51(4): 171–175.

McGuire, J. (1983) *The Effects of a Child's Gender on the Nature of Parent–Child Interactions in the Home During the Third Year of Life*, Unpublished PhD Thesis, London University.

McGurk, H. and Glachan, M. (1988) Children's conversation with adults, *Children and Society* 2: 20–34.

McKnight, A. and Merrett, D. (1987) Alcohol consumption in pregnancy: a health education problem, *Journal of the Royal College of General Practitioners* February: 73–76.

McLoone, P. and Boddy, F.A. (1994) Deprivation and mortality in Scotland, *British Medical Journal* 309: 1465–1470.

McNeill, A.D. (1991) The development of dependence on smoking in children, *British Journal of Addiction* 86: 589–592.

McNeill, A.D., Jarvis, M.J., Stapleton, J.A., Russell, M.A.H., Eiser, J.R., Gammage, P. and Gray, E.M. (1988) Prospective study of factors predicting uptake of smoking in adolescents, *Journal of Epidemiology and Community Health* 43: 72–78.

McWhinney, I.R. (1989) Family dynamics in the achievement of symptom control, *Journal of Palliative Care* 5(2): 37–39.

Meier, K.S. (1991) Tobacco truths: the impact of role models on children's attitudes towards smoking, *Health Education Quarterly* 18(2): 173–182.

Middleton, S., Ashworth, K. and Walker, R. (1994) *Family Fortunes: Pressures on Parents and Children in the 1990s*, Child Poverty Action Group, London.

Miles, A. (1991) Women, Health and Medicine, Open University Press, Milton Keynes.

Millar, F.E. and Rogers, L.E. (1988) Power dynamics in marital relationships. In Noller, P. and Fitzpatrick, M.A. (eds) *Perspectives on Marital Interaction, Multilingual Matters*, Cleveland and Philadelphia.

Miller, J.B. and Lane, M. (1991) Relations between young adults and their parents, *Journal of Adolescence* 14(2): 179–194.

Miller, S., Nunnally, E. and Wackman, D.B. (1975) *Alive and Aware*, Interpersonal Communications Programs, Minneapolis.

Minuchin, P. (1988) Relationships within the family: a systems perspective on development. In Hinde, R.A. and Hinde, J.S. (eds) *Relationships Within Families: Mutual Influences*, Oxford University Press, Oxford.

Mitchell, L. (1990) *Growing up in Smoke*, Pluto Press, London.

Mitchell, L. and Stenning, K. (1989) The family atmosphere: growing up in smoke, *Health Education Journal* 48(3): 103–109.

Mitic, W.R., McGuire, D.P. and Neumann, B. (1985) Perceived stress and adolescents' cigarette use, *Psychological Reports* 57: 1043–1048.

Mittelmark, M.B., Pallonen, V.E., Murray, D.M., Luepker, R.V., Pechacek, T.F. and Pirie, P.L. (1988) Predictors of non-adoption of cigarette smoking following experimentation, *Scandinavian Journal of Primary Health Care* 6(3): 131–135.

Montemayor, R. and Hanson, E. (1985) A naturalistic view of conflict between adolescents and their parents and siblings, *Journal of Early Adolescence* 5: 23–30.

Moore, L, Smith, C. and Catford, J. (1994) Binge drinking: prevalence, patterns and policy, *Health Education Research* 9(4): 497–505.

Moreno, C., Laniado-Laborin, R., Sallis, J.F., Elder, J.P., De Moor, C., Castro, F.G. and Deosaransingh, K. (1994) Parental influences to smoke in Latino youth, *Preventive Medicine* 23, 48–53.

Morgan, D.L. (1986) *Focus Groups as Qualitative Research*, Sage, London.

MORI (1989) *Teenage Health and Lifestyles*, HEA, London.

MORI (1990) *Young Adults, Health and Lifestyle: Sexual Behaviour*, HEA, London.

MORI (1991) *Teenage Smoking: Fourth Tracking Survey,* HEA, London.

Morris, J.K., Cook, D.G. and Shaper, A.G (1994) Loss of employment and mortality, *British Medical Journal* 308: 1135–1152.

Morrison, M. (1995) Sharing food at home and school: exploring commensality, Paper presented at *The Nation's Diet Conference*, ESRC, 14 November.

Moser, K.A., Fox, A.J. and Jones, D.R. (1986b) Unemployment and mortality in the OPCS longitudinal study. In Wilkinson, R.G. (ed) *Class and Health*, Tavistock, London.

Moser, K.A. *et al.* (1986a) Unemployment and mortality, *The Lancet*: 365–367.

Moskowitz, R. (1984) The case against immunisation, *The Homeopath: The Journal of the Society of Homeopathy* 4(4): 3–13

Moskowitz, R. (1992) Vaccination: a sacrament of modern medicine, *The Journal of the Society of Homeopathy* 12(1): 134–140

Moss, K.E. (1988) New reproductive technologies: concerns of feminists and researchers, *AFFILIA – Journal of Women and Social Work* 3(4): 38–49.

Murcott, A. (1983a) 'It's a pleasure to cook for him...': food, mealtimes and gender in some South households. In Gamarnikow, E., Morgan, D., Purvis, J. and Taylorson, D. (eds) *The Public and the Private*, Heinemann, London.

Murcott, A. (1983b) Cooking and the cooked. In Murcott, A. (ed) *The Sociology of Food and Eating*, Gower, Aldershot.

Murcott, A. (1995) Social influences on food choice and dietary change: a sociological attitude, Symposium on 'Psycho-social influences on food choice: implications for dietary change', *Proceedings of the Nutrition Society* 54: 759–769.

Murray, M., Kiryluk, S. and Swan, A.V. (1985) Relations between parents' and children's smoking behaviour and attitudes, *Journal of Epidemiology and Community Health* 39: 169–174.

Nader, P. *et al.* (1983) The Family Health Project: cardiovascular risk reduction for children and their parents, *Developmental and Behavioural Paediatrics* 41: 3–10.

Naidoo, J. and Wills, J. (1994) *Health Promotion: Foundations for Practice*, Bailliere Tindall, London.

Needle, R., McGubbin, H., Wilson, M. Peneck, R., Lezar, A. and Mederer, H. (1986) Interpersonal influences in adolescent drug use – the role of older siblings, parents and peers, *International Journal of Addiction* 21(7): 739–766.

Nelson, M. (1994) Children's diets: problems and solutions. In Buttiss, J. and Human, K. (eds) *Making Sense of Food: Children in Focus,* National Dairy Council, London.

Nelson, S.C., Budd, R.J., Eiser, J.R., Morgan, M., Gammage, P. and Gray, E. (1985) The Avon prevalence study: a survey of cigarette smoking in secondary school children, *Health Education Journal* 44(1): 12–14.

New, S. and Senior, M. (1991) "I don't believe in needles": Qualitative aspects of a study into the uptake of infant immunisation in two English health authorities, *Social Science and Medicine* 33(4): 509–518.

Newcombe, R. *et al.* (1995) A survey of drinking and deviant behaviour among 14–15 year-olds in North West England, *Addiction Research* 2(4): 319–341.

Newcomer, S.F. and Udry, R.J. (1985) Parent–child communication and adolescent sexual behaviour, *Family Planning Perspectives* 17: 169–174.

Newman, I.M. and Ward, J.M. (1989) The influence of parental attitude and behaviour in early adolescent cigarette smoking, *Journal of School Health* 59(4): 150–152.

NFER/HEA (1994) *Parents, Schools and Sex Education*, HEA, London.

Nicklas, T.A., Arbeit, M.L., Johnson, C.C., Franklin, F.A. and Berenson, G.S. (1988) 'Heart Smart' program: a family intervention program for eating behaviour of children at high risk of cardiovascular disease, *Journal of Nutrition Education* 20(3): 128–131.

Nolin, M.J. (1988) *Parent–child communication about sexuality*, unpublished PhD dissertation, the American University.

Noller, P. (1984) *Non-Verbal Communication and Marital Interaction*, Pergamon, Oxford.

Noller, P. and Bagi, S. (1985) Parent–adolescent communication, *Journal of Adolescence* 8: 125–144

Noller, P. and Callan, V.J. (1988) Understanding parent–adolescent interactions: perceptions of family members and outsiders, *Developmental Psychology* 24: 707–714.

Noller, P. and Callan, V.J. (1990) Adolescents' perceptions of the nature of their communication with parents, *Journal of Youth and Adolescence* 19(4): 349–362.

Noller, P. and Callan, V.J. (1991) *The Adolescent in the Family*, Routledge, London.

Noller, P. and Fitzpatrick, M.A. (eds) (1988) *Perspectives on Marital Interaction*, Multilingual Matters, Cleveland and Philadelphia.

Noller, P. and Gallois, C. (1986) Sending emotional messages in marriage: non-verbal behaviour: sex and communication clarity, *British Journal of Social Psychology* 25: 287–297.

Northouse, P.G. and Northouse, L.L. (1987) Communication and cancer: issues confronting patients, health professionals, and family members, *Journal of Psychosocial Oncology* 5(3): 17–46.

Nutbeam, D. (1987) Smoking prevalence among schoolchildren: the effects of transfer to secondary education. In Campbell, G. *et al.* (eds) *Health Education: Youth and Community*, Falmer Press, Lewes.

Nutbeam, D. (1995) Exposing the myth – what schools can and cannot do to prevent tobacco use by young people, *Promotion and Education* 2(1): 11–14.

Nutbeam, D. and Aaro, L.E. (1991) Smoking and pupils' attitudes towards school: the implications for health education with young people, *Health Education Research* 6: 415–421.

Nutbeam, D. *et al.* (1993) Evaluation of two school smoking programmes under normal classroom conditions, *British Medical Journal* 102–107.

Nye, F.I. (1979) Choice, exchange and the family. In Burr, W.R., Hill, R., Nye, F.I. and Reiss, I.L. (eds) *Contemporary Theories About the Family* Vol.2, The Free Press, New York.

O'Brien, M. and Jones, D. (1994) Young people's attitudes to fatherhood, Paper presented at the *Father Figures: A Conference for the International Year of the Family*, Glasgow.

O'Byrne, D.J. (1983) A study of smoking in the Greater Dublin Area, Proceedings of the *Fifth World Conference on Smoking and Health*, Winnipeg, Canadian Council on Smoking and Health.

Oakley, A. (1980) *Women Confined: Towards a Sociology of Childbirth*, Martin Robertson, Oxford.

Oakley, A. (1981) Interviewing women: a contradiction in terms. In Roberts, H. (ed) *Doing Feminist Research*, Routledge, London.

Oakley, A. (1990) Who's afraid of the randomised controlled trial? Some dilemmas of the scientific method and 'good' research practice. In Roberts, H. (ed) *Women's Health Counts*, Routledge, London.

Oakley, A. (1993) *Essays on Women, Medicine and Health*, Edinburgh University Press, Edinburgh.

Oakley, A. (1994) Who cares for health? Social relations, gender, and the public health, *Journal of Epidemiology and Community Health* 48: 427–434.

Oakley, A., Brannen, J. and Dodd, K. (1992) Young people, gender and smoking in the United Kingdom, *Health Promotion International* 7(2):75–88.

Oakley, A. and Fullerton, D. (1995) *Young People and Smoking*, A Report for the North Thames Health Authority, Social Science Research Unit, London.

Oechsli, F.W. and Seltzer, C.C. (1984) Teenage smoking and antecedent parental characteristics: a prospective study, *Public Health London* 98: 103–108.

Ogden, J. and Fox, P. (1994) Examination of the use of smoking for weight control in restrained and unrestrained eaters, *International Journal of Eating Disorders* 16: 177–185.

OHE (1987) *Women's Health Today*, Office of Health Economics, London.

OHE (1992) Compendium of Health Statistics, 8th edition, Office of Health Economics, London.

Olson, D.H. and Rabunsky, C. (1972) Validity of four measures of family power, *Journal of Marriage and the Family* 34: 224–234.

OPCS (1986) *General Household Survey 1984*, HMSO, London.

OPCS (1990a) *Mortality Statistics by Cause*, HMSO, London.

OPCS (1990b) *Cigarette Smoking 1972–1988*, Monitor, April.

OPCS (1991a) *Mortality Statistics by Cause*, HMSO, London

OPCS (1991b) *General Household Survey 1989*, HMSO, London.

OPCS (1992a) *Mortality Statistics by Cause*, HMSO, London.

OPCS (1992b) *General Household Survey 1990*, HMSO, London.

OPCS (1993) *General Household Survey 1991*, HMSO, London.

OPCS (1994a) *Mortality Statistics: Childhood*, HMSO, London.

OPCS (1994b) *General Household Survey 1992*, HMSO, London.

OPCS (1995a) *Living in Britain: Preliminary Results from the 1994 General Household Survey*, HMSO, London.

OPCS (1995b) *The Health of Our Children*, HMSO, London.

Orford, J. (1992) Control, confront or collude: how family and society respond to excessive drinking, *British Journal of Addiction* 87(11): 1513–1525.

Orford, J. and Velleman, R. (1990) Offspring of parents with drinking problems: drinking and drug taking as young adults, *British Journal of Addiction* 85(6): 779–794.

Owen, L. and Bolling, K. (1995) *Tracking Teenage Smoking*, National Smoking Education Campaign, HEA, London.

Packer, C.N., Stewart-Brown, S. and Fowle, S.E. (1994) Damp housing and adult health: results from a lifestyle study in Worcester, England, *Journal of Epidemiology and Community Health* 48: 555–559.

Paolozzi, H., (1994) Looking after your kit, *Nursing Times* 90(5): 30–31.

Parker, H. and Measham, F. (1994) Pick'n mix: changing patterns of illicit drug use amongst 1990s adolescents, *Drugs, Education, Prevention and Policy* 1(1): 5–13.

Parsons, L. (1991) Homeless families in Hackney, *Public Health* 105(4): 287–296.

Parsons, L. and Day, S. (1992) Improving obstetric outcomes in ethnic minorities: an evaluation of health advocacy in Hackney, *Journal of Public Health Medicine* 14(2): 183–191.

Parsons, T. (1952) *The Social System*, Tavistock, London.

Pearson, M. *et al.* (1993) Primary immunisations in Liverpool I: who holds consent? *Archives of Diseases in Childhood* 69: 110–114.

Perelberg, R.J. and Miller, A.C. (1990) *Gender and Power in Families*, Routledge, London.

Perry, C.L. and Silvis, G.L. (1987) Smoking prevention: behavioural prescriptions for the paediatrician, *Paediatrics* 79(5): 790–799.

Perry, C.L. *et al.* (1988) Parent involvement with children's health promotion, *Health Education Quarterly* 16: 171–180.

Petchesky, R.P. (1987) Fetal images: the power of visual culture in the politics of reproduction, *Feminist Studies* 13(2): 263–292.

Phillimore, P. *et al.* (1994) Widening inequality of health in Northern England, 1981–91, *British Medical Journal* 308: 1125–1128.

Phoenix, A. (1991) *Young Mothers*, Polity Press, London.

Phoenix, A., Woolett, A. and Lloyd, E. (eds) (1991) *Motherhood: Meanings, Practices and Ideologies*, Saga, London.

Piepe, T., Cattermole, B., Charlton, P., Morley, F., Morey, J. and Yerrell, P. (1988) Girls' smoking and self-esteem – the adolescent context, *Health Education Journal* 47: 83–85.

Pill, R. and Stott, N. (1986) Concepts of illness causation and responsibility: some preliminary data from a sample of working class mothers. In Currer, C. and Stacey, M. (eds) *Concepts of Health, Illness and Disease: a Comparative Perspective*, Berg, Leamington Spa.

Pisano, S. and Rooney, J.F. (1988) Children's changing attitudes regarding alcohol: a cross-sectional study, *Journal of Drug Education* 18(1): 1–11.

Plant, M.A., Peck, D.F. and Samuel, E. (1985) *Alcohol, Drugs and School Leavers*, Tavistock, London.

Plant, M.A. *et al.* (1989) The effects on children and adolescents of parents' excessive drinking: an international review, *Public Health Reports* 104(5): 433–442.

Plant, M.A. *et al.* (1990) Young people and drinking: results of an English national survey, *Alcohol and Addiction* 25(6): 685–690.

Popay, J. and Bartley, M. (1989) Conditions of labour and women's health. In Martin, C. and McQueen, D. (eds) *Readings for a New Public Health*, Edinburgh University Press, Edinburgh.

Popay, J. and Young, A. (1993) *Reducing Accidental Death and Injury in Children*, Report Produced for NWRHA Pubic Health Working Group of Child Accidents, June.

Popay, J. *et al.* (1993) Gender inequalities in health: social position, affective disorders and minor physical morbidity, *Social Science and Medicine* 36(1): 21–32.

Power, C. (1994) Health and social inequality in Europe, *British Medical Journal* 308: 1153–1156.

Pratt, L. (1976) *Family Structure and Effective Health Behaviour*, Houghton, Mifflin, Boston.

Prendergast, S. and Prout, A. (1987) *Knowing and Learning About Parenthood*, Research Report No.17, HEA, London.

Prendergast, S. and Prout, A. (1990) Learning about birth: parenthood and sex education in English secondary schools. In Garcia, J., Kilpatrick, R. and Richards, M. (eds) *The Politics of Maternity Care*, Clarendon Press, Oxford.

Prochaska, J. and Di Clemente, C. (1984) *The Transtheoretical Approach: Crossing Traditional Foundations of Change*, Harnewood II, Don Jones/Irwin.

Prout, A. (1986) Wet children and little actresses, *Sociology of Health and Illness* 8: 11–36.

Prout, A. (1996) *Families, Cultural Bias and Health Promotion: Implications of an Ethnographic Study*, HEA, London.

Pugh, G. (1994) *Effective Parenting Programme for Schools: a Pilot Study*, NCB, London.

Pugh, G. and Poulton, L. (1987) *Parenting as a Job for Life: a Local Development Project in Hampshire*, National Children's Bureau, London.

Pugh, G. *et al.* (1994) *Confident Parents, Confident Children: Policy and Practice in Parent Education and Support*, NCB, London.

Puska, P., Vertainen, E., Pallonen, U., Salonen, J.T., Poyhia, P., Koskela, K. and McAlister, A.L. (1982) *The North Karelia Youth Project*, *Preventive Medicine* 11: 550–570.

Puska, P. *et al.* (1983) Change in risk factors for coronary heart disease during 10 years of a community intervention (North Karelia Project), *British Medical Journal* 287: 1840–1844.

Quirk, M.E., Godkin, M.A. and Schwenzfeir, E. (1993) Evaluation of two AIDS prevention interventions for inner city adolescents and young adult women, *American Journal of Preventive Medicine* 9: 21–26.

Qureshi, B. (1985) Obstetric problems in multi-ethnic women, *Maternal and Child Health*, 303–307.

Qvortrup, J. (1985) Placing children in the division of labour. In Close, P. and Collins, R. (eds) *Family and Economy in Modern Society*, Macmillan, London.

Raats, M.M. and Sparks, P. (1995) Unrealistic optimism about diet-related risks: implications for interventions, Symposium on 'Psycho–social influences on food choice: implications for dietary change', *Proceedings of the Nutrition Society* 54: 737–745.

Raitakari, O.T. *et al.* (1994) Effects of persistent physical activity and inactivity on coronary risk factors in children and young adults, *American Journal of Epidemiology* 140: 195–205.

Ramazanoglu, C. (1990) *Methods of Working as a Research Team*, WRAP Paper 3, Tufnell Press, London.

Ranson, R. (1987) *Home Safety: The Challenge to Public Health*, University of Warwick, Coventry.

Reader, E.G., Carter, R.P. and Crawford, A. (1988) AIDS – knowledge, attitudes and behaviour: a study with university students, *Health Education Journal* 47(4): 125–128.

Reid, D. J. *et al.* (1995) Reducing the prevalence of smoking in youth in Western countries: an international review, *Tobacco Control* 4: 266–277.

Rhodes, J. E. *et al.* (1994) Risk and protective factors for alcohol use among pregnant African-American, Hispanic, and white adolescents: the influence of peers, sexual partners, family members and mentors, *Addictive Behaviors* 19: 555–564.

Ribbens, J. and Edwards, R. (1995) Introducing qualitative research on women in families and households, *Women's Studies International Forum* 18(3): 271–284.

Roberts, H. (1991) Child protection – accident prevention: a community approach, *Health Visitor* 64(7): 219–220.

Roberts, H. (1992) Safety as a social value: a community approach to child accidents, Paper presented to the *Childcare and Development Group Seminar*, Faculty of Social and Political Science, Cambridge University, May.

Roberts, H., Smith, S. and Lloyd, M. (1991) *Safety as a Social Value*, Public Health Research Unit, Glasgow.

Roberts, K. (1988) Young people's drinking habits: evidence from the ESRC 16–19 Initiative, Paper presented at the ESRC Conference, *Alcohol Abuse and Young People*, ESRC, December, London.

Robertson, S. (1995) Men's health promotion in the UK: a hidden problem, *British Journal of Nursing* 4(7): 382–401.

Robinson, T.N. *et al.* (1993) Does television viewing increase obesity and reduce physical activity? Cross-sectional and longitudinal analyses among adolescent girls *Paediatrics* 91: 273–280.

Roche, A. (1991) Making better use of qualitative research: illustrations from medical education research, *Health Education Journal* 50(3): 131–137.

Rocheron, Y. (1988) The Asian Mother and Baby Campaign: the reconstruction of ethnic minorities' health needs, *Critical Social Policy* 22: 4–23.

Rocheron, Y. and Dickinson, R. (1990) The Asian Mother and Baby Campaign; a way forward in health promotion for Asian women? *Health Education Journal* 49(3): 128–133.

Rocheron, Y., Dickinson, R. and Khan, S. (1989) *Evaluation of the Asian Mother and Baby Campaign*, Centre for Mass Communication Research, University of Leicester, Leicester.

Rogers, A. and Pilgrim, D. (1993) *Rational Non-Compliance with Childhood Immunisation: Personal Accounts of Parent and Primary Health Care Professionals*, Unpublished report for HEA.

Rogers, A. *et al.* (1996) *Understanding and Promoting Mental Health in the Family*, HEA, London.

Romanus, V. *et al.* (1987) Pertussis in Sweden after the cessation of general immunisation in 1979, *Paediaric Infectious Disease* 6: 364–371.

Rose, H. (1990) Activists, gender and the community health movement, *Health Promotion International* 5: 209–218.

Rosenbaum, E. and Rosenbaum, I. (1986) Achieving open communication with cancer patients through audio and videotapes, *Journal of Psychosocial Oncology* 4(4): 91–105.

Rousseau, N. (1983) Give us a playpiece, please; not lectures!, Journal of the Royal Society of Health 3: 105–109.

Rowland, N. and Maynard, A. (1991) Putting patients' drinking histories in context, *Health Education Journal* 50(2): 82–83.

Royal College of Psychiatrists (1993) *Anorexia and Bulimia*, RCP, London.

Royal College of Physicians (1992) *Smoking and the Young: A Report of the Working Party of the Royal College of Physicians*, RCP, London.

Rushing, B. *et al.* (1992) Race differences in the effects of multiple roles on health: longitudinal evidence from a national sample of older men, *Journal of Health and Social Behaviour* 33(2): 126–139.

Rutter, M. and Smith, D. (1995) (eds) *Psychosocial Disorders in Young People: Time Trends and Their Causes*, published for Academia Europea by John Wiley, Chichester.

Rutter, M., Taylor, E. and Herzov, V. (eds) (1994) *Child and Adolescent Psychiatry: Modern Approaches*, Blackwell Scientific, London.

Ruzek, S. (1987) Feminist visions of health: an international perspective. In Mitchell, J. and Oakley, A. (eds) *What is Feminism?* Blackwell, Oxford.

Sallis, J.F. and Nader, P.R. (1988) *Family Determinants of Health Behaviours*. In Gochman, D. S. (ed) *Health Behaviour*, Plenum Press, New York.

Saltonstall, R. (1993) 'Healthy Bodies, Social Bodies'. Men's and women's concepts and practices of health in everyday life, *Social Science and Medicine* 36(1): 7–14.

Sanders, G.F. and Mullis, R.L. (1988) Family influences on sexual attitudes and knowledge as reported by college students, *Adolescence* 23(92): 837–846.

Schinke, S.P., Gilchrist, L.D., Schilling, R.F., Snow, W.H. and Bobo, J.K. (1986) Skills methods to prevent smoking, *Health Education Quarterly* 13(1): 23–27.

Schofield, M. (1965) *The Sexual Behaviour of Young People*, Longman, London.

Scott, P. (1995a) *Ethnicity, Lay Beliefs and the Management of Disease Among Diabetics*, Report to the ESRC, SSRU, Insitute of Education, London University.

Scott, P. (1995b) Factors affecting cooperation with medical advice among West Indians with diabetes. *In Diabetes, Choice and Control: Consent Conference Series* No. 8, SSRU, Institute of Education, London University, July.

Sebes, J. (1983) *Determining the Risk for Abuse in Families with Adolescents: the Development of a Criterion Measure*, Unpublished PhD dissertation, Pennsylvania State University, Pennsylvania.

Senior, P.A. and Bopal, R. (1994) Ethnicity as a variable in epidemiological research, *British Medical Journal* 30: 327–330.

Shapiro, J. and Shumaker, S. (1987) Differences in emotional well-being and communication styles between mothers and fathers of pediatric cancer patients, *Journal of Psychosocial Oncology* 5(3): 121–131.

Sharma, U. (1991) *Complementary Medicine Today: Practitioners and Patients*, Routledge, London.

Sharp, D. and Lowe, G. (1989) Adolescents and alcohol – a review of the recent British research, *Journal of Adolescence* 12: 295–307.

Sharpe, R.M. and Skakkeback, N.E. (1993) Are oestrogens involved in falling sperm counts and disorder of the male reproductive tract? *The Lancet* 341: 1392–1395.

Sharpe, S. (1987) *Falling For Love: Teenage Mothers Talk*, Virago, London.

Sharpe, S. (1994) *Fathers and Daughters*, Routledge, London.

Sharpe, S. and Oakley, A. (1992) *Parental Influences on Young People's Smoking Behaviour: a Review of the Literature*, SSRU, Insitute of Education, London University.

SHE (1994) *What's your Drinking Style? A Survey of Drinking Habits Amongst 1006 Women Readers of SHE*, The National Magazine Company Ltd., London.

Sheldon, T.A. and Parker, H. (1994) Race and ethnicity in health research, *Journal of Public Health Medicine* 14(2): 104–110.

Shisslak, C.M., McKeon, R.T. and Crago, M. (1990) Family dysfunction in normal weight bulimic and bulimic anorexic families, *Journal of Clinical Psychology* 46(2): 185–189.

Siegel, J.H., Hardoff, D., Golden, N.H. and Shenker, R. (1995) Medical complications in male adolescents with anorexia nervosa, *Journal of Adolescent Health* 16(6): 448–453.

Silverman, D. and Perakyla, A. (1990) AIDS counselling: the interactional organisation of talk about 'delicate' issues, *Sociology of Health and Illness* 12(3): 293–318.

Silverstein, M. and Bengtson, V.L. (1991) Do close parent–child relations reduce the mortality of older parents?, *Journal of Health and Social Behaviour* 322(4): 382–395.

Silvestri, B. and Flay, B.R. (1989) Smoking education: comparison of practice and state of the art, *Preventive Medicine* 18: 257–266.

Sinnott, R. and Jackson, H. (1990) *Developments in House and Home Safety*, University of Warwick, Coventry.

Skelton, R. (1988) Man's role in society and its effect on health, *Nursing* 3: 26.

Sloggett, A. and Joshi, H. (1994) Higher mortality in deprived areas: community or personal disadvantage? *British Medical Journal* 309: 1470–1474.

Smith, C. (1996) *Developing Parenting Programmes*, National Children's Bureau, London.

Smith, C. and Pugh, G. (1996) *Learning to be a Parent,* Family Policy Studies Centre, London.

Smith, C. *et al.* (1992) Health behaviour research with adolescents: a perspective from the WHO cross-national health behaviour in school-aged children study, *Health Promotion Journal of Australia* 2: 41–44.

Spencer, L., Faulkner, A. and Keegan, J. (1988) *Talking About Sex: Asking the Public About Sexual Behaviour and Attitudes*, Social and Community Planning Research, London.

Spitzack, C. (1990) *Confessing Excess: Women and the Politics of Body Reduction*, State University of New York Press, Albany, New York.

Spray, J. and Greenwood, K. (1989) From street work to district policy. In Martin, C and McQueen, D. (eds) *Readings for a New Public Health*, Edinburgh University Press, Edinburgh.

Stacey, M. (1986) Concepts of health and illness and the division of labour in health care. In Currer, C. and Stacey, M. (eds.) *Concepts of Health, Illness and Disease: a Comparative Perspective*, Berg, Leamington Spa.

Stacey, M. (1988) *The Sociology of Health and Healing – a Textbook*, Unwin Hyman, London.

Stacey, M. (1991) *Sociology of Health and Healing*, Routledge, London.

Stafford, E.M. *et al.* (1980) Employment, work involvement and mental health in less qualified young people, *Journal of Occupational Psychology* 53(4): 291–304.

Stanley, L. (ed) (1990) *Feminist Praxis: Research, Theory and Epistemology in Feminist Sociology*, Routledge, London.

Stanley, L. and Wise, S. (1983) *Breaking Out: Feminist Consciousness and Feminist Research*, Routledge, London.

Statham, J. (1986) *Daughters and Sons*, Blackwell, Oxford.

Steinglass, P. (1987) Psychoeducational family therapy for schizophrenia: a review essay, *Psychiatry* 50(1): 14–23.

Stenbakken, R.O. (1989) *Parents and Sex Education at Home: the Expressed Needs of Thirteen Parents*, Unpublished PhD dissertation, Columbia University Teachers College.

Stockley, L. (1993) *The Promotion of Healthier Eating: a Basis for Action – A Discussion Paper for Those Concerned With Promoting Healthier Eating*, HEA, London.

Stone, D.H. (1993) *Costs and Benefits of Accident Prevention: a Selective Review of the Literature*, Public Health Research Unit, University of Glasgow.

Straussner, S.L.A. (1994) The impact of alcohol and other drug abuse on the American family, *Drug and Alcohol Review* 13: 393–399.

Striegel-Moore, R.H., Silberstein, L.R. and Rodin, J. (1986) Toward an understanding of the risk factors for bulimia, *American Psychologist* 41: 246–63.

Sunseri, A.J., Alberti, J.M., Kent, N.O. *et al.* (1983) Reading, demographic and social and psychological factors related to pre-adolescent smoking and nonsmoking behaviours and attitudes, *Journal of School Health* 53: 257–263.

Swan, A.V. *et al.* (1988) *Why do Children Smoke and Why have Girls become More Likely to Smoke than Boys? – a Review of the Scientific Literature 1970–1987*, School Medicine and Health Services Research Unit and Division of Community Medicine, St. Thomas' Campus.

Swan, A.V., Meila, R.J.W., Fitzsimons, B., Breeze, E. and Murray, M. (1989) Why do more girls than boys smoke cigarettes? *Health Education Journal* 48(2): 59–64.

Swan, A.V., Creeser, R. and Murray, M. (1990) When and why children first start to smoke, *International Journal of Epidemiology* 19(2): 323–330.

Sweeting, H. and West, P. (1995) Family life and health in adolescence: a role for culture in the health inequalities debate? *Social Science and Medicine* 40(2): 163–175.

Tacade (1985) *Alcohol Education,* Syllabus 11–19, Tacade, Manchester.

Tannen, D. (1991) *You Just Don't Understand: Women and Men in Conversation*, Virago, London.

Tannen, D. (1995) *Talking from Nine to Five: How Women's and Men's Conversational Styles affect Who gets Heard, Who gets Credit and What gets Done at Work*, Virago, London.

Tether, P. and Harrison, L. (1986) Alcohol-related fires and drownings, *British Journal of Addiction* 81: 425–431.

Textor, M.R. (1989) The 'healthy' family, *Journal of Family Therapy* 11(1): 59–75.

Thom, B. and Edmondson, K. (1989) *Women, Family and Drugs: Women Talking*, Unpublished report of a workshop, Commonwealth Secretariat and Addiction Research Unit, Institute of Psychiatry, London, June.

Thomas, M. *et al.* (1993) *Smoking among Secondary School Chidren in 1992*, HMSO, London.

Thompson, B. and Illsley, R. (1969) Family growth in Aberdeen, *Journal of Biosocial Science* 1: 23.

Thomson, R. and Scott, S. (1990) *Researching Sexuality in the Light of AIDS: Historical and Methodological Issues*, WRAP Paper 5, Tufnell Press, London.

Thomson, R. and Scott, S. (1991) *Learning About Sex: Young Women and the Social Construction of Sexual Identity*, WRAP Paper 4, Tufnell Press, London.

Thorogood, N. (1988) *Health and Management of Daily Life Amongst Women of Afro-Caribbean origin Living in Hackney*, Unpublished PhD thesis, Goldsmith's College, London University.

Thorogood, M., Coulter, A., Jones, L., Yudkin, P., Muir, J. and Mant, D. (1993) Factors affecting response to an invitation to attend for a health check, *Journal of Epidemiology and Community Health* 47: 224–228.

Throwe, A.N. (1986) Families and alcohol, *Critical Care Quarterly* 8(4): 79–88.

Tones, B.K. (1987) Devising strategies for preventing drug misuse: the role of the Health Action Model, *Health Education Research* 2: 305–317

Torkington, P.K. (1991) *Black Health – a Political Issue: The Health and Race Issue*, Catholic Association for Racial Justice and Liverpool Institute of Higher Education, London.

Towner, E., Dowswell, T. and Jarvis, S. (1993) *Reducing Childhood Accidents – the Effectiveness of Health Promotion Interventions: a Literature Review*, HEA, London.

Townsend, P. and Davidson, N. (1982) *Inequalities in Health: The Black Report*, Penguin, Harmondsworth.

Townsend, P., Davidson, N. and Whitehead, M. (1988) *Inequalities in Health: The Black Report and the Health Divide*, Penguin, Harmondsworth.

Townsend, J., Wilkes, H., Haines, A. and Jarvis, M. (1991) Adolescent smokers seen in general practice: health, lifestyle, physical measurements, and response to antismoking advice, *British Medical Journal* 303: 947–950.

Tuakli, N., Smith, M.A. and Heaton, C. (1990) Smoking in adolescence: methods for health education and smoking cessation: a MIRNET study, *Journal of Family Practice* 31(4): 369–374.

Turner, S., Mayall, B. and Mauthner, M. (1995) One big rush – dinner time at school, *Health Education Journal* 54: 18–27.

Umberson, D. (1987) Family status and health behaviours: social control as a dimension of social integration, *Journal of Health and Social Behaviour* 28(3): 306–319.

University of Exeter School of Education, Exercise and Sport Behaviour Research and Promotion, and HEA (1994) *Physical Activity Promotion in Primary Health Care in England: Final Research Report*, HEA, London.

Urberg, K. and Robbins, R.L. (1981) Adolescents' perceptions of the costs and benefits associated with cigarette smoking: sex differences and peer influence, *Journal of Youth and Adolescence* 10(5): 353–361.

Urberg K. A. *et al.* (1990) Peer influence in adolescent cigarette smoking, *Addictive Behaviours* 15: 247–255.

Valentich, M. and Gripton, J. (1989) Teaching children about AIDS, *Journal of Sex Education and Therapy* 15(2): 92–102.

van Dalen, H., Williams, A. and Gudex, C. (1994) Lay people's evaluations of health: are there variations between different sub-groups? *Journal of Epidemiology and Community Health* 48: 248–253.

VanEvery, J. (1995) *Heterosexual Women Changing the Family: Refusing to be a Wife*, Taylor and Francis, London.

Vartiainen, E., Pallonen, V., McAlister, A., Koskela, K. and Puska, P. (1986) Four year follow-up results of the smoking prevention program in the North Karelia Youth Project, *Preventive Medicine* 15(6): 692–698.

Verbrugge, L.M. (1985) Gender and health: an update on hypotheses and evidence, *Journal of Health and Social Behaviour* 26: 156–182.

Vineis, P., Fornero, G., Magnino, A., Giacometti, R. and Ciccone, G. (1993) Diagnostic delay, clinical stage, and social class: a hospital based study, *Journal of Epidemiology and Community Health* 47: 229–231.

Waddell, C. and Floate, P. (1986) Gender and the Utilisation of Health Care Services in Perth Australia, *Social Health Illness* 8(2): 170–177.

Wadsworth, J. *et al.* (1987) Family type and accidents in pre-school children, *Journal of Epidemiology and Community Health* 37: 100–104.

Waldby, C. *et al.* (1990) Theory in the bedroom: a report from the Macquarie University AIDS and Heterosexuality Project, *Australian Journal of Social Issues* 25(3): 177–185.

Waldron, I. (1991) Patterns and causes of gender differences in smoking, *Social Science and Medicine* 32(9): 989–1005.

Waldron, I. (1993) Recent trends in sex mortality ratios for adults in developing countries, *Social Science and Medicine* 36(4): 451–62.

Walker, D. (1990) Immunisation in Fife Part I – Health professional attitudes towards MMR vaccine two years on, *Health Education Journal* 49(3): 101–102.

Wallace, P.G. and Haines, A.P. (1984) General practitioners and health promotion: what patients think, *British Medical Journal* 289: 534–436.

Wang, M.Q. *et al.* (1995) Family and peer influence on smoking behaviour among American adolescents: an age trend, *Journal of Adolescent Health* 16(3): 200.

Wardle, J. (1995) Parental influences on children's diets, Symposium on 'Psycho-social influences on food choice: implications for dietary change', *Proceedings of the Nutrition Society* 54: 747–758.

Warman, D.W. (1986) *Father–adolescent son communication about sexuality*, Unpublished PhD dissertation, Syracuse University.

Warner, J. (1981) Family therapy: a search for foundations, II – communications, boundaries and control, *Journal of Family Therapy*, 3(2): 201–209.

Warren, C. and Neer, M. (1986) Family sex communication orientation, *Journal of Applied Communication Research*, 14(2): 86–107.

Warwick, I., Aggleton, P. and Homans, H. (1988a) Young people's health beliefs and AIDS. In Aggleton, P. and Homans, H. (eds) *Social Aspects of AIDS*, Falmer Press, Lewes.

Warwick, I., Aggleton, P. and Homans, H. (1988b) Constructing commonsense – young people's beliefs about AIDS, *Sociology of Health and Illness* 10(3): 213–233.

Waterson, E. J. *et al.* (1989) It's a woman's world – fathers' participation in smoking and drinking in pregnancy, *Health Education Journal* 48(2): 163–173.

Waterson, E. J. and Murray-Lyon, I. M. (1990) Preventing alcohol-related birth damage: a review. *Social Science and Medicine*, 30(3): 349–364.

Watson, E. (1984) Health of infants and use of health services by mothers of different ethnic groups in East London, *Community Medicine* 6: 127–135.

Watson, J. (1993) Male body image and health beliefs: a qualitative study and implications for health promotion practice, *Health Education Journal* 52 (4): 246–252.

Watt, I.S., Howel, D. and Lo, L. (1993) The health care experience and health behaviour of the Chinese: a survey based in Hull, *Journal of Public Health Medicine* 15(2): 129–136.

Weatherburn, P. *et al.* (1992) *The Sexual Lifestyles of Gay and Bisexual Men in England and Wales*, Project Sigma, London.

Webb, J.A. and Baer, P.E. (1995) Influence of family disharmony and parental alcohol use on adolescent social skills, self-efficiency, and alcohol use, *Addictive Behaviours* 20(1): 127–135.

Welin, L. *et al.* (1992) Social network and activities in relation to mortality from cardiovascular diseases, cancer and other causes: a 12 year follow-up of the study of men born in 1913 and 1923, *Journal of Epidemiology and Community Health* 46: 127–132.

Wellings, K. *et al.* (1994) *Sexual Behaviour in Britain (UK National Survey of Sexual Attitudes and Lifestyles)*, Penguin, Harmondsworth.

Wells, J. and Batten, L. (1990) Women smoking and coping: an analysis of women's exprience of stress, *Health Education Journal* 49: 57–60.

Werch, C.E. *et al.* (1991) Effects of a take-home drug prevention program on drug-related communication and beliefs of parents and children, *Journal of School Health* 61(8): 346–350.

West, P. (1988) Inequalities? Social class differences in health in British youth, *Social Science and Medicine* 27: 291.

West, P. *et al.* (1990) Social class and health in youth: findings from the West of Scotland Twenty 0–7 study, *Social Science and Medicine* 30: 665.

West, R. (1990) Alternative medicine: prospects and speculations. In Black, N. (eds) *Health and Disease: a Reader*, Open University Press, Milton Keynes.

Wheelock, J. (1990) *Husbands at Home: the Domestic Economy in a Post-Industrial Society*, Routledge, London.

White, A. *et al.* (1992) *Infant Feeding*, HMSO, London.

Whitehead, M. (1987) *Inequalities of Health: The Health Divide*, HEC, London.

Whitfield, R. (1990) Sex education, families and public policy, *Sexual and Marital Therapy* (UK) 5(1): 5–24.

Wight, D. (1990) *The Impact of HIV/AIDS on young People's Heterosexual Behaviour in Britain: a Literature Review*, Working Paper #20, Medical Sociology Unit, MRC, Glasgow, December.

Wight, D. (1991) Communicating about sex: studying the sexuality of 14–16 year–old males and salience of HIV, Paper presented at the *Royal Society of Medicine Forum on Medical Communications: Delicate Discussions*, November.

Wight, D. (1992) *Boys' Thoughts and Talk about Sex in a Working Class Locality of Glasgow*, Paper prepared for MRC Sociology Unit, Glasgow.

Wight, D. (1993) Constraints or Cognition: Factors Affecting Young Men's Practice of Safe Heterosexual Sex. In Aggleton, P., Davies, P., and Hart, G. (eds) *AIDS: The Second Decade*, Falmer Press, Lewes.

Wilkinson, R.G. (1994) *Unfair Shares: The Effects of Widening Income differences on the Welfare of the Young*, A Report for Barnados, Trafford Centre for Medical Research, University of Sussex, Brighton.

Wilkinson, S.R. (1988) *The Child's World of Illness*, Cambridge University Press, Cambridge.

Wilks, J. and Callan, V. (1984) Similarity of university students and their parents' attitudes towards alcohol, *Journal of Studies on Alcohol* 45(4): 326–333.

Wilks, J. *et al.* (1989) Parent, peer and personal determinants of adolescent drinking, *British Journal of Addiction* 84: 619–630

Willett, W.C. *et al.* (1987) Moderate alcohol consumption and the risk of breast cancer, *New England Journal of Medicine* 316: 1174–1180.

Williams, T.W.N. and Moon, A. (1987) *A Picture of Health: Health Education in Primary Schools Project*, HEA/Health Education Unit, University of Southampton.

Wilsnack, S.C. *et al.* (1994) How women drink: epidemiology of women's drinking and problem drinking, *Alcohol Health and Research World* 18(3): 173–181.

Wilson, M. (1983) Health care for ethnic groups: networking for health, *Health and Social Service Journal* Vol. 93, No. 4846, pp 565-567.

Wingard, D.L. (1984) The sex differential in morbidity, mortality and lifestyle, *Annual Review of Public Health*, 5: 433–458.

Witschi, J.C. *et al.* (1978) Family cooperation in a cholestrol lowering diet, *Journal of American Diet Association* 72: 384–388.

Woodhouse, A. and Nicholson, M. (1994) *Parents' Information Needs on Immunisation*, Strategic Research Group, London.

Woods, A. *et al.* (1994) Safety practices among parents and children in a primary care setting, *Health Education Journal* 53(4): 397–408.

World Health Organization (WHO) (1985) IARC Monographs of the Evaluation of the Carcinogenic Risks of Chemicals to Humans: *Tobacco Smoking, International Agency for Research on Cancer* 38.

Wright, D.W., Peterson, L.R. and Barnes, H.L. (1990) The relation of parental employment and contextual variables with sexual permissiveness and gender role attitudes of rural early adolescents, *Journal of Early Adolescence* 10(3): 382–398.

Wright, L. and Buczkiewicz, M. (1995) *Awaaz: Asian Young Women and Alcohol*, Tacade, Salford.

Yarber, W.L. and Greer, J.M. (1986) The relationship between the sexual attitudes of parents and their college daughters' or sons' sexual attitudes and sexual behaviour, *Journal of School Health* 56: 68–72.

Young, A. (1986) Internalising and externalising medical belief systems: an Ethiopian example. In Currer, C. and Stacey, M. (eds) *Concepts of Health, Illness and Disease: a Comparative Perspective*, Berg, Leamington Spa.

Youniss, J. and Ketterlinus, R.D. (1987) Communication and connectedness in mother and father adolescent relationships, *Journal of Youth and Adolescence* 16: 265–282.

Youniss, J. and Smollar, J. (1985) *Adolescent Relations with Mothers, Fathers and Friends*, University of Chicago Press, Chicago.

Zani, B. (1991) Male and female patterns in the discovery of sexuality during adolescence, *Journal of Adolescence* 14(2): 163–178.

Zarb, G. and Steele, J. (1993) *Evaluation of Low Uptake Immunisation Projects*, Policy Studies Insitute, June.